SUBURBAN GRIDLOCK

SUBURBAN GRIDLOCK

Robert Cervero

Copyright 1986, Rutgers, The State University of New Jersey
All rights reserved.

Published in the United States of America
by the Center for Urban Policy Research
Building 4051-Kilmer Campus
New Brunswick, New Jersey 08903

Library of Congress Cataloging-in-Publication Data

Cervero, Robert.
    Suburban gridlock.

        Bibliography: p. 235
        Includes index.
        1. Traffic congestion—United States.
2. Traffic flow—United States.   3. Land use—United
States— Planning.   4. Suburbs—United States.
I. Title.
HE355.3.C64C47   1986   388.4'13142'0973   86-2628
ISBN 0-88285-115-2

To Montyne

Contents

Photographs

Chapter 4.   Suburban Traffic Management: Approaches and Prospects

Tables

Figures

Maps

Preface

The transportation planning profession has historically focused its attention and resources on downtown access and mobility problems. Indeed, since the first appearance of the motorized four-wheel buggy, the overwhelming majority of urban transport investments—from minor arteries to rapid transit systems—have sought to accommodate the convergence of regional trips into spatially constrained downtown cores. Suburbs, and places beyond, on the other hand, have long been considered havens for travel, free from frustrating traffic jams and ideal for leisurely weekend excursions. To a large extent, transportation planning in suburbia has over the years involved little more than adding new projects to five-year capital improvement programs for the pouring of concrete and pavement along developing corridors.

Within the past five to ten years, however, traffic conditions along many fringe corridors have begun to change markedly for the worse. Recent surges in white-collar employment triggered by the relocation of downtown offices to outlying locales have swamped many suburban thoroughfares with traffic they were never designed to handle. As far as 20 miles from main downtown cores of expanding metropolises like Houston, Los Angeles, and Washington, D.C., rush-hour traffic has gone from free-flow to gridlock conditions in a span of five years along some stretches. The situation has reached such epic proportions that some watchful observers have issued warnings that congestion could become the number one problem within the suburbs as well as the transportation field by the 1990s and into the twenty-first century unless drastic action is taken.

For most Americans, the idea of congestion in the suburbs almost seems like a contradiction in terms. Suburbia has come to represent an important slice of Americana over the post-WWII era, a place where families can maintain a rural-like lifestyle while residing close enough to big cities to enjoy the same occupational choices as urban dwellers. The image of the suburbs as predominantly bedroom communities is forevermore being redrawn by the steady influx of offices and businesses, and the urban kinds of problems they bring along. As America's suburbs continue to mature, traffic congestion, pollution, and other unpleasantries are apt to become a way of life that both planners and transportation professionals must quickly learn to deal with.

This book explores the scope of mobility and congestion problems posed by rapid office and business growth on America's urban fringes. Emphasis is placed on illuminating the many behavioral, institutional, and logistical dilemmas planners can expect to face in battling congestion in suburbia. The potential roles that various design, land use, and management strategies might play in attenuating traffic's presence and protecting natural environments are also closely examined. Because so many large-scale developments are currently being discussed, planned, and built in suburbia, considerable attention is given to highlighting what are considered to be exemplary design and management practices presently underway that others might follow. Above all, this book aims to call the looming mobility crisis facing our suburbs to the attention of the nation's developers, city planners, and transportation professionals in hopes of stimulating both dialogue and creative responses.

Much of the inspiration for this manuscript has come from the rich body of writings by students of suburban problems and issues over the past 25 years. While suburbia has only begun to capture the serious attention of transportation planners since the mid-seventies, important groundwork on employer and developer involvement in safeguarding suburban mobility has been laid in recent years that this work was able to build upon. Some of the ideas and case accounts presented in this book were drawn from panel discussions and workshops that took place at the conference on "Mobility for Major Metropolitan Growth Centers" held in Los Angeles in November 1984. Several hundred developers, politicians, federal administrators, planners, and scholars attended this conference, arriving at a general consensus that protecting suburbs from downtown-like traffic jams will become an increasingly difficult challenge that deserves priority attention on all fronts.

I owe debts of appreciation to many for their support of this work. The Institute of Transportation Studies, University of California, Berkeley, provided both financial backing and outstanding staff assistance. Julia Perez and Charlie Anderson collaborated as research assistants, helping with the collection and analysis of both census and survey information as well as with the conduct of several case studies. I am also thankful to the many local and regional transportation planners, too numerous to list here, who went beyond the call of duty in assisting us gather supporting materials for this work. I am particularly grateful to the dozens of developers and private individuals who gave their time unsparingly and shared their many insights on a wide array of suburban mobility issues during field interviews. Without their assistance and commitment to improving transportation in suburban growth settings, this work could never have been completed. Finally, my heartfelt thanks to my wife Montyne for sacrificing a summer while I wrote this manuscript.

Robert Cervero
August 1985

1

The Suburban Office Boom

MOBILITY IMPLICATIONS

Suburban Office and Development Trends

Many American cities have witnessed an explosion of new office construction on their outskirts. Low-lying, campus-style office projects are popping up in areas that only ten years earlier were inhabited by cows and fruit groves. In some suburban locales, what can only be described as "second downtowns"—complete with office towers and the finest shops, hotels, and restaurants—are mushrooming skyward, dwarfing surrounding tree-lined residential neighborhoods. Combined with shopping malls, recreational theme parks, new subdivisions, and other mammoth land developments, outlying office parks and mixed-use complexes are permanently reshaping the landscapes of suburban America.

The rapidity of recent suburban office development has been staggering. Over 80 percent of all office floorspace in America's suburbs has been built since 1970.[1] By comparison, only 36 percent of all downtown office buildings have gone up over the past 15 years. Nationwide, the share of total office space outside central cities jumped from 25 percent in 1970 to 57 percent in 1984. In some areas of the country, a tripling of current suburban office inventories has been projected by century's end.[2]

While examples of the "suburban office boom" can be found almost anywhere, new construction has been particularly feverish on the fringes of rapidly growing sunbelt and western metropolises like Dallas, Houston, Atlanta, Denver, and Orange County, California. Maps 1.1 and 1.2 show where office growth is heading in two of these areas. In Dallas, the LBJ Freeway corridor north of downtown and the 1700-acre, master-planned community of Las Colinas west of downtown have recently emerged as major new markets for office development, absorbing roughly 50 percent of all office construction since the mid-seventies.[3] In Atlanta, despite a concerted effort to centralize economic activity by building a downtown-focused rapid transit system, office space grew 30 percent faster in the suburbs than in downtown during the seventies.[4] Between 1978 and 1983, the share of regional office space in Atlanta's core shrunk from 34 percent to 26 percent (see Photo 1.1).

Houston's suburban office growth has been even more startling. In 1970, only 39 percent of all office construction was outside of downtown Houston; by 1982, the share had catapulted to 87 percent.[5] Already, one suburban area known as City Post Oak contains more office space than the entire city of San Antonio. Recently, a 65-story suburban skyscraper was

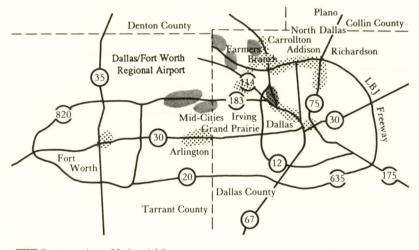

▰▰ Concentrations of Industrial Space
⋮⋮⋮⋮ Concentrations of Office Space

Map 1.1. Locations of Recent Office and Industrial Growth in Dallas and Fort Worth, Texas.
(Sources: Robert Cervero, "Managing the Traffic Impacts of Suburban Office Growth," *Transportation Quarterly*, Vol. 38, No. 4, 1984, p. 535; and Peat, Marwick, Mitchell & Co., "Dallas/Fort Worth Metropolitan Area Market," *Development Review and Outlook 1983–1984* [Washington, D.C.: Urban Land Institute, 1983], p. 160, Figure 11–4.)

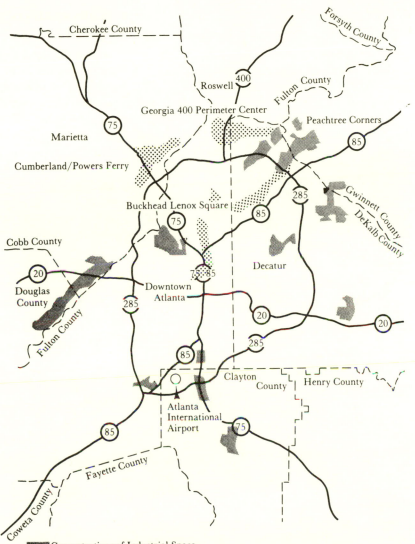

Cherokee County

Forsyth County

Roswell 400

Georgia 400 Perimeter Center

Fulton County

Peachtree Corners

75

Marietta

85

Cumberland/Powers Ferry

285

Gwinnett County

DeKalb County

Buckhead Lenox Square

75

85

Cobb County

Decatur

20

75·85

Douglas County

Downtown Atlanta

285

20

Fulton County

285

20

85

Clayton County

Henry County

Atlanta International Airport

75

85

Fayette County

Coweta County

■■■ Concentrations of Industrial Space
∴∴∴ Concentrations of Office Space/Activity

Map 1.2. Locations of Recent Office and Industrial Growth in Atlanta, Georgia.
(Sources: Robert Cervero, "Managing the Traffic Impacts of Suburban Office Growth," *Transportation Quarterly*, Vol. 38, No. 4, 1984, p. 536; and Hammer, Siler, George Associates, "Atlanta Metropolitan Area Market," *Development Review and Outlook 1983–1984* [Washington, D.C.: Urban Land Institute, 1983], p. 129, Figure 8–4.)

**Photo 1.1. Office Towers Springing up Along Atlanta's North
Perimeter.**
Above, mid- to high-rise towers flanking the I-285 beltway.
Below, new glassed office structures surrounding Georgia's
400 Perimeter Center. (Photos by the author.)

erected—the Transco Tower—reputedly the world's largest building outside of a CBD (Central Business District). Moreover, several behemoth office buildings of over one million square feet each have recently gone up in west Houston. An estimated ten million square feet of office floorspace is currently being built outside of downtown Houston annually.[6]

In the Rocky Mountain states, while Denver has emerged as the undisputed regional hub, most office building activities have actually taken place outside of its downtown. The suburbs' share of annual office construction erupted from just 15 percent in 1970 to 73 percent in 1981.[7] Along Denver's southeast I-25 corridor, a stretch dotted with office, high-tech,[8] and business-executive parks, more office space has already been produced than in all of downtown Denver. One complex situated ten miles from downtown, the Denver Technological Center, already has 4.2 million square feet of office space in place, along with a number of freestanding restaurants, small retail shopping areas, gas stations, banks, a 620-room hotel, and indoor recreational facilities[9] (see Photos 1.2 a and b).

Photo 1.2a. Rapid Transformation of the Southeast Denver I-25 Corridor.
Photo taken in 1962 when the area was predominantly farmland. (Photo by Roach Photos, Inc., provided courtesy of the Denver Technological Center.)

Photo 1.2b.   By 1985, over 4 million square feet of commercial and office space concentrated in the master-planned Denver Technological Center. (Photo by Landis Aerial Photos, Inc., provided courtesy of the Denver Technological Center.)

On the west coast, central Orange County, the airport area of west Los Angeles, and the eastern and southern perimeters of the San Francisco Bay Area have become major catchments for new regional office construction. The Irvine Spectrum and South Coast Metro projects, both still being developed, will add an expected 60 million square feet of office, light industrial, commercial, and other mixed-use space to central Orange County when completed. An estimated 80,000 daily workers will be drawn to these two "super complexes" at buildout[10] (see Photo 1.3). A comparable employment agglomeration has taken form in west Los Angeles County where a 40 million square foot mix of office, hotel, light manufacturing, and commercial space already exists around the international airport, and another 40 million is scheduled for the next decade. Development within this 16-square mile area will eclipse the entire floorspace of downtown Los Angeles. And to the north in the Bay Area, two major business parks some 35 miles east of downtown San Francisco are slated for 45,000 new employees by 1990—far more than will be added to the CBDs of San Francisco and Oakland combined.

Even more mature eastern U.S. cities and snowbelt metropolises are undergoing visible suburban facelifts. In New York City, for instance, the number of Fortune 500 firms headquartered in Manhattan dropped from 136 in the late sixties to about 65 today.[11] Many have fled to such areas as Stamford, CT., White Plains, N.Y., and Bergen County, N.J. Within the next few years, more prime office space will exist in northeastern New Jersey than in midtown Manhattan.[12] In the nation's capital, most office growth is concentrating not around new Metrorail transit stations but rather in burgeoning suburban communities, best exemplified by the Tysons Corner area of northern Virginia, a nine million square foot office–hotel–shopping complex. And in Hamilton Lakes, Illinois, outside of Chicago, a 33-story skyscraper will soon tower over eight million square feet of office space, engulfing a surrounding suburban subdivision.[13]

There has been more going on in suburbia, of course, than merely office construction. Notably, individuals and families are continuing to arrive from cities, small towns, and rural areas in record numbers. From 1950 to 1980, the population of America's suburbs nearly tripled, from 35.2

Photo 1.3.   South Coast Metro in Central Orange County, California.
(Photo courtesy of the South Coast Metro Alliance.)

million to 101.5 million—representing about 45 percent of the nation's total population. During the same period, central cities grew only modestly, from about 50 million to 68 million, or 30 percent of total U.S. population. Suburbs, moreover, are beginning to shatter their traditional stereotype as sterile, culturally deprived bedroom communities. Today, there is scarcely an urban function that cannot also be found in suburbia. Performing arts centers, dinner theaters, nightclubs, professional sports stadia, and other large drawing cards are beginning to crop up in areas once considered "the boonies." The activities found at some recently opened suburban complexes read like inventories of traditional downtown facilities—corporate headquarters, hotels, boutiques, specialty shops, convention halls, and government offices. In the words of one observer: "Suburbs are no longer a monolith but rather a kaleidoscope."[14]

Factors Behind Suburban Office Growth

A potpourri of reasons has been given for the suburbs' sudden popularity with office developers.[15] It is insightful to first, however, look at just who the tenants of these new developments are. Many represent the nation's fastest growing industries, such as service- and information-based companies (e.g., data processing and research firms) and businesses involved with advanced technologies (e.g., manufacturers of electronic components and precision instruments). The ascendancy of such firms has reflected the larger postindustrialization of America's economy—the change from a heavy "smokestack" manufacturing base to one devoted more to the production of ideas and information.

Employment statistics clearly reveal this shift. Over the last 30 years, office-based occupations have been the fastest growing employment sectors in the United States. Nationally, the share of jobs in manufacturing has fallen from 32 percent right after WWII to 24 percent in the early 1980s. The service sector, including jobs in office, retail, government, education, and entertainment, grew from 49 percent to 66 percent of total employment during this same period.

It has been this "white-collarization" of America's employment sector that has prompted many businesses to relocate their offices in suburbia. No longer are most firms today tied to rail spurs and waterports. Rather, they have become, in economists' parlance, "footloose"—i.e., able to make locational decisions on the basis of factors other than proximity to raw materials and goods. Particularly in the case of high-tech industries, the miniaturization of product lines has drastically reduced the cost of shipping goods to the point where firms are virtually free to move to wherever they can maximize their net advantage.

Today's checklist of desirable attributes for an office location tends to be long and varied.[16] Among high-tech firms, the existence of high-skilled labor usually tops the list. To help recruit and maintain engineers and professional staff, many firms have been attracted to the aesthetics and roominess of a campus office park setting. Moreover, the steady flight of families to the suburbs throughout the 1960s and 1970s has created vast pools of workers, particularly married women, who are often available for a wide assortment of clerical and staff support positions. Concerns over rising inner-city crime rates, congestion, and the lack of affordable housing for workers have also influenced corporate relocation decisions. The generally lower cost-of-living levels in suburban areas, moreover, have meant potential salary savings to businesses who locate there.

Skyrocketing land and rental costs in many downtown areas have likewise prompted corporations to relocate their mid-management and back office staffs to outlying locations where real estate is comparatively cheap and easy to assemble.[17] The rapid acceleration of telecommunications technologies has enabled many businesses to spin off portions of their operations (e.g., computer functions) to less expensive suburban environs. Furthermore, some suburban communities have successfully lured office investors from central cities by offering various incentives (e.g., relaxed zoning or building code requirements) and improving public works (e.g., widening major roadways or building recreational facilities). New office developments invariably fatten public treasuries, so not surprisingly the competition for these projects is usually spirited.

Suburban Mobility Challenges

The flight of office workers to the suburbs portends a future of frustrating traffic tie-ups along major arteries and freeway stretches that have historically operated smoothly. As jobs have continued to scatter along the urban fringes, regional commutesheds are taking on amoeba-like forms, fanning out as much as 100 miles in places like Los Angeles, Houston, and San Francisco. No longer does the dominant commute pattern resemble the radial spokes of a wheel focused on a downtown hub. Rather, trips are becoming increasingly dispersed and cross-town in direction. Table 1.1 underscores this. In 1975, about twice as many work trips were from suburb

TABLE 1.1

Trends in Origin–Destination Mixes of Work Trips
Within All U.S. Urbanized Areas, 1975 and 1980

	1975		1980	
Commute Pattern[1]	Total Trips (in 1000s)	Percent	Total Trips (in 1000s)	Percent
Central City to Central City	16,528	33.4	20,879	33.0
Suburb to Central City	9,592	19.6	12,691	20.1
Suburb to Suburb	19,261	38.9	25,329	40.1
Central City to Suburb (reverse commute)	4,040	8.1	4,226	6.8
TOTAL	49,421	100.0	63,125	100.0

[1]These are estimates extracted from data on place of residence, by place of work in both 1975 and 1980 censuses. Data are only for trips within SMSAs, not those to other SMSAs or to non-SMSA areas. 1975 data include workers 14 years of age and older, while 1980 data include workers 16 years of age and older. See Chapter Two for the definition of SMSAs and further discussions of geographic commuting patterns in the United States.

Sources: U.S. Department of Commerce, Bureau of the Census, *1980 Census of Population. Journey to Work – Metropolitan Commuting Flows* (Washington: U.S. Government Printing Office, 1984); and adapted from U.S. Department of Commerce, Bureau of the Census, *Journey to Work in the United States: 1975* (Washington: U.S. Government Printing Office, 1979).

to suburb (38.9%) as from suburban to central city locations (19.6%). By 1980, intrasuburban travel widened this margin, accounting for over 40 percent of all metropolitan work trips. Average commuting distances also jumped over this period—from a nationwide average of 11.1 miles in 1975 to 12.1 miles in 1980. In general, as American cities have sprawled, so have trip patterns.

Unfortunately, this trend does not square well with the current transportation networks of many American cities. Most metropolitan highway systems were built to funnel commuters from the outskirts to downtowns. Many radial thoroughfares are simply incapable of handling large volumes of lateral and peripherally oriented trips. Moreover, conventional fixed-route transit and ridesharing services, such as vanpools, will be hard-pressed to survive in an environment of regionally scattered trip ends. Of equal concern, money is drying up for new road building, with priority usually given to the maintenance and restoration of facilities already in place. Even if there was available funding, it is questionable whether politically potent suburban constituencies would allow their idyllic neighborhoods to be disrupted by new highway construction.[18]

One does not have to look very far to find evidence of suburban traffic snarls even today. A recent *Wall Street Journal* editorial described one suburbanite's daily plight as follows:

> Every weekday morning, Gretchen Davis drives down Fairfax Farms Road on the way to work at the Ayr Hill Country Store in nearby Vienna. Sounds pastoral, doesn't it? But a short way down the road, Mrs. Davis reaches Route 50, a major arterial highway through this Washington, D.C. suburb. There, a river of cars roars through the suburban calm. Sometimes you have to wait 20 minutes just for a gap in traffic big enough to get out—and even then you have to take a chance, the shopkeeper says. For Mrs. Davis, stop-and-go traffic often stretches what used to be a pleasant 20-minute commute into a nerve-wracking hour.[19]

Adds another observer:

> Congestion has lost its directional bias: people commuting from one suburb to another . . . are just as likely to run into heavy traffic as are commuters on their way downtown. In some metropolitan areas, such as Houston and Santa Clara County, California, traffic congestion no longer is confined to main radial corridors leading toward the central city; it pervades the entire highway system.[20]

The suburbanization of congestion is also reflected by growing regionwide dissatisfaction with commuting. For the past two years, residents of the San Francisco Bay Area have ranked transportation as the region's number one problem; a full 28 percent put transportation at the top of their list, up from just a 10 percent rating in the early 1980s. The greatest concern was expressed in rapidly developing Santa Clara County, home of the world renowned Silicon Valley, where 39 percent of those polled cited transportation as the number one problem. No other issue area in the Bay region garnered more than a 10 percent response. Congestion is today cited as the number one regional problem by residents, not only from the Bay Area, moreover, but from Phoenix, Houston, Atlanta, and Washington, D.C. as well.

Some residents are threatening to express their outrage toward suburban congestion at the ballot box. In the Bay Area, riled motorists in several outlying counties are blaming their elected leaders for allowing more growth than roads can handle, and many are pushing initiatives so that voters can set limits of their own.[21] Forewarns the mayor of one of the fastest-growing Bay Area suburbs: "We're going to get the living daylights kicked out of us by an absolutely irate, indignant electorate. No one's out there trying to hang politicians yet, but the public is a sleeping giant on this issue, and they're incensed."[22] So much so, in fact, that five Bay Area suburbs experiencing tremendous growth pressures have recently passed sweeping traffic control initiatives that effectively ban all new development for the foreseeable future. The political stakes posed by rampant suburban office and commercial growth are indeed high, and the rising ground swell of resentment to mounting traffic jams can only be expected to spawn even more confrontations among builders, residents, and city councils in coming years.

Of course, there has been more behind suburban traffic congestion than just the arrival of office jobs from CBDs. Notably, a number of widely publicized demographic and lifestyle "megatrends" are continually altering Americans' commuting habits. Perhaps most telling have been the changes in family composition. Today's households are far more atomistic than in the past—they are smaller and more diverse. Since 1950, the average American family has shrunk from 3.4 to 2.7 persons. No longer does the two-parent, two-child household represent the norm; rather, nontraditional families are on the rise. For instance, single-parent female-headed households increased by over 55 percent during the seventies, while single-parent male-headed households rose 39 percent.[23] We are also witnessing a feminization of the labor force—more than two-thirds of married women between the ages of 25 and 44 now work, compared to only one-third 25 years ago.

These changes, coupled with the dispersal of jobs and housing, give every reason to believe that Americans will become more and more reliant upon private, flexible modes of urban travel in the future, namely the automobile. The splintering of traditional nuclear households is likely to make private vehicular usage more imperative in the future since more single, independent adults will be around. Table 1.2 indicates this trend is well under way. Since 1970, the automobile has strengthened its dominance in the commuting market. In contrast, despite the multibillion dollar subsidies public transit received during the seventies, its share of journey-to-work trips actually dropped to just 6 percent.[24] Transit's standing could slip even more since buses operating on fixed routes and set schedules are usually ill suited for delivering workers to dispersed suburban addresses. Surveys of office employees in Orange County and San Francisco suburbs, for example, reveal that fewer than 5 percent currently patronize transit. Even workers in suburban office towers located around rail transit stations are almost entirely dependent on the automobile. Travel surveys at Washington's New Carrollton Metrorail station and San Francisco BART's Pleasant Hill station show that fewer than 4 percent of all employees commute to work by rail.[25] Regardless of how conveniently rail transit serves suburban office centers, if only a fraction of the workforce lives near a line, most employees will end up driving to work.

Coping With Impending Congestion Problems

Congestion in the suburbs presents a whole new milieu for transportation planning. Over the years, an arsenal of techniques have been used by engineers and planners to accommodate traffic generated by new land development. Road widenings, improved signal timings, carpool matching programs, and expanded bus services have been typical responses. "Non-pavement" strategies—i.e., those aimed at modifying travel demand, popularly called "transportation system management" (TSM)—have particularly been in vogue since the mid-seventies. But a host of factors—some social and institutional, others contextual—make many traditional engineering and traffic management solutions either ineffective or unworkable in suburbia.

Ridesharing, for instance, is an oft-cited prescription for relieving rush-hour congestion. Carpools and vanpools, however, become difficult to arrange in outlying office settings since they restrict participants from tending to midday personal business or running job errands. Upscale, white-collar workers find little incentive to bunch into vans, moreover, when ample free parking—a trademark of most office parks—is readily available. In addition, the residences of employees and individual office destinations tend to be so widely scattered in suburbia that matching carpool participants can seem like an exercise in futility. Indeed, many master-planned suburban office and industrial park developments are being built on such large, expansive scales that they are effectively preordained for drive-alone auto commuting.

Integration of new suburban housing projects with large office complexes could promote other alternatives to solo driving, including ridesharing, cycling, and walking. However, there is often resistance among

TABLE 1.2

Percentage Changes in Principal Means of Travel to Work in the U.S., 1970–80

	Percent of Trips by Mode[1]		Change in Percentage Share
	1970	1980	
Means of Transportation:			
Car, Truck or Van	82.2	84.5	+2.3
Drive Alone	67.2	64.6	−2.6
Carpool[2]	15.0	19.9	+4.9
Public Transportation[3]	7.2	6.0	−1.2
Walk to Work	5.8	5.6	−0.2
Other Means[4]	2.1	1.6	−0.5
Worked at Home	2.7	2.3	−0.4
TOTAL	100.0	100.0	

[1] 1970 census data represent workers 14 years and older. 1980 census data represent workers 16 years of age and over.

[2] Carpool represents private vehicular trips with one or more passengers.

[3] Includes bus, streetcar, rapid rail transit, commuter railroad, and taxicab.

[4] Includes cycling, boat, and air transportation.

Sources: U.S. Department of Commerce, Bureau of the Census, *Census of Population: Journey to Work — Characteristics of Workers in Metropolitan Areas* (Washington: U.S. Bureau of the Census, 1973 and 1984 publications). 1970 data adapted from: U.S. Department of Transportation, Federal Highway Administration, *1969 Nationwide Personal Transportation Study: Mode of Transportation and Personal Characteristics of Tripmakers* (Washington: Federal Highway Administration, Report No. 9, 1973).

developers, some public officials, and even residential neighborhoods to siting homes and workplaces side by side. Traditional Euclidean zoning, whereby land uses are strictly segregated, remains firmly entrenched in suburbia.[26] Moreover, many office park developers are simply not in the housing business, expecting other builders and investors to respond to the housing needs of their tenants' workers. Additionally, while some suburban communities openly embrace new office developments that will beef up local tax coffers, others have been less than receptive to "affordable" housing projects, the popular perception being that they are major drains on public services. Consequently, some suburban municipalities have evolved into major work centers while others have become principally bedroom communities. In many parts of the country, this jobs-housing imbalance is the root cause of rampant increases in intersuburban commuting.

Given the paucity of public funds to build new highways and expand transit services, private-sector financing of major infrastructural improvements could be pursued. While important precedents have recently surfaced in this area, the legal authority for exacting cash contributions from private developers to finance off-site highway construction remains clouded in some states. Developers and businesses certainly realize the vested interest they have in safeguarding the mobility of their employees and customers in addition to promoting orderly suburban growth. However, hammering out a fair and mutually agreeable cost-sharing arrangement between multiple public and private interests can be a Herculean undertaking.

Institutional inertia sometimes also hampers progress in suburbia. Jurisdictional responsibilities among state highway departments, municipal public works offices, regional planning bodies, areawide transit authorities, and other public agencies, for instance, often become blurred in outlying settings. Where they are clearly defined, red tape and project approval delays can discourage even the most strident investors from attempting fresh and imaginative approaches to transportation problem solving. Furthermore, traffic engineering departments and county offices in unincorporated areas and smaller communities are sometimes ill-equipped, in both staff resources and management experience, to take on the traffic problems posed by new large-scale office and industrial developments.

While solving mounting suburban congestion problems will clearly be no simple task, there is cause for optimism. Notably, several exemplary programs are currently underway in suburbia to design office parks with alternatives to the automobile in mind, to build village-like developments that integrate homes and workplaces, to aggressively promote ridesharing, and to spread the burden of costly infrastructure improvements equitably among both private and public interests. Important lessons can be gained by looking closely at these experiences. Without question, suburban office settings represent a new, unexplored frontier for the city planning profession, posing unique challenges as well as unprecedented opportunities to be both proactive and creative. The intent of this book is to contribute in this regard.

Road Map: What's Ahead

The foci of the following chapters are on defining the scope of access and mobility problems posed by large-scale suburban employment growth, and examining what appear to be the most promising approaches toward traffic management in outlying settings. Strategies discussed include: fashioning creative approaches to project site design and land use planning that promote commuting alternatives; introducing assorted transportation management programs, such as ridesharing, flexible work hours, and commuter bus operations; designing appropriate institutional and regulatory responses, such as employer associations and traffic impact ordinances; and exploiting opportunities for joint public-private partnerships for financing highway and transit improvements in suburban growth corridors. Economic, political, and general contextual problems associated with these and other strategies are elaborated upon throughout. In addition, an effort is made to showcase what are considered to be noteworthy examples of progressive site designs, integrated land use planning, and traffic management in suburban office settings.

A balance of empirical and interpretative approaches are used throughout this volume. Recent literature in the fields of land use planning, transportation policy, and economic development offer a rich perspective on a range of suburban mobility topics. These writings form much of the basis for the following work, and are supplemented by both a national survey and in-depth case studies of several large suburban office developments in the United States.

The national survey, conducted in late 1984, sought to elicit firsthand responses from suburban office developers on a range of land use, tenant, and mobility issues related to their projects.[27] Questionnaires were targeted primarily at large suburban office complexes of at least one-half million square feet of floor space from all parts of the United States. Around two-thirds of the office centers surveyed were already completed while the remaining one-third were either being expanded or still under construction. The average size of the 120 office parks from which reasonably complete questionnaires were returned was 2.43 million square feet on a land area of 230 acres.[28] Among the completed projects surveyed, the average labor force was 9,985 employees.[29] The average distance of the surveyed parks to their regional CBDs was 10.7 miles, and the mean population size of the metropolitan areas housing these office complexes was 2.197 million.[30] Thus, although it is difficult to generalize because of considerable sample variation, fairly mammoth developments on the fringes of major U.S. metropolitan areas were largely captured in the survey.

Case studies were also carried out among major suburban office developments in Los Angeles and Orange Counties in Southern California and the San Francisco Bay Area of Northern California. Case sites consisted primarily of "megaprojects," generally much larger and more diversified than suburban office developments found in most areas of the country. While the national survey aimed to describe the scope of office park activities and suburban mobility issues in general terms, the case examinations sought to provide a finer-grain, more focused perspective of what is going on in the field. Interviews with key public and private sector informants, in addition to numerous agency and company reports, provided most of the background materials for case examinations.

Definitional Caveats

When discussing suburban mobility issues, it soon becomes apparent that our existing vocabulary leaves something to be desired. The distinction between what is "suburban" versus what is "urban" has blurred with the passage of time. While some office developments outside of traditional CBDs are on the metropolitan fringes and have distinct suburban characters, others are in fairly built-out areas, sometimes in-filling vacant urban spaces. Still others could be more accurately defined as "exurban"—either situated in the hinterlands or straddled between two expanding metropolises. Partly for convenience, the term "suburban" has been chosen here. It is used loosely, however, and is meant to suggest the location of any land activity outside of a regional CBD, generally at least five or more radial miles away.

Still other definitional shortcomings should be mentioned. There really is no standard, universally accepted term for describing large suburban workplaces occupied by tenants made up of professional and technical employees. Today, expressions like "business park," "executive park," "office park," "R&D park," "technology park," "science park," and even "industrial park" are often used interchangeably. This is, in part, because many developments have a little bit of all of these activities going on. Office complexes often provide sites not only for tenants involved with "paper processing" but also for research and development (R&D), light manufacturing, and business-support services.[31] In the following chapters, the term "office park" is used liberally, and is meant to encompass a wide range of large-scale suburban developments catering to the fastest growing sectors of the nation's economy.[32]

Several distinctions in the types of suburban office developments being built should also be made at the outset. As discussed in Chapter Three, some projects could best be described as large master-planned, campus-style parks. These generally cater to high-technology and R&D firms, and place a high premium on amenities and aesthetics. Others consist of fairly loosely organized collections of individual office buildings, typically with multiple ownerships. Still, the cumulative traffic impacts of these unrelated developments can be every bit as troublesome as their larger, master-planned counterparts, and therefore should not be overlooked. New office developments can also be distinguished on the basis of whether they engage strictly in single-purpose functions, or in multiuse activities. Finally, suburban office complexes often vary in terms of land ownership. Some are under single title while in other cases, multiple interests hold the deed to the land. Many large master-planned projects are owned and operated by development divisions within large corporations, such as insurance companies, or by special joint ventures. Others may be owned by individual land developers, investment companies, or private realtors. Moreover, in some instances developers lease their properties to businesses while in others land is sold outright to individual companies.

In closing, a mosaic of office developments now populates America's suburban landscape. Some are on the far outskirts while others lie in the gray area between city and suburb. Some are massive campuses while others are collectivities of individual buildings. Perhaps the most generic phrase for describing the location and composition of these developments would be "non-CBD employment centers." For simplicity, however, expressions like "suburban office complex" and "office park" are generally used.

Notes

1. Institute of Real Estate Management, *Office Buildings: Income/Expense Analysis, Downtown and Suburban* (Chicago: Institute of Real Estate Management, 1984).
2. Ibid.
3. Peat, Marwick, Mitchell & Co., "Dallas/Fort Worth Metropolitan Area Market," *Development Review and Outlook 1983-1984* (Washington, D.C.: Urban Land Institute, 1983), p. 163.
4. Jerry Schneider, *Transit and the Polycentric City* (Washington, D.C.: Urban Mass Transportation Administration, U.S. Department of Transportation, 1981).
5. Rice Center, "Houston Metropolitan Area," *Development Review and Outlook 1983-1984* (Washington, D.C.: Urban Land Institute, 1983), p. 182.
6. Thomas Hazlett, "They Built Their Own Highway . . . and Other Tales of Private Land-Use Planning," *Reason* (November 1983), pp. 28-29.
7. Gladstone Associates Inc., "Denver Metropolitan Area Market," *Development Review and Outlook 1983-1984* (Washington, D.C.: Urban Land Institute, 1983), p. 173.

8. "High tech" has become a favorite buzzword of the 1980s. These firms represent the nation's growth industries, sought after by every business park developer in the country. High tech generally refers to light, clean industries, such as those involved in the manufacture of computers, measuring instruments, telecommunications equipment, drugs, electronic components, and laboratory equipment. See: Urban Land Institute, *Development Review and Outlook 1983–1984* (Washington, D.C.: Urban Land Institute, 1983), p. 86.

9. Richard F. Galehouse, "Mixed-Use Centers in Suburban Office Parks," *Urban Land*, Vol. 43, No. 8 (1984), pp. 11–12.

10. C. Kenneth Orski, "Suburban Mobility: The Coming Transportation Crisis?" *Transportation Quarterly*, Vol. 39, No. 2 (1985), p. 286.

11. Lawrence D. Maloney, "America's Suburbs Still Alive and Doing Fine," *U.S. News & World Report* (March 12, 1984), p. 60.

12. Joann S. Lublin, "The Suburban Life: Trees, Grass Plus Noise, Traffic and Pollution," *The Wall Street Journal* (June 20, 1985), p. 29.

13. Neal R. Peirce, "Instant 'Cities' in the Suburbs," *The Boston Globe* (August 19, 1985).

14. Maloney, "America's Suburbs Still Alive and Doing Fine," p. 61.

15. See: Douglas R. Porter, "Research Parks: An Emerging Phenomenon," *Urban Land*, Vol. 43, No. 9 (1984), p. 9; Urban Land Institute, *Development Review and Outlook 1983–1984*, pp. 86–87.

16. One study by the staff of the Congressional Joint Economic Committee ranked factors influencing the location choices of high-technology firms within regions as follows: availability of workers (96.1%); state and local tax structure (85.5%); community attitudes toward business (81.9%); cost of property and construction (78.8%); and good transportation for people (76.1%). Percentages represent the share of respondents that rated the factor either significant or very significant. Good access for materials and products was ranked ninth and proximity to customers was ranked tenth. See: Joint Economic Committee, *Location of High Technology Firms and Regional Economics* (Washington, D.C.: U.S. Government Printing Office, 1982).

17. Office rental rates are generally one-quarter to one-third lower in suburban areas than comparable downtown locations. See: Urban Land Institute, *Development Review and Outlook 1983–1984*, pp. 84–90.

18. Orski, "Suburban Mobility," p. 287.

19. Christopher Conte, "The Explosive Growth of Suburbia Leads to Bumper-to-Bumper Blues," *Wall Street Journal* (April 16, 1985), p. 37.

20. Orski, "Suburban Mobility," pp. 283–84.

21. Elliot Diringer and George Snyder, "Suburbs in Uproar Over Growth-Snarled Traffic," *The San Francisco Chronicle* (October 21, 1985), pp. 1, 4.

22. Ibid., p. 1.

23. U.S. Department of Commerce, Bureau of the Census, *State and Metropolitan Area Data Book* (Washington, D.C.: U.S. Government Printing Office, 1982).

24. Outside of the central city of U.S. metropolitan areas, transit's share of total commuter trips was even lower—4.1 percent. Within central cities, around 9 percent of all journeys to work were by transit in 1980.
25. Orski, "Suburban Mobility," p. 287; and Carole W. Baker, "Tracking Washington's Metro," *American Demographics,* Vol. 5, No. 11 (1983), p. 35.
26. For discussions on standard zoning practices in suburban areas, see: Anthony Downs, *Opening Up the Suburbs* (Washington, D.C.: The Brookings Institution, 1973); and David E. Dowall, *The Suburban Squeeze* (Berkeley: University of California Press, 1984).
27. A total of 310 questionnaires were sent out in the fall of 1984 and 120 were returned, for a respectable response rate of 39 percent. Most survey respondents were either developers, property managers, or leasing agents. Over one-quarter of all surveyed parks were from the states of California and Texas, with other large response rates from North Carolina (9%), Florida (7%), Illinois (7%), Colorado (6%), and Michigan (5%). A little over one-third of all surveyed parks were comprised solely of office uses. The remainder tended to be predominantly office functions, with some light industrial and research and development (R&D) uses. Only 10 percent of the parks had a majority of their floorspace devoted to R&D.
28. The variation in both of these statistics was significant. The standard deviations for building space and land area were 5.25 million square feet and 335 acres, respectively.
29. Variation in this statistic was also high. The standard deviation was 17,460 employees.
30. These statistics were also quite variable, with standard deviations of 7.4 miles (from the regional CBD) and 1.985 million persons (population size).
31. The major differences between high-technology parks and office/mixed-use complexes are mainly qualitative. In the former, site plans, conditions, and covenants are usually rigorous and designed for development appropriate for scientific pursuits. Office/mixed-use parks, on the other hand, are usually designed to appeal to a broad range of tenants, including certain high-technology firms. See: Porter, "Research Parks: An Emerging Phenomenon," p. 7.
32. The word "park" generally suggests an openness in the spacing of buildings within a project. Not all suburban office developments are park-like, although the clear design trend over the past decade has been in this direction. See Chapter Three for a discussion of office park design issues.

2

America's Growth Regions

DEMOGRAPHIC, ECONOMIC, AND COMMUTING TRENDS

Burgeoning Metropolises

For the past two decades, the nation's economic epicenter has been drifting in a southerly and westerly direction. The lower cost of doing business coupled with favorable weather and environmental conditions have lured thousands of companies, investors, and job seekers to America's sunbelt crescent. Major metropolises in Texas, Florida, and California have enjoyed particularly prosperous times. Interregional shifts in labor, capital, and investments to these states since the sixties have produced extremely healthy and vibrant local economies, exemplified by the meteoric rise in white-collar, office employment. America's political power base has likewise swung to the South and West. The states of Florida, Texas, and California, for example, picked up nine representatives in the 1982 reapportionment of congressional seats. In total, the nation's southern and western tier states took away 16 congressional votes from the snowbelt that year.

Moreover, sunbelt cities seem to be sustaining this growth posture during the eighties. Between 1980 and 1983, population growth in all 17 of the major metropolitan areas located in the South and West, with the exception of Portland, Oregon, outpaced all major areas in the North.[1] The only two metropolitan areas outside of the South and West to grow faster than the national average during the early 1980s were Washington, D.C. and Minneapolis/St. Paul.

Within booming sunbelt and western regions, the suburbs, and accretions beyond, have been the major recipients of growth in general, and prodigious office and new home building in particular. To further probe how this could affect regional mobility, this chapter examines pertinent demo-

graphic, economic, and commuting trends in the suburban spheres of 12 of
the nation's fastest growing standard metropolitan statistical areas
(SMSAs):[2] Atlanta; Dallas-Ft. Worth; Denver; Houston; Los Angeles-Long
Beach; Orange County, California; Phoenix; San Diego; San Francisco-
Oakland; San Jose; Seattle; and Tampa-St. Petersburg. All 12 have metropolitan populations above one million, and represent the very largest
SMSAs in the South and West.[3] It should be noted that there really is no
clean distinction between what is a suburb and what is not in any of these
areas. The U.S. Census Bureau simply designates parts of an SMSA either
as "central city" or "not in central city," the former comprising the official
boundaries of the most populous municipality and in the case of twin cities,
the second largest municipality as well. This dichotomy unfortunately does
not always provide an accurate portrayal of what is urban versus suburban.
The Los Angeles SMSA offers a case in point. Open fields in the San Fernando Valley some thirty miles from downtown Los Angeles are counted as
part of the "central city" in census tabulations because they are within the
corporate limits. Beverly Hills and Culver City, however, are treated as
being outside of the central city because they are separate jurisdictions,
despite the fact that both are highly urbanized and closer to Los Angeles's
CBD than most of the city's own neighborhoods.

Notwithstanding these definitional problems, useful insights into mobility issues can still be gained by examining assorted demographic and commuting trends taking place on the fringes of these twelve SMSAs. This is
followed by a discussion of current traffic conditions around major suburban
office parks throughout the United States. Modal preferences of today's
suburban office workers are also examined.

The Demography of Suburbia

Table 2.1 highlights the explosive suburban growth experienced by the 12
selected southern and western SMSAs during the seventies. On average,
total population increased three times faster in these metropolitan areas
between 1970 and 1980 than for the nation as a whole. Tampa and Phoenix
grew the most percentage-wise, while Houston outgained all others in absolute terms (nearly one million new residents).

With the exceptions of Los Angeles and San Francisco, moreover, all
these areas decentralized more rapidly during the seventies than the nation
at large. When one considers the relatively large suburban population base
that already existed in 1970 in these areas, recent gains are all the more

TABLE 2.1

Population Changes: 1970–1980
Total SMSA and Suburban Populations

SMSA	Total Population			Percent Living Outside of Central City		
	1970	1980	% Change	1970	1980	Change in %
Atlanta	1,390,164	2,029,710	+46.00	58.6	74.6	+16.0
Dallas	2,318,036	2,974,805	+28.33	46.6	56.7	+10.1
Denver	1,227,529	1,620,902	+32.15	58.1	64.9	+6.8
Houston	1,985,031	2,905,353	+46.42	38.0	45.1	+7.1
Los Angeles	7,037,075	7,477,503	+6.30	54.2	54.3	+0.1
Orange County	1,420,386	1,932,709	+36.12	68.3	76.5	+8.2
Phoenix	956,572	1,509,052	+56.07	35.7	45.1	+9.4
San Diego	1,357,854	1,861,846	+37.10	45.4	51.2	+5.8
San Jose	1,064,714	1,295,071	+21.64	50.3	57.2	+6.9
San Francisco	3,109,519	3,250,630	+4.57	65.4	65.7	+0.3
Seattle	1,421,869	1,607,469	+13.11	58.9	65.9	+7.0
Tampa	1,012,594	1,569,134	+58.00	51.2	67.5	+16.3
12 SMSA Average [1]	2,117,159	2,587,732	+32.15	52.7	60.4	+7.7
U.S. [2]	203,211,916	226,545,805	+11.54	42.3	44.2	+1.9

[1] Nonweighted average of 12 SMSAs.

[2] Total U.S. population and percentage of population living outside of central cities.

Source: U.S. Department of Commerce, Bureau of the Census, *Census of Population: General Population Characteristics, United States Summary* (Washington: U.S. Government Printing Office, 1973 and 1983).

impressive. The most dramatic suburban growth occurred in Tampa, Atlanta, and Dallas. On average, over 60 percent of the total SMSA population currently lives outside of the central city in all 12 case areas, compared to a national figure of 44 percent.

This suburbanization wave has continued unabated into the 1980s. The five fastest growing large metropolitan areas in the country between 1980 and 1983 have been Houston, Dallas, Tampa, Phoenix, and Denver, all with annual growth rates over 2.7 percent and all exploding on their urban perimeters. Suburbanization, moreover, seems to have picked up momentum in most sections of the country during the eighties. Among the 36 U.S. metropolitan areas over one million population, their suburbs grew at an annual rate of 1.25 percent from 1980 to 1983; by comparison, their major central cities grew at a much slower 0.42 percent pace.[4]

In terms of other demographic characteristics—such as population density, household size, and family income levels—the 12 metropolises appear quite similar to other urbanized areas around the country.[5] Table 2.2 indicates that these case areas are slightly denser than their urbanized counterparts to the north and east, partly because most have comparatively large average household sizes and partly because, as with most big cities, they have sizable numbers of apartment dwellers. The urbanized portion of Los Angeles County is actually the second most densely settled area of the country, ahead of places like Chicago, Philadelphia, and Detroit.[6] Median family incomes of these 12 areas generally also exceed the national average, although a fair amount of variation exists even among sunbelt cities. At

TABLE 2.2

Summary of 1980 Demographic
Characteristics for Urbanized Areas of SMSAs[1]

SMSA	Population Density[2]	Vehicles/ Household[3]	Persons/ Household	Median Income
Atlanta	1,783	1.6	2.8	$21,509
Dallas	1,915	1.8	2.7	$24,463
Denver	3,080	1.8	2.6	$18,622
Houston	2,300	1.9	2.8	$24,463
Los Angeles & Orange County	5,188	1.7	2.8	$22,049
Phoenix	2,198	1.8	2.7	$20,545
San Diego	2,790	1.7	2.7	$20,095
San Francisco	4,009	1.5	2.5	$24,599
San Jose	3,816	1.9	2.8	$26,695
Seattle	2,874	1.7	2.6	$24,930
Tampa	2,621	1.5	2.5	$16,543
11 SMSA Average[4]	2,961	1.7	2.7	$22,228
U.S. Average	2,676	1.5	2.8	$21,243

[1] An urbanized area consists of a central city or cities, and surrounding closely settled territory ("urban fringe"), as defined by the U.S. Census Bureau.

[2] Total population per square mile of urbanized land.

[3] Total vehicles, including automobiles, trucks, vans, and motorcycles.

[4] Nonweighted average for 11 SMSAs.

Source: Carlos G. Rodriguez, et al., *Transportation Planning Data for Urbanized Areas* (Washington: Federal Highway Administration, U.S. Department of Transportation, 1985).

the lower end of the earnings scale is Tampa-St. Petersburg, where median yearly annual household income falls nearly $5,000 below the national average. The high proportion of retirees and pensioners living on Florida's gulf coast heavily skews this figure, however.

Since 1970, it should be added, suburban populations throughout America have become increasingly heterogeneous. No longer do middle-age, middle-class, Anglo families characterize America's urban outskirts. A 1979 Urban Institute study called "The Graying of Suburbia" reported that the number of elderly households in suburbia rose by nearly one-third between 1970 and 1976 while the number in central cities grew by only 10 percent.[7] And contrary to popular myth, the study found that most retirees are not flocking to sunbelt states, but rather they are moving across town in search of tranquil suburbs, just as other Americans. By 1980, 48 percent of Americans 62 or older resided in the suburbs.[8] The Urban Institute report projected that, under these trends, America's suburbs would have as many elderly residents as its central cities by the mid-eighties.

The ethnic composition of suburbia, moreover, is becoming as diverse as many older core cities. From 1970 to 1980, black population in the suburbs rose by 1.84 million (59.1%), outstripping the rates of suburban white increase (24.0%) and black increase in central cities (5.3%) over the same period.[9] Today, over one-quarter of America's nonrural blacks live along the urban fringes. Several suburbs collaring both Chicago and Los Angeles, in fact, have become predominantly minority communities over the past 15 years. For instance, Harvey, Illinois, a minority enclave west of Chicago, grew from a black population of 6.8 percent in 1960 to 65.6 percent in 1980. More often than not, however, minority-dominated suburbs have failed to attain the same level of affluency as their largely white counterparts.[10] All 20 of the most economically distressed suburbs outside of Los Angeles, for example, are predominantly minority enclaves. Among the many factors fueling the changing ethnic mix of suburban communities have been the availability of inexpensive housing, displacement of families from gentrified inner city neighborhoods, racial steering, panic peddling by realtors, and exurban white flight.[11]

In general, suburbs are undergoing a "second wave" of in-migration radically different from the movement that gave them birth in the 1940s and 1950s. Since the early 1970s, we have been witnessing a citification of the suburbs.[12] Some older, close-in suburbs, in fact, are virtually indistinguishable from their central city neighbors, beset with similar problems of crime, unemployment, blight, and disaffection. Many of the traditional, large-lot residential suburbs of yesteryear have been pushed out onto a fairly amorphous outer ring beyond the older, inner-tier ones. In some cases, close-in, middle-class, predominantly white enclaves have managed to preserve their cultural homogeneity through exclusionary zoning practices and political maneuvering. Although there are no firm statistics available, many new suburban complexes, like executive parks, seem to be favoring these outer-tier, more affluent suburban settings.

Employment in Growth Regions

Employment growth in the 12 case SMSAs has been just as impressive as population gains (Table 2.3). Overall, the number of jobs grew about twice as fast during the seventies in the 12 areas as it did for the nation as a

TABLE 2.3

Employment Totals and Concentrations
Outside of Central Cities, 1970–80

SMSA	Total Employment			Percent of Employment Outside of Central City		
	1970	1980	% Change	1970	1980	Change in %
Atlanta	587,708	966,935	64.53	64.4	81.9	+17.5
Dallas	976,077	1,488,947	52.54	45.2	56.7	+11.5
Denver	492,961	819,770	66.30	51.3	65.1	+13.8
Houston	797,421	1,448,657	81.67	35.3	42.9	+7.6
Los Angeles	2,826,565	3,471,764	22.83	54.3	55.1	+0.8
Orange County	544,313	974,845	79.10	67.8	72.1	+4.3
Phoenix	362,156	663,624	83.24	36.4	44.7	+8.3
San Diego	430,495	756,400	75.70	41.2	52.6	+5.4
San Francisco	1,267,643	1,592,892	25.66	63.9	69.5	+5.6
San Jose	409,077	661,063	61.60	60.5	53.4	−7.1
Seattle	556,755	791,049	42.08	55.7	65.4	+9.7
Tampa	346,353	613,308	77.08	50.1	66.4	+16.3
12 SMSA Average [1]	841,016	1,239,631	59.57	52.2	60.5	+8.3
U.S.	76,852,389	96,617,296	25.73	35.6	47.7	+12.1

[1] Nonweighted average of 12 SMSAs.

Source: U.S. Department of Commerce, Bureau of the Census, *Census of Population: Social and Economic Characteristics* (Washington: U.S. Government Printing Office, 1973 and 1983).

whole. Phoenix, Houston, and Orange County enjoyed the healthiest gains. Moreover, the share of total regional jobs outside the central city rose in all but one of the 12 SMSAs, the exception being San Jose. There, the shrinkage in suburban share of jobs can be attributed to the ongoing high-tech employment boom of the Silicon Valley, much of which has occurred within San Jose's northern city limits. The vast majority of San Jose's growth since the early seventies, however, could nonetheless be characterized as sprawling, low-rise office development.[13]

Table 2.4 further highlights the ascendancy of suburbia as the preferred office employment location in most of the 12 SMSAs. Particularly in

TABLE 2.4

Changes in Office-Related Employment
In and Outside of Central City, 1970–80

SMSA	Percent of Change in Office-Related[1] Employment, 1970–80	
	Inside of Central City	*Outside of Central City*
Atlanta	−16.4	109.2
Dallas	20.5	91.3
Denver	19.4	110.8
Houston	60.4	120.6
Los Angeles	20.7	24.6
Orange County	55.7	90.5
Phoenix	59.5	124.7
San Diego	57.8	95.7
San Francisco	6.1	36.7
San Jose	90.7	42.6
Seattle	10.9	66.9
Tampa	19.2	134.8
12 SMSA Average[2]	33.7	87.8
U.S.[3]	15.0	115.9

[1] Office-related is defined as those Standard Industrial Classification (SIC) codes in services, retail, light manufacturing, and associated industries.

[2] Nonweighted average of 12 SMSAs.

[3] All U.S. SMSAs.

Source: U.S. Department of Commerce, Bureau of the Census, *Census of Population: Social and Economic Characteristics* (Washington: U.S. Government Printing Office, 1973 and 1983).

Tampa-St. Petersburg, Atlanta, Denver, Houston, and Phoenix, suburban office employment flourished throughout the seventies at the expense of their respective downtowns. In the case of Phoenix, of the SMSA's 21 million square feet of privately owned, multitenant office space, only two million square feet have been built downtown. Although the city of Phoenix has actively pursued downtown redevelopment, no new office buildings were constructed during the late seventies or early eighties. In contrast, Phoenix's northern suburban corridor witnessed the addition of four new office towers, totaling 1.3 million square feet during 1982–83.

While these statistics bode favorably for the economic future of suburbia in these 12 metropolises, it should be noted that office employment grew even more precipitously in other nondowntown settings across the country. New white-collar jobs were particularly plentiful on the fringes of a number of smaller metropolitan areas in the 250,000 to one million range. For example, office employment in the suburbs of Des Moines, Norfolk-Virginia Beach, Memphis, and Tulsa rose by 112 percent, 126 percent, 154 percent, and 166 percent respectively during the seventies. The most sensational gains were in Austin—from 15,000 to 86,000 jobs in just ten years, a 465 percent increase. Among the 36 U.S. metropolitan areas of one million or more population, however, the suburban work force of the 12 case areas grew substantially more than the rest. Additionally, it should be noted that the averages shown in Table 2.4 are suppressed by the inclusion of California cities, in particular Los Angeles and San Francisco, both of which have reached fairly mature stages of their growth cycles compared to the other case areas. Excluding west coast cities from Table 2.4, the average change in suburban office-related employment during the seventies was 125 percent, above the national average.

The Geography of Suburban Commuting

As discussed in the previous chapter, the bulk of work trips within SMSAs both begin and end in the suburbs. Table 2.5 shows that this preeminence in suburb-to-suburb commuting holds for all four regions of the country. Intersuburban travel is actually most prominent in the Northeast, owing largely to the enormous amount of cross-town and interstate travel throughout the greater New York metropolitan area. The South has the highest share of the traditional suburb-to-central city radial commuting, while the highest incidences of reverse commuting can be found in the Pacific states.

Table 2.6 discloses trends from 1970 through 1980 in intrametropolitan as well as suprametropolitan travel for the 12 case areas, broken down by place of residence within each SMSA.[14] The table reveals that the shares of trips destined to suburbs—reverse commutes and suburb-to-suburb journeys—rose in nearly all of the 12 case areas. Long haul trips from suburbia to places outside of SMSAs likewise jumped during the seventies in most places. Correspondingly, the role of inner-city trip making dropped sharply in almost all study areas. Only in the cases of Atlanta and Tampa did commuting shares within central cities rise.

Several areas recorded particularly significant increases in reverse commuting, notably Dallas, Orange County, and San Jose. Orange County also sustained high rates of intermetropolitan commuting during the seventies. In 1980, nearly 25 percent of Orange County's employed residents commuted to surrounding counties, with 18 percent going to neighboring Los Angeles County. Atlanta, Dallas, and San Jose experienced the greatest gains in suburb-to-suburb commuting during the decade. The Atlanta region also stands out for its increasingly insular pattern of commuting—residents within Atlanta's city limits are making relatively more intraurban journeys whereas those living outside of the city proper have stepped up their intersuburban travels. Dallas, moreover, witnessed the largest increases in commuting between its suburbs and exurbs (i.e., areas outside of the SMSA), while Los Angeles registered equally dramatic declines in suprametropolitan travel (i.e., to and from different SMSAs).

TABLE 2.5

1980 Work Trip Patterns Within SMSAs
for Different Regions of the U.S.

Region of U.S.	Percentage of Total Work Trips within SMSA			
	Central City to Central City	Central City to Suburb[1]	Suburb to Central City	Suburb to Suburb[1]
Northeast	32.2	4.7	15.3	47.8
North Central	30.7	7.0	20.3	49.0
South	36.1	6.1	23.7	40.1
West	32.4	9.3	19.9	38.4
Total U.S.	33.1	6.7	20.1	40.1

[1] Suburb represents all areas in SMSA outside of the central city.

Source: U.S. Department of Commerce, Bureau of the Census, *1980 Census of Population: Journey to Work – Metropolitan Commuting Flows* (Washington: U.S. Government Printing Office, 1984).

TABLE 2.6

Changes in Commuting Patterns Within and Between Central City and Other Locations, 1970-80

SMSA	Percent of Central City Residents Commuting						Percent of Residents Living Outside of Central City Commuting					
	Inside Central City		to Outside of Central City[1]		to Outside of SMSA		to Central City		Outside Central City[1]		to Outside of SMSA	
	1970	1980	1970	1980	1970	1980	1970	1980	1970	1980	1970	1980
Atlanta	69.2	73.3	18.4	14.6	12.4	12.1	36.2	26.9	62.7	68.3	1.1	4.8
Dallas	81.2	74.9	11.1	18.7	7.7	6.4	41.7	30.9	54.7	60.1	3.6	9.0
Denver	78.3	75.5	14.9	16.4	6.8	8.1	41.2	38.6	58.7	61.0	0.1	0.4
Houston	78.4	77.5	7.4	8.2	14.2	14.3	40.4	43.8	59.5	54.0	0.1	2.2
Los Angeles	63.5	63.8	22.9	24.2	13.6	12.0	16.3	19.4	76.0	79.8	7.7	0.8
Orange County	44.5	40.9	29.0	34.8	26.5	24.3	19.9	19.2	65.0	69.3	15.1	11.5
Phoenix	78.6	74.5	13.0	14.9	8.4	10.6	26.8	26.4	73.2	72.9	.0	0.7
San Diego	78.2	73.1	14.0	12.7	7.8	14.2	29.5	30.2	70.4	69.4	0.1	0.4
San Francisco	75.6	73.4	11.1	13.2	13.3	13.4	25.8	28.7	67.6	66.0	6.6	5.3
San Jose	46.5	42.6	36.2	41.5	17.3	15.9	15.7	8.2	84.2	91.5	0.1	8.5
Seattle	80.8	77.4	12.6	15.3	6.6	7.3	41.4	36.1	58.2	60.8	0.4	3.1
Tampa	73.3	75.2	16.3	18.9	10.4	5.9	32.3	29.6	67.4	66.9	0.3	3.5
12 SMSA Average[2]	70.7	68.5	17.2	19.5	12.1	12.0	30.4	27.3	66.4	68.5	3.2	4.2
U.S.[3]	80.7	71.8	15.2	14.5	4.1	13.7	32.8	28.0	59.4	55.8	7.8	16.2

[1] Outside of the central city but within the SMSA.

[2] Nonweighted average of the 12 SMSAs.

[3] All U.S. SMSAs.

Source: U.S. Department of Commerce, Bureau of the Census, *Census of Population: Journey to Work – Metropolitan Commuting Flows* (Washington: U.S. Government Printing Office, 1973 and 1984).

Combined, these trends suggest that trip patterns in America's most prosperous regions are becoming much more varied and complex. Symmetric, star-shaped commute paths, long a hallmark of America's cities, have been replaced by a patchwork quilt of intrametropolitan travel. No longer does commuting follow a distinct directional orientation; heavy rush traffic, once the dubious privilege of downtown motorists, now impinges everyone to some degree. For many, the days of a leisurely contra-flow commute are fast coming to a close. Along the Katy (I-10W) and Gulf Freeways (I-45S) in Houston, for instance, inbound and outbound traffic volumes are today virtually identical during both the A.M. and P.M. peaks.[15] With over 400 new automobiles being added to the streets of Houston each day, clogged arteries and congested freeways are virtually assured during rush hours in almost any part of the SMSA.

Not only are Houstonians plagued with "ubiquitous congestion," they, along with Dallas commuters, are chalking up more miles to get to and from work than anywhere in the country. The per capita miles of daily vehicular travel in Houston and Dallas were 20.7 and 21.6 respectively in 1980. This compares to a per capita average of 16.5 miles for all 12 case areas and 14.2 miles for all 366 U.S. urbanized areas.

The trend toward trip diffusion is most graphically shown by tracing changes in the origins and destinations of journeys over time. Figures 2.1 and 2.2 show that the web-like commuting pattern for work trips destined to the burgeoning community of Pleasanton, California, 35 miles east of San Francisco, has expanded noticeably in just three years. In 1981, most journeys to work originated in the nearby Livermore Valley to the east (Figure 2.1). The second figure reveals that by 1984, commuting patterns to Pleasanton's Hacienda Business Park—a mammoth 860 acre mixed-use complex that employed 3,000 workers at the time—were much more spread out and multidirectional. Notably, the outer boundaries of Pleasanton's commute-shed has spilled over into Marin County and other North Bay locales. Although only around one-third of all Pleasanton workers were captured in the 1984 travel survey, it is clear that commute trips destined there increasingly resemble what physicists call Brownian motion—they are geographically random and go in all directions.[16]

Urban Versus Suburban Commuting: Which is Faster?

Accompanying the sprawl of U.S. cities over the past several decades has been a lengthening of average commuter travel times. Between 1970 and 1980, for instance, the mean time to get to work increased from 23 minutes

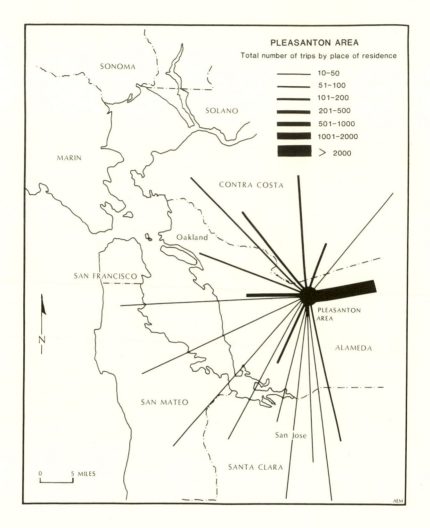

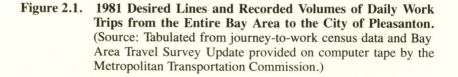

Figure 2.1.   1981 Desired Lines and Recorded Volumes of Daily Work Trips from the Entire Bay Area to the City of Pleasanton. (Source: Tabulated from journey-to-work census data and Bay Area Travel Survey Update provided on computer tape by the Metropolitan Transportation Commission.)

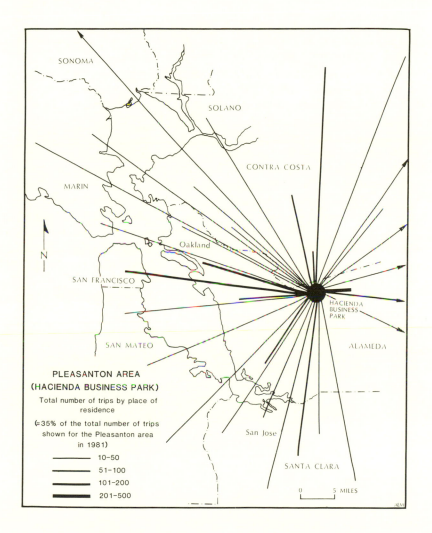

Figure 2.2. 1984 Desired Lines and Recorded Volumes of Daily Work Trips from the Entire Bay Area to the Hacienda Business Park.
(Source: Employee travel survey data provided by the Hacienda Business Park Owners Association.)

to 26 minutes (14%) in Atlanta, and from 21 minutes to 26 minutes in the San Francisco Bay Area (24%). Nationwide, average commuting times rose from 22 minutes to 24 minutes (9%) during the seventies.

Although suburbanites generally commute longer distances than their central city coworkers, they often do so at faster average speeds so that the total time both groups spend behind the wheel is nearly equal. Table 2.7 shows that, in 1980, for the nation as a whole, the typical surburban motorist traveled over three miles farther to get to work than the average city-dweller, but at speeds of over 5 mph faster. On average, urban commuters beat their suburban counterparts to work by only one minute. (Within any single modal category, however, central city residents generally got to work at least three minutes faster than suburbanites; the comparability of travel time for all modes combined largely reflects the fact that urban commuters patronize slower bus transit modes far more frequently than suburbanites.) The longest commuting times were experienced by those suburbanites who opted for public transportation, reflecting the lengthy waits associated with scheduled bus service in low-density areas.

TABLE 2.7

1980 Journey-to-Work Distance, Travel Time, and Speed Statistics for the United States, by Place of Residence Within SMSAs

	Average Distance (miles)		Average Travel Time (minutes)		Average Travel Speed (mph)	
	Central City	Noncentral City	Central City	Noncentral City	Central City	Noncentral City
Automobile/Truck	9.4	12.7	20.5	23.4	27.5	32.6
Drive Alone	8.8	11.8	24.7	29.0	21.4	24.4
Carpool	11.7	16.4	19.5	22.0	36.0	44.7
Public Transportation	9.0	20.0	39.9	48.7	13.5	24.6
All Modes[1]	8.8	12.6	23.1	24.2	22.9	31.2

[1] In addition to automobile/truck and public transportation modes, this category includes cycling, motorcycle, walk, and other means of travel.

Sources: U.S. Department of Commerce, Bureau of the Census, *1980 Census of Population: Journey to Work — Characteristics of Workers in Metropolitan Areas* (Washington: U.S. Government Printing Office, 1984). 1980 distance and speed data were adapted from: U.S. Department of Commerce, Bureau of the Census, *The Journey to Work in the United States* (Washington: U.S. Government Printing Office, Current Population Reports, 1982).

On the whole, the regional dispersal of trips has been a mixed blessing to the average commuter. He tends to travel farther, however a smaller share of his time is generally being spent in frustrating, slow-moving traffic. The disadvantage of traditional downtown-focused radial commuting is that it results in "trip convergence"—motorists from the outskirts are funneled into the same geographically limited space, producing traffic standstills. With dispersal, trips tend to be more circuitous, however the multidestinational commute patterns help to free up downtown traffic snarls. Yet, as employment activities continue to intensify along the urban fringes, many new confluence points will emerge. And with this, the speed advantages of intersuburban commuting could quickly become a relic of the past. With time, new traffic equilibriums are likely to be reached whereby the shorter commute distances afforded by the relocation of jobs to close-by suburban residences will be offset by slower home-to-office travel speeds.

Modal Commuting Trends

With the steady decentralization of jobs and housing, it is no surprise that the private automobile reigns supreme as the preferred mode of passenger travel in the nation's most rapidly growing metropolises, and by a wide margin (Table 2.8). Unlike most other areas of the country, however, the share of total trips has actually been shifting slightly from the automobile to public transportation modes in Los Angeles, Orange County, San Jose, and Seattle. In contrast, every SMSA in the North Central region of the country lost transit patrons during the seventies, the only exception being Minneapolis-St. Paul. This is not to suggest that diesel buses have won the affections of southerners and westerners, however. Slight gains in transit's modal share, although against the grain of national trends, are fairly inconsequential in real terms since ridership levels have historically been low in the South and West to begin with. Among the 12 case areas, only San Francisco and Atlanta (both of which have modern rapid rail systems), along with Seattle, presently have transit usage rates appreciably above the national average.

At the other end of the modal spectrum are Houston, Dallas, and Tampa—each with more than 90 percent of all commuter trips made by the private automobile and rapidly dwindling transit ridership levels. Annual bus patronage declined by over 15 million riders in these three areas during the 1970s. Houston does, however, enjoy comparatively high rates of carpooling, with 22 percent of its daily vehicular work trips involving one or more passengers (compared to a national average of 18 percent for urban-

TABLE 2.8
Modal Breakdowns
Of Commuter Trips, 1970–80

SMSA	Private Vehicle			Public Transportation[1]			Other[2]		
	1970	1980	Change in %	1970	1980	Change in %	1970	1980	Change in %
Atlanta	84.6	88.3	+3.7	9.4	7.6	-1.8	6.0	4.1	-1.9
Dallas	88.0	91.8	+3.8	5.2	3.4	-1.8	6.8	4.8	-2.0
Denver	85.2	85.5	+0.3	4.4	6.1	+1.7	10.4	8.4	-2.0
Houston	86.9	91.9	+5.0	5.4	3.0	-2.4	7.7	5.1	-2.4
Los Angeles	85.9	85.5	-0.4	5.5	7.0	+1.5	8.6	7.5	-1.1
Orange County	92.5	90.9	-1.6	0.3	2.1	+1.8	7.2	7.0	-0.2
Phoenix	88.9	89.1	+0.2	1.2	2.0	+0.8	9.9	8.9	-1.0
San Diego	75.8	81.2	+5.4	4.2	3.3	-0.9	20.0	15.5	-4.5
San Francisco	73.5	73.7	+0.2	15.2	16.4	+1.2	11.3	9.9	-1.4
San Jose	88.7	89.0	-0.3	2.3	3.1	+0.8	9.0	7.9	-1.1
Seattle	83.5	82.1	-1.4	7.1	9.6	+2.5	9.4	8.3	-1.1
Tampa	87.6	90.4	+2.8	3.1	1.8	-1.3	9.3	7.8	-1.5
12 SMSA Average[3]	84.8	86.2	+1.4	5.5	5.8	+0.3	9.7	7.9	-1.8
U.S.[4]	77.7	84.1	+6.4	8.9	6.4	-2.5	9.4	7.9	-1.2

[1] Includes bus, rail transit, railroads, and taxicab modes.

[2] Includes bicycle, walk, and other modes as well as residents who work at home.

[3] Nonweighted average of 12 SMSAs.

[4] All U.S. SMSAs.

Sources: U.S. Department of Commerce, Bureau of the Census, *Census of Population: Journey to Work – Characteristics of Workers in Metropolitan Areas* (Washington: U.S. Government Printing Office, 1973 and 1984).

ized areas). Still, carpooling rates seem to be either declining or stabilizing in almost all the 12 case areas. On average, peak hour vehicle occupancy levels dropped from 1.14 to 1.13 (0.2%) during the seventies in these 12 areas, compared to a decline among all the nation's SMSAs from 1.18 to 1.15 (2.5%).

Table 2.8 also reveals that cycling and walking to work consistently declined in all 12 areas during the seventies. The largest drop-off was in San Diego. Still, more than 15 percent of all journeys to work there are made by nonvehicular modes. The popularity of walking and cycling among San Diegans can be partly attributed to the area's large concentration of enlisted personnel, many of whom live either on a military base or close by.

Finally, changes in the geographic distribution of different commuter modes within SMSAs are also worth noting. In most places, both auto and transit usage have risen in the suburbs and remained fairly stagnant (or declined) elsewhere.[17] Nationwide, the percent of transit users who live in the suburbs rose from 25 percent to 30 percent during the seventies. Every large SMSA in the South and West, with the exceptions of San Antonio, Ft. Lauderdale, and New Orleans, experienced a drop in central city ridership and a corresponding increase in suburban usage during the seventies.[18] This flip-flop largely reflects the redeployment of bus services from central cities to outlying areas by many regional transit authorities during the seventies, a maneuver used to gain the taxing support of wealthier suburban communities.

The shifting of transit's market to the South and West as well as the metropolitan fringes provides new, untapped frontiers for industrywide innovation. Traditionally, America's transit bosses have viewed suburbia as forbidden territory. The vast majority of bus operators in this country continue to offer fixed-route, radial services focusing on downtown hubs, with an occasional foray to an outlying shopping mall. Yet, the congregation of employment and retail activities along the urban fringes of many booming metropolises presents a unique opportunity for the transit industry to carve out a new niche for itself. In particular, employment subcenters offer natural intercept points for building coordinated networks of converging transit routes. The potential role transit could play in vitiating suburban traffic problems is discussed in more detail in Chapter Four.

Traffic Conditions Around Suburban Office Complexes

While census statistics offer useful insights into suburban travel trends in general, they do not really say much specifically about traffic conditions and access issues around major outlying employment centers, such as business and office parks. Indeed, there are plenty of anecdotal accounts of chronic "arterialsclerosis" around mushrooming suburban office complexes. Words like "nightmarish" and "nerve-wrenching" have become part of the lexicon used to describe spot rush-hour traffic conditions around outlying mini-CBDs such as Tysons Corner, Virginia and west Los Angeles.[19] In Houston, "Texas-size traffic jams" has become a favorite cliche, both downtown and on the outskirts.[20] Do such conditions characterize most of the nation's suburban office settings today?

The national survey of 120 large-scale suburban office developments sheds some light on this. Around two-thirds of surveyed office developers and managers described current rush-hour traffic conditions on nearby roadways as either moderately or heavily congested. Nearly 25 percent felt traffic was fairly light, while 9 percent perceived there were no access or circulation problems at all. Overall, it seems that as of the mid-eighties, most suburban office park settings are operating at tolerable congestion levels during peak hours, what traffic engineers typically call the gray zone between Level of Service D and E—i.e., somewhere between 85 percent and 95 percent of roadway capacity. In that nearly one-third of the surveyed complexes have yet to reach buildout and the vast majority expect higher future employment levels both on-site and nearby, traffic conditions can only be expected to deteriorate over time in many of these settings.

Congestion levels, of course, primarily reflect the quality of existing roadway facilities surrounding suburban work centers, in addition to factors such as the incidence of employee ridesharing and transit usage. Among the surveyed developments, either controlled-access freeways or major four-lane arterials[21] provided the primary access linkage to two-thirds of the office parks' entrances. Almost one-half of those sampled indicated there was a major freeway nearby, regardless whether or not it served as the main thoroughfare leading into the complex. Overall, 80 percent of the developers/managers surveyed felt that current roadway access was generally adequate. Most did, however, indicate that some additional highway improvements would likely be necessary to handle future ingress and egress to their complexes.

To no surprise, the survey revealed that the overwhelming majority of employees commuting to suburban office developments drive alone to work. On average, 85 percent are solo commuters, with the remaining 15 percent generally pooling with coworkers. As discussed in Chapter Four, there are a number of significant exceptions to this dominance in single-occupancy commuting to suburban work centers, such as the Fluor Corporation compound in Irvine, California where company-sponsored vanpool services prosper. Still, the vast majority of suburban workplaces today are reached almost exclusively by employees driving alone.

Summary

Census trends over the decade of the seventies offer graphic evidence of the suburbs' emergence as a veritable beehive of business and commerce. Particularly within fast growing sunbelt and west coast metropolises, the urban fringes have become powerful magnets for luring new start-up industries as well as longstanding corporate giants seeking more attractive working environments. Socially and culturally, suburbs have also matured, attracting a wider cross-section of Americana and replacing its squeaky-clean, antiseptic image of years past with a more contemporary, urbane persona. No longer can they be called, as one author put it sixty years ago, merely "a footnote to urban civilization."[22] Indeed, many of the same problems plaguing our urban centers have transcended city boundaries. The "urbanization of the suburbs," a topic that inspired an exploratory volume of writing in the early 1970s,[23] seems to have fully blossomed in the mid-eighties.

The mobility implications of urbanized suburbs are profound. A labyrinth of commute patterns now characterizes our cityscapes, casting serious doubts over the future of conventional bus transit and other shared-ride modes of transportation. Despite some recent gains in transit usage in the western United States, all signs point to greater auto reliance in the future. Only a ubiquitous transportation mode that emulates the interconnectivity of a telephone network, some argue, can thrive in an environment of scattered trip ends, namely the auto-highway combination.[24] Around a growing list of suburban office parks, congestion already seems to be approaching barely tolerable levels. This situation can only be expected to worsen as the suburban building craze continues unabated throughout the eighties and into the nineties. As to what policies and programs might be introduced to safeguard suburban mobility, we turn to the next two chapters.

Notes

1. Richard L. Forstall and Donald E. Starsinic, "The Largest U.S. Metropolitan Areas," *Urban Land*, Vol. 43, No. 9 (1984), pp. 32–33; and U.S. Department of Commerce, Bureau of the Census, *Statistical Abstracts of the United States: 1985* (Washington, D.C.: U.S. Government Printing Office, 1984), p. 21.

2. SMSA, or Standard Metropolitan Statistical Area, represents the U.S. Bureau of the Census's classification of a large population nucleus and those adjacent communities that are economically and socially integrated with that nucleus. Each SMSA has one or more central counties containing the area's main urbanized concentration of at least 50,000 inhabitants. Outlying counties with close social and economic ties are also considered part of SMSAs where certain minimal standards regarding population density and urban population are met.

3. The only other southern and western SMSAs above one million population in 1980 not included in this list are Miami and New Orleans, both fairly mature metropolises by sunbelt standards.

4. Forstall and Starsinic, "The Largest U.S. Metropolitan Areas," p. 33; and U.S. Department of Commerce, Bureau of the Census, *Statistical Abstracts of the United States: 1985*, p. 21.

5. An urbanized area comprises central cities and their surrounding closely settled territories, in most cases reflecting the vast majority of an SMSA's total population. In 1980, there were 366 officially designated urbanized areas. The 12 listed in Table 2.1 account for twenty percent of the United States' total urbanized population.

6. In 1980, urbanized Los Angeles had 5,189 persons per square mile, compared to 4,526, 4,052, and 3,649 persons per square mile in Chicago, Philadelphia, and Detroit respectively. See: Carlos G. Rodriquez, et al., *Transportation Planning Data for Urbanized Areas* (Washington: Federal Highway Administration, U.S. Department of Transportation).

7. Michael Gutowski and Tracey Field, *The Graying of Suburbia* (Washington, D.C.: The Urban Institute, Paper on Social Services, 1979).

8. U.S. Department of Commerce, Bureau of the Census, *1980 Census of Population, General Population Characteristics: United States Summary* (Washington: U.S. Government Printing Office, 1983); also, 1973 publication of the 1970 United States Summary.

9. Ibid. Also, see: Robert W. Lake, *The New Suburbanites: Race and Housing in the Suburbs* (New Brunswick, N.J.: Center for Urban Policy Research, Rutgers University, 1981).

10. Lowell W. Culver, "The Politics of Suburban Distress," *Journal of Urban Affairs*, Vol. 4, No. 1 (1982), pp. 1–18.

11. Ibid., p. 10.

12. For a discussion of the citification of suburbs, see: Harlan Hahn, "Ethnic Minorities: Politics and Family in Suburbia," *The Urbanization of the Suburbs*, L.H. Masotti and J.K. Hadden, eds. (Beverly Hills, Calif.: Sage Publications, 1973), pp. 194–96.

13. See Chapter Six for a case study discussion of office development in San Jose and the Silicon Valley.

14. Four-way breakdowns of intrametropolitan commuting, such as in Table 2.5, are not published at the SMSA level.

15. Rice Center, "Mobility and Congestion: Office Location Issues in Houston," *Research Brief*, No. 1, (April 1979), p. 4.

16. This analogy to the Brownian movement principle has been made by C. Kenneth Orski, in "Suburban Mobility: The Coming Transportation Crisis?" *Transportation Quarterly*, Vol. 39, No. 2 (1985), p. 287.

17. In 1980, among all SMSAs, automobile commuting dominated by the widest margin outside of the central cities (90 percent of all work trips), whereas transit's mode split was far higher in the central cities (14.5%) than the suburbs (4.0%). See: Philip N. Fulton, "Public Transportation: Solving the Commuting Problem?" (Washington, D.C.: Paper presented at the Annual Meeting of the Transportation Research Board, January 1983).

18. Fulton, "Public Transportation," p. 14.

19. See: Christopher Conte, "The Explosive Growth of Suburbia Leads to Bumper-to-Bumper Blues," *Wall Street Journal* (April 16, 1985), p. 37; and William Trombley, "Suburbs Gear Up to Beat Traffic," *Los Angeles Times* (December 28, 1984), p. 24.

20. Thomas Hazlett, "They Built Their Own Highway . . . and Other Tales of Private Land-Use Planning," *Reason* (November 1983), p. 28.

21. A major arterial is usually defined as a thoroughfare of four to six lanes that has limited, although not full, control of access.

22. H.P. Douglass, *The Suburban Trend* (New York: Century Press, 1925). Quoted in *The Urbanization of the Suburbs*, L.H. Masotti and J.K. Hadden, eds. (Beverly Hills, Calif.: Sage Publications, 1973), p. 7.

23. L.H. Masotti and J.K. Hadden, eds. *The Urbanization of the Suburbs* (Beverly Hills, Calif: Sage Publications, 1973).

24. Melvin Webber, "Trends and Trepidations" (Los Angeles: Paper presented at the Conference on Mobility of Major Metropolitan Areas, Urban Mass Transportation Administration, U.S. Department of Transportation, November 1984).

3

Design and Land Use Considerations in Suburban Office Development

Suburban Office Complexes: Physical Context

Perhaps the first thing taught in any introductory transportation course is that traffic, whether in the city core or suburban fringe, is, in the most generic sense, a manifestation of people attempting to overcome physical space. People do not hop into cars for the sake of traveling per se, but rather for the purpose of accessing physical places. Any travel between two points is inexorably tied to how metropolises are spatially organized—that is, where we choose to locate residences, jobs, schools, shops, and other land activities. Massive new suburban employment complexes certainly are no exception to this rule. The physical layout and land use composition of outlying office developments directly define what kinds of traffic conditions will exist, including the fluidity of on-site circulation, the relative ease of site ingress and egress, and even the modal preferences of employees commuting to and from work.

The physical makeup of satellite employment centers offers a logical launching point for framing strategies aimed at safeguarding suburban mobility. Nationally, hundreds of office developers are attempting to design-in features that promote alternatives to solo driving. Strategies have focused on both *macro-scale* considerations governing the overall layout of a site as well as *micro-level* design treatments such as on-site bus shelters, cycling trails, and staging areas for carpools and vanpools. More and more, developers are realizing, sometimes from past mistakes, that the best way to avert future congestion problems around any office development is to carefully consider access and circulation issues from the very onset, especially when important design decisions influencing project scale and density are being made.

Contemporary suburban office complexes are far more varied than their central city counterparts, ranging from low-rise, freestanding, single-purpose structures to towering clusters of multifunction high-rises fully interconnected by pedestrian walkways. In between these polar extremes lies a fairly wide spectrum of office, executive, and R&D complexes, all of which have been indelibly shaped by powerful market forces calling for highly specialized working environments. Still, most large suburban office developments generally conform to one of three basic types: (1) campus-style office and business parks; (2) freestanding, independent office structures; and (3) clustered towers and "urban villages."

Campus-Style Office Parks

The master-planned suburban office park form is now over three decades old. It finds its genesis in the early 1950s when America's interstate highway system opened up vast expanses of land outside of metropolitan areas to realtors and speculators. Over the past three decades, most suburban office parks have nestled close to one or more freeway interchanges, oftentimes off a regional circumferential, where visibility, exposure, and property access are generally good. The role of post-WWII freeways and superhighways in spawning office parks, it might be noted, was not at all unlike that of the trolley lines at the turn of the century when real estate magnates such as Henry Huntington and Cornelius Vanderbilt extended streetcar lines to lure America's middle class to the suburbs for the purpose of reaping windfalls from the sale of land. What streetcars did for residential dispersal during the first half of the century, freeways have done for the office park boom during the latter half.

The nation's first office park was, appropriately enough, Office Park, a 70-acre complex constructed five miles from downtown Birmingham, Alabama during the early 1950s.[1] Office Park served as the prototype for most master-planned suburban workplaces to follow. The design emphasis was to create a spacious and appealing campus-like working environment characterized by low-rise buildings of one to three stories and open, heavily landscaped grounds accented by trees and lawn plantings. The project's developer made it clear from the outset that Office Park was meant to provide companies an attractive alternative to congested inner-city environs:

> Office Park [offers] . . . spacious surroundings and a calm, park-like atmosphere ideally suited to creative business planning, free from downtown noise,

smoke, traffic and other distractions; no tiring traffic tangles in the morning or evening rush hours; [and] ample, paved, free parking at the office door.[2]

Over the years, the park-like, campus style has not only become the predominant form of suburban office construction, it has generally served as the design template for most large-scale commercial, industrial, and even residential projects built in outlying settings where land can be readily assembled. The term "park" itself is highly suggestive of the environmentally soft, low-profile design philosophy behind most master-planned, campus-style developments. More recent projects have dwarfed their predecessors, covering as much as 2,000 acres of land (approximately three square miles) and containing low to mid-rise buildings of one million square feet or more (see Photo 3.1). Today, individual office buildings can be quite impressive, some featuring two-story rooms, with lofts, vaulted ceilings, balconies, and other embellishments tailored to the discriminating tastes of executives and high-skilled professionals.

Freestanding, Independent Office Structures

A second characteristic type of non-CBD office development, found primarily where land tracts are physically restricted, is the speculative, freestanding building. A large share of suburban office structures built during the 1960s and 1970s were single, physically unrelated buildings situated in mixed-use surroundings. Typically, these projects have been financed by a single developer who offers long-term leases, although in some instances groups of investors have built series of nearly identical freestanding structures of ten stories or more, usually with each building boasting a total floor area of one-half to one million square feet.

The Oak Brook corridor in western Chicago is the archetype of suburban freestanding design. Office space along this corridor presently totals over three million square feet spread over eight mid-rise structures, each six to 12 stories in height. Similar ribbons of physically disjointed, mid-rise office towers can be found in fairly built-up non-CBD settings of most large American cities, particularly in the vicinity of regional airports. Most of these projects lack the ornamental landscaping of their campus-style counterparts, with the wide spaces between towers often devoted to surface parking instead (see Photo 3.2). The overall organization of land found at many freestanding suburban office developments is reminiscent of the city planning genre, popularized by Le Corbusier, which featured series of

Photo 3.1. A Master-Planned, Campus-Style Office Park in San Ramon, California, with Nearby Housing.
(Photos by the author.)

Photo 3.2.   Mid-Rise, Independent Office Structures, Enveloped by Surface Parking.
Above, freestanding towers in Orange County, California. Below, new freestanding structure in Alameda County, California. (Photos by the author.)

imposing, isolated towers situated within superblocks.[3] Over time, designers criticized these schemes for their barrenness and absence of human scale. Indeed, today most of these freestanding developments are characterized by such wide spacing that virtually any physical interaction with the outside world requires the use of an automobile.

Clustered Towers and Urban Villages

In diametric contrast to freestanding structures, a recent and growing trend has been the clustering of high-rise buildings on the fringes of rapidly expanding metropolitan areas, producing a form that has been referred to variously as "urban villages" and "megacenters."[4] Many of these satellite centers are mini-downtowns in their own right, with daytime populations upwards of 60,000, densities far above typical suburban spreads, and often permanent residential populations, as high as 10,000.[5] The trademark of suburban megacenters is their distinct high-rise, mixed-use character—typically featuring a wide assortment of office, hotels, retail shops, theaters, restaurants, and other professional and service establishments.

The most notable examples of suburban megacenters are: the City Post Oak and the Greenway Plaza near Houston; Las Colinas Urban Center midway between Dallas and Ft. Worth; Century City, Warner Center, and Howard Hughes Center in Los Angeles County; South Coast Metro, Newport Center, and Irvine Spectrum in central Orange County, California; the Denver Technological Center; Tysons Corner in suburban Washington, D.C.; the Meadowlands in northeastern New Jersey; and the North York and Scarborough Town Centres 15 miles from downtown Toronto. Intense development pressures and rapidly escalating land values have spawned an unprecedented densification of structures in all these suburban settings, with office floorspace stacked vertically rather than spread horizontally. Each of these projects either currently or will eventually have buildings of at least 20 stories and total floor areas of over ten million square feet, massive concentrations of office employees, and a highly integrated urban character punctuated by extensive networks of pedestrian skyways. In most cases, the tallest structures will be centrally located as prominent landmarks, with building heights and densities gradually tapered toward a site's perimeter so that only low-rise offices border neighboring properties. Photo 3.3 offers an oblique angle view of this kind of density gradation at the burgeoning Warner Center complex in Los Angeles's west San Fernando Valley. The first of six 20- to 28-story office towers has already been erected in the core plaza of Warner Center, ringed by low-rise business suites, light manufac-

Photo 3.3. First Phase of the Warner Plaza Development in Los Angeles's San Fernando Valley.
Densities are tapered from the high-rise core to the low-rise periphery. (Photo by the author.)

turing, and townhouses. Typically, specific floor area ratio requirements (FARs) are established to achieve this conical skyline effect, as illustrated by the site covenant shown in Map 3.1 for Toronto's Scarborough Town Centre.[6] In Scarborough, 20-story structures will occupy the core while predominantly low-rise residential and retail uses are slated for the project's perimeter. At many of these megacomplexes, core structures have become prestigious addresses, in some cases featuring atrium lobbyways and companion restaurants, escalator connections to second-story offices, lavish landscaping, and surrounding fountains, artwork, and water sculptures.

The rapidity at which some of these suburban megacenters have sprung up has earned them the title of "instant downtowns." It is not uncommon for suburban high-rise projects of five million square feet or more to be completed within a span of five years.[7] This dizzying pace of new construction has more often than not overwhelmed the local supporting infrastructure, with nearby roadways perhaps strained the most. By contrast, most traditional CBDs have evolved gradually over time, allowing a more carefully paced approach to transportation service delivery.[8] As many suburbanites are beginning to find out, all too often "instant downtown" has also meant "instant congestion."

Density and Site Layout Considerations

The ability to aggregate commute trips into buses, vanpools, and other forms of ridesharing is directly related to the intensity of activities taking place at new suburban developments. Residential densities of at least eight dwelling units per acre, for instance, are normally considered necessary to economically justify fixed bus routes operating on one-half hour headways.[9] Similarly, reasonably dense clusters of suburban employees are essential if public transit, private commuter buses, and carpools are to assemble trips without excessive route deviations and time delays. While the service features of transit and vanpools, along with population densities at the residential ends of trips, are equally important determinants of which modes commuters choose, the physical site design and layout of suburban employment centers is the one area developers themselves have direct control of.

Almost without exception, employment and land use densities of suburban office developments fall far below those of their CBD counterparts. Table 3.1 gives a sense of this. On average, floor area ratios (FARs)—the gross floorspace divided by total land area—for suburban office developments are roughly one-twenty-fifth of downtown office FARs. This obviously reflects the difference in massing of CBD versus suburban office structures—downtown buildings usually reach towering heights on relatively small plots of land, while buildings found in suburban office parks are typically low-rise on generous size land parcels. Within buildings themselves, suburban office employees generally enjoy twice as much elbow room as downtown workers: on average, around 380 square feet of gross floorspace per worker in the suburbs versus 175 to 200 square feet in downtown settings. Thus, not only are downtown buildings much taller, they are used more intensively floor by floor. The mammoth scale of most suburban office spreads is reflected in the final density measure shown in Table 3.1. Generally, there is over 30 times as much land area per worker in suburban versus downtown office settings, indicating that the roominess advantages of suburban workplaces are even greater once a worker steps outside of his or her building. In sum, not only are office structures much closer to the ground in suburbia, they are more spacious and remote. All of this adds up, of course, to extremely low project employment densities.

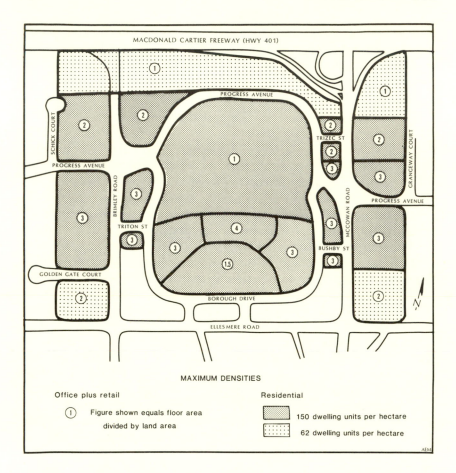

Map 3.1. Tapered Floor Area Ratios at the Developing Scarborough Town Centre on the Fringes of the Toronto Metropolitan Area.
(Source: Municipality of Scarborough, Scarborough Official Plan: Town Centre Plan, 1982.)

The implications of this on what modes suburban commutes will usually opt for are unequivocal. Most contemporary suburban office developments, for all intents and purposes, are effectively preordained for automobile usage. Particularly in the case of sprawling office parks where liberally spaced, horizontally scaled buildings dominate the landscape, the private automobile faces no serious competition to speak of (see Photo 3.4). In that virtually any movement between buildings must be made by car, most employees find few realistic alternatives to driving their own vehicles to work.

Building placement also influences on-site movement and mode choice. Normally, suburban office compounds are subdivided into individual parcels that are then sold to single corporate tenants or developed by park owners into leasable space. All too often, individual structures are sited within land parcels without reference to neighboring buildings or properties. As a result, many office buildings tend to be introverted, focusing on themselves rather than the complex as a whole, producing long walking distances (see Photo 3.5). This inward focus, chided by some critics as bordering on egocentricity,[10] is particularly prevalent among large corporate headquarters and estates.

High surface parking ratios, with 3.5 to 4.0 spaces per 1,000 square feet of net space usually the norm, also serve to spread out many complexes, separating structures by the length of several football fields in some cases (see Photo 3.6). Compounding matters even more, some office parks lack any physical integration or direct provisions for foot traffic. A normally

TABLE 3.1

Comparison of Suburban and CBD Office Density Characteristics

	Suburban Office Complexes[2]			CBD Range[3]	Approximate Difference Ratio of Suburbs to CBD
	Average	Low	High		
Floor Area Ratio[1]	0.29	0.06	1.48	5–10 (varies widely)	.04:1
Gross Square Feet of Floorspace per Employee	380	140	970	175–200	2:1
Total Square Feet of Land per Employee	1;410	230	3,360	35–50	33:1

[1] Floor area ratio represents gross floorspace of all buildings divided by the total land area of the office development.

[2] Based on national survey of 120 suburban office developments.

[3] *Sources:* F. So, ed., *The Practice of Local Government Planning* (Washington: International City Management Association), 1979; and B. Cohen, "A Look at Suburban Office Space," *Skyscraper Management* (February 1971), p. 8.

Photo 3.4.   Horizontally Scaled Suburban Office Structures in North Atlanta (above) and Alameda County, California (below). Design profiles discourage pedestrianization. (Photos by the author.)

casual walk from an off-site bus stop to one's office, for instance, might be mired by a sea of parked cars obstructing an otherwise clear passageway. Where few on-site sidewalk and pedestrian amenities are provided, transit and foot travel generally are relegated to a second-class status.

The clear trend seems to be toward even greater expansiveness of suburban workplaces, and thus greater auto-dependency in the future. Notably, the tract areas of America's office parks have grown markedly over the past several decades. Several surveys in the mid-sixties and early seventies, for instance, found the average park size to be around 70 acres, with the very largest complexes spanning 185 acres.[11] By the mid-eighties, the average suburban office park had grown to around 230 acres. Presently, roughly 15 percent of all U.S. office and business parks exceed 500 acres in area.[12] Five hundred acres are slightly less than one square mile in area and, depending on the layout of individual parcels, can result in one-way walking distances between on-site destinations of two miles or farther. With spreads of this magnitude, how sites are organized and buildings juxtaposed in rela-

Photo 3.5. An Insular Office Site in Santa Clara County, California.
It is a long trek from the bus stop (on far left side of photo) through an open field to the office building. (Photo by the author.)

**Photo 3.6.   Surface Parking at Business Parks in Atlanta's North Pe-
rimeter (above) and in San Ramon, California (below).**
Both complexes designed at four parking spaces per 1,000 net
square feet. (Photos by the author.)

tion to one another will cast the die as to whether foot travel and mass commuting are viable possibilities or not.

The overarching theme of recent suburban office park designs, of course, has been shaped less by utilitarian principles than by aesthetics. Most developers hope that the emphasis on landscaping, symmetry, spaciousness, and visual amenities will tip the scales in their favor in luring widely sought tenants, such as high-tech firms. As both a marketing strategy and an appeasement to long-time area residents, architects of several of the nation's largest office parks have attempted, as outlined in their design guides, to recreate the original rural ambience of the land on which they are building, which in a number of cases first consisted of orchard groves or graze land.[13] Additionally, the vocal resistance of many suburbanites to the threats posed by more urban-like businesses and industries has often pressured developers to reduce densities, restrict heights, and spread buildings laterally, all adding to circulation distances. Large-parcel industrial zoning has frequently been invoked by suburban policymakers to enforce this public will.

Moreover, office park developers themselves normally attach private covenants to individual property sales in order to maintain some control over what is done within specific land parcels sold to companies. Typically, covenants govern lotting practices and building lines to not only ensure access, privacy, light, and air, but also to achieve visual continuity and certain aesthetic ends. Lotting patterns of suburban office parks usually consist of five-acre tracts that can be assembled into 25-acre parcels.[14] For each parcel, landowners are generally allowed to build upon as much as 30 percent of a site, with a total impervious coverage restricted to no more than 60 percent to maintain an open, park-like atmosphere. Controls over building lines almost always require front, rear, and side setbacks of at least 40 to 50 feet. Imposed height limits more often than not produce squatty, land-hungry buildings—43 percent of all suburban office structures are currently one or two stories high, and only 8.9 percent exceed ten stories.[15] In addition, covenants invariably dictate street design, entrance identities, signage, lighting, and exterior appearances of individual buildings as well.

Besides zoning controls and restrictive deeds on land, the trend toward insular building designs and detachedness has also been reinforced by corporate dictum. Particularly in settings where major headquarter offices are housed, mid-rise towers are typically spaced far apart to visually accent a company's individualism and perhaps make a statement about its corporate mission. Notes one industry observer: "The corporation wants a building tagged with its own name to augment its image."[16]

The net effect of all of these factors—zoning controls, aestheticism, and corporate image making—has been to create highly auto-dependent suburban working environments. This trend has not gone unnoticed by the design profession, however. In a 1984 *Boston Globe* article, architectural critic Robert Campbell referred to many office and business park forms as resembling "Cities for Cars and Towers" rather than "Cities for People":

> Here, buildings do not gather sociably into anything larger than themselves, do not shape spaces for people. Each one stands separately surrounded by unformed, unshaped space of meaningless grass areas and asphalt parking. A reversal of figure and ground takes place. It is the building that occupies space, [and] you who are peripheral.[17]

On the west coast, a leading Bay Area architectural firm recently challenged the profession to discard popular suburban office styles of the post-WWII era:

> The business park consists of low buildings just gobbling up land. What should be built are clusters of tall buildings and mixtures of office, residential and entertainment on one site. . . . In the future, zoning ordinances should be written to permit developers to build taller buildings if they agree to preserve open space. . . . The solution is to make suburbs more like old-fashioned cities by giving them well-defined centers and buildings located for pedestrians rather than autos.[18]

Any movement toward creating "urban villages" versus sprawling office complexes could go a long way toward attenuating the automobile's domineering presence in suburban work settings. The emergence of physically integrated megacenters such as City Post Oak in Houston and Tysons Corner in Fairfax County certainly offer outstanding exemplars in this regard. However, given the overwhelming preference for low-density forms, more attention needs to be devoted toward strengthening the pedestrian orientations of traditional campus-style developments. Grouping buildings into "community clusters," each well connected by walkway, trails, and plazas, could allow developers to maintain low-scale structural profiles while also encouraging nonvehicular circulation. Campus clusters have become particularly vogue in R&D and high-tech parks where tenants prefer community atmospheres conducive to face-to-face contacts and the exchange of ideas. Similarly, community-like work settings in office and business parks, not just R&D ones, should be laid out (see Photo 3.7). The key, however, is not only to group buildings and stress propinquity, but also

Photo 3.7. **Campus Cluster Designs Focusing on Interior People Space Rather than on Parking Lots.**
Nicely landscaped grounds attract noon-hour lunch crowds. (Photos by the author.)

to interconnect each campus cluster with pathways and possibly shuttle circulators.

A number of recently constructed office parks stand out as paragons of pedestrian-oriented, cluster designs. The Harbor Bay Business Park, a 325-acre office complex in Alameda, California, uses a cluster building arrangement to promote worker interaction (see Photo 3.8). Landscaped walkways, outdoor concourses, and on-site bus connections lace the campus plazas. Two commercial areas, complete with restaurants, shops, and several hotels, are also being constructed within easy walking distance. Developers believe the chosen site layout and design elements will measurably reduce on-site auto-dependency.

Current low-profile, physically fragmented office parks are by no means locked into this form in perpetuity. In several instances, sprawling complexes have been converted to denser, community designs over incremental phases. One notable example is the Denver Technological Center. There, the expansive 850-acre compound first built in the early 1960s has been transformed into a village-like development by architecturally integrating buildings using extensive walkways and traditional urban squares. Over time, the Tech Center's developers have proceeded to raise early suburban densities of FAR .25 to more urban densities of 1.0 to 2.0[19] (see Photo 3.9). All future buildings will range from four to 24 stories, configured around campus clusters. Through a conscientious redirection in design strategy, the Tech Center's metamorphosis from a suburban office spread to a fully integrated urban village has allowed it, in the words of the developer, to "survive and regenerate."[20]

In most instances, market pressures alone will likely drive the eventual densification of office and business park complexes. Over time, as suburban land prices soar, many developers will be forced to put land to more efficient use, perhaps compromising their original aesthetic intentions somewhat in the process. From both an architectural and space utilization standpoint, there really are few constraints on how suburban office structures are laid out. Designers have far greater flexibility in building office towers, for instance, than factories. While industrial parks normally require single-story plants for assembling, distributing, and warehousing products, office functions can be just as efficiently carried out on a vertical scale as on a horizontal one. Where land is cheap enough, however, developers can slash construction costs by spreading buildings laterally since elevators and extra foundation supports can be eliminated. When the marketplace commands land to be used more productively though, retrofits of original park-like designs to denser clusters, such as at the Denver Technological Center, will become more commonplace.

Photo 3.8. **Landscaped Grounds at the Harbor Bay Business Park in Alameda, California.**
(Photos by the author.)

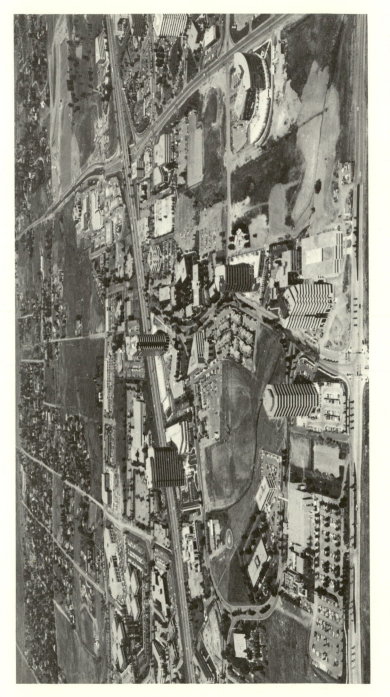

Photo 3.9. High-Rise Profile of the Denver Technological Center in the Foreground, Flanked by I-25 and I-225. Strong emphasis has been placed on in-filling in the recent expansion of the center. (Photo by Landis Aerial Photos, provided courtesy of the Denver Technological Center.)

Transportation Design Features

In addition to project scale and layout considerations, attention to more micro-design details—such as the segregation of vehicular and pedestrian traffic and the provision of convenient transit shelters and preferential parking—can influence how suburban employees choose to travel. The design of internal roadways and circulation systems not only defines the movement patterns of cars, pedestrians, and bicycles, it also determines the degree of potential conflict and safety implications of getting from point A to point B via one mode versus another. The geographic proximity of employee parking to building entrances relative to how close bus stops are, moreover, can be an important barometer of modal preferences. Although by themselves specific design treatments might appear somewhat trivial, their collective influences can be every bit as important as more macro-scale decisions.

Pathways and Circulation Facilities

The physical channels for circulating within any office complex are defined by the natural contours, dimensions, and physical features of a site. Notwithstanding these constraints, circulation systems are often also used to reinforce certain design themes, such as visually separating various campus clusters or segregating land uses, like traditional office functions from warehousing.

Roadway networks within some office parks follow curvilinear designs while others are laid out as standard grids, with many variants in between.[21] Almost all office parks have a functional hierarchy of passageways, usually involving a system of collectors and frontage roads that feed into a main entrance thoroughfare. One popular layout is a spine-and-loop network,[22] illustrated in Figure 3.1. Here, a main spinal street penetrates the core of the project and is connected by minor loops flanked on both sides, providing two continuous paths, one major and direct, the other local and sinuous. Loops offer alternate exits as well as channels for unimpeded circulation of cars and service vehicles. The Opus 2 industrial and office park, situated nine miles southwest of downtown Minneapolis, has adopted this kind of extended loop configuration. There, a one-way loop system snakes through the 554-acre compound, funneling cars in a "figure eight" type of movement pattern (see Photo 3.10). Stop signs are absent from the Opus 2 development since one-way flows virtually eliminate any vehicle-to-vehicle confrontations. Although the one-way primary system required some fine-

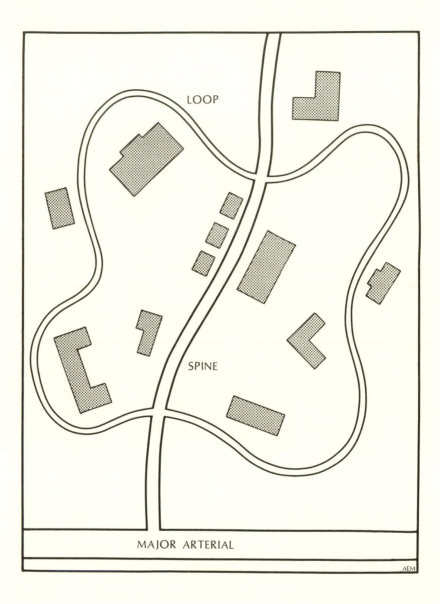

LOOP

SPINE

MAJOR ARTERIAL

**Figure 3.1.   Layout of a Spine-and-Loop Roadway Common to Many
Office and Industrial Parks.**

Photo 3.10. **Overhead View of the Non-Stop, One-Way Loop Road System at the Opus 2 Business Park in Southwest Minneapolis.**
Photo by Markhurd Corporation, provided courtesy of the Opus Corporation.)

tuning of directional signage to orient first-time visitors, the project's developers feel the free-flow circulation system has been a tremendous boon to attracting efficiency-minded companies.[23]

While undulating roadways might appeal to motorists, they have their drawbacks as far as transit and pedestrian circulation. As any walker knows, a straight line is the shortest distance between two points. If all sidewalks within a business park hug a serpentine roadway system, walking distances can increase by a factor of two over those of a simple grid-iron system. Accordingly, at some complexes, office designers have superimposed more lineal footpaths onto their loop networks, in most instances providing pedestrians grade-separated skybridges as well. In the case of the Opus 2 project, for instance, a secondary pedestrian and bicycle system follows several linear parks throughout the development. Not only have more direct trails been provided, the dissociation of foot and vehicular traffic has enhanced both pedestrian safety and the walking experience. Additionally, buses can have a difficult time negotiating tight curves along winding roads, especially where traffic lanes are the traditional 12 feet or narrower. Some office park developers have begun providing wide 15-foot lanes and shaving intersection curbs in recognition of the restrictive maneuverability of buses.[24]

For office parks with grids and other less sinuous street systems, pedestrian and cycling facilities, as a rule, parallel roadways. Photo 3.11 illustrates joint use of rights-of-way at the Hacienda Business Park in Pleasanton, California, where sidewalks flank all arteries and reserved four-foot bikepaths occupy exterior lanes. Such designs are less expensive than specially segregated pathways. However, since the scale of shared right-of-way facilities are circumscribed by the needs of the motor vehicle, they are not always practicable for walkers. Where block faces are long and skybridges absent, some pedestrians may risk jaywalking in order to access neighboring offices (see Photo 3.12). Mid-block walkways with yellow-blinking overhead caution signals could be used in such instances, albeit at the expense of impeding vehicular traffic and possibly detracting from the aesthetics of an office park.

Perhaps equally important to the provision of on-site sidewalks and cycling paths is the integration of facilities with those off-site so as to create a coordinated trail system. Pathways that end abruptly at property lines certainly do little to promote pedestrian or bicycle commuting. An attractively landscaped, gently winding bikepath that ties directly into a comprehensive trail system can greatly enhance the cycle-to-work experience. Similarly, wide sidewalks buffered from main arteries by plantings and berms and linked to nearby residential and commercial pathways can invite foot travel.

On-site Terminuses and Connection Points

Once traffic circulates through a compound, adequate terminuses and staging areas are needed for daytime storage of vehicles and to serve workers arriving by buses and vanpools. The amount and location of on-site parking, transit stops, carpool drop-off zones, and various ridesharing amenities can doubtlessly sway the commuting allegiances of suburban workers.

Parking. One prominent feature of suburban office parks is the abundance of free off-street parking. Next to environmental quality, surveys show free parking to be the most important factor in drawing tenant-occupants.[25] Currently, the average suburban office development provides 3.9 spaces per 1,000 square feet (or nearly one space per employee),[26] more than what is required under most suburban zoning ordinances. Local governments set minimum parking ratios to prevent an undersupply situation that could lead to a spillover of cars into surrounding neighborhoods. Many developers have voluntarily opted to exceed the normal ratio of 3.5 spaces per 1,000 square feet as a strategic marketing ploy.[27] Opines one Orange County, California office developer, "always overbuild the parking . . . this is a must as far as R&D is concerned."[28] This predisposition toward parking perhaps reflects a skepticism over the possible success of alternative travel modes in suburban work settings as much as it does a belief in parking's salesmanship value.

Providing bountiful, free parking can nevertheless be a costly proposition. A single parking space consumes roughly 350 square feet of real estate, and can cost from $1,500 to $3,000, including land.[29] With today's liberal standard of nearly a space per worker, suburban parking lots can actually gobble up as much area as the buildings they serve and cost large businesses well over $5 million in capital outlays. Sprawling lots can also create long walking distances to building entrances, not to mention the isolating, patulous effects they have on building placements and access to street-side pathways and transit stops. The general rule of thumb for the maximum acceptable walking distance from a parking spot to an office's front door is about 300 feet. The survey of 120 U.S. office parks revealed that in most cases walking distances tend to be far below this maximum: for over two-thirds of the parks, average walking distances from parking lots to

Photo 3.11.   Joint Use of Right-of-Way for Sequestered Bikelanes and Motoring at the Hacienda Business Park in Pleasanton, California.
Lower photo shows a traffic signal monument, representative of the ceremonial designs found at some complexes. (Photos by the author.)

Photo 3.12. Pedestrian–Auto Conflict at Outlying Office Centers.
Long block faces produced by large project scales encourage jaywalking. (Photo by the author.)

building entrances are under 100 feet, and for 95 percent of them, distances are shorter than 200 feet. In the case of multistory office towers with more than 1,000 employees, the only way to ensure that all surface parking is within a 300-foot radius is to completely envelop a building with asphalt. Protective covenants, however, sometimes preclude this.

In view of parking's price tag and space consumption, some suburban office developers have begun building decked facilities, particularly in settings where land costs are escalating. Multilevel parking structures can be found, for instance, at Tysons Corner in Fairfax County, Warner Center in Los Angeles's San Fernando Valley, Orange County's South Coast Metro, and the Denver Technological Center (see Photo 3.13). In all these cases, commercial fees are collected to defray building and debt expenses. Some developers feel covered parking can be a marketing asset since many tenants coming from downtown locations are accustomed to accessible parking garages.[30] Additionally, multilevel parking generally consumes around 8 percent less space than equivalent surface facilities because tenants accept narrower aisles and smaller stalls in return for closer proxim-

Photo 3.13. Tri-Level Parking Structures at the Warner Center Plaza in Los Angeles's San Fernando Valley (above) and at the North Perimeter Office Complex in Suburban Atlanta (below).
Warner Center's decked structure (on photo's left) is connected to office buildings by a pedestrian skybridge (on photo's right). A manned kiosk is used for collecting parking fees. In contrast, the parking structure in Atlanta's North Perimeter is free to office workers and clients. (Photos by the author.)

ity to their offices.[31] Still, decked parking structures are economical only when land costs reach $8 per square foot (in 1982 currency), which is rare in the suburbs.[32] Some office developers eschew parking structures on aesthetic grounds, moreover, noting that one of the reasons many companies move to the suburbs in the first place is to escape the "parking garage image" and the congestion associated with it.[33]

Several important parking design features should always be considered as inducements to ridesharing regardless. Ideally, the most convenient parking spaces should be set aside for carpools and vanpools, with some reserved stalls wide enough for vans (see Photo 3.14). An estimated 40 percent of all American suburban office parks presently offer some preferential parking. On average, around 7 percent of all stalls are reserved for carpools and vanpools at these office parks, and the mean walking distance to building entrances for preferred parkers is about 50 feet, only around one-half as far as most solo drivers must trek. In places with decked parking, structures should be designed to ensure that there is adequate overhead clearance for van entry. At several suburban developments that have multitier, enclosed parking, ceiling heights are under seven feet, generally too low to accommodate a vanpool. The cost difference of building, say, 7'6" versus 6'6" ceilings is fairly negligible when stretched out over the life of a structure, and certainly worth the additional expenditure when one considers the potential road construction savings frequent vanpooling could offer. Moreover, in that a preferential parking scheme might concentrate all vanpool spaces on the first floor of a garage anyway, the actual cost differential might involve raising a structure's total height by only an extra foot or so.

Mass Transit and Other Commuting Amenities. Equally convenient terminuses for buses and cyclists should also be designed into suburban office complexes. A growing roster of suburban office parks nationwide are being built with some of the special operating needs of mass transportation in mind. Gentle street grades, bus turnouts, designated stops, passenger shelters, generous road geometrics, and large-vehicle turnarounds have made transit a welcomed member of the overall transportation system in places like Bishop Ranch and the Hacienda Business Park east of San Francisco-Oakland, the Denver Tech Center, and the new town of Aliso Viejo in Orange County, California.[34] In California, the state government has been instrumental in encouraging these kinds of improvements through the passage of legislation requiring Planned Unit Developments (PUDs) with 200 or more dwelling units to dedicate land for bus turnouts, benches,

Photo 3.14. Preferential Parking for Car/Vanpools at the Hacienda Business Park in Pleasanton, California.
(Photos by the author.)

and shelters.[35] Some California developers have begun extending this practice to office parks as well, particularly in recognition of the fact that 20 bus shelters serving 500 workers opting for transit can be a lot cheaper than providing them with 500 free parking spaces.

Based on the national survey, around one-quarter of all suburban parks presently have some type of on-site transit amenity, ranging from specially designated transit drop-off zones to the provision of several dozen plexiglas-covered bus shelters with benches. The siting of convenient bus stops is particularly important if transit users are to receive a fair shake in relation to motorists (see Photos 3.15 and 3.16). To date, they have not fared particularly well. From the survey and site investigation of 32 centers, average walking distance between main building entrances and on-site bus stops is around 480 feet, over four times as far as the average parker has to walk to her desk.[36] For office parks without any on-site transit services, the average walking distances from the nearest off-premises bus stop to the main building entrance is nearly two-thirds of a mile, roughly 30 times farther than most motorists have to jaunt. In several cases, access to off-site bus stops has been confounded by the presence of residential soundwalls, freeway interchanges, and other physical barriers. Despite the availability of assorted transit amenities, in most suburban office park settings public transit still takes a backseat in deference to the needs of motorists.

Allowing transit vehicles front-door access could obviate the need for roadside bus stops. Loading and disembarking zones reserved for both buses as well as vanpools would make the office connection for mass commuters almost effortless. Where front-door boarding and drop-off areas are provided, designers need to make sure connecting driveways can accommodate the wide turning radii of buses and that no obstructions, such as overhead canopies, bar vehicle entry.

Finally, terminuses should also be provided for cyclists, such as convenient bike racks. Perhaps one of the biggest deterrents to cycling is, understandably, the aversion many have toward arriving at one's desk after working up a sweat. Accordingly, several large office parks, such as the Bay Area's Bishop Ranch, have introduced covenants specifically requiring all buildings with large concentrations of employees to contain showers and lockers.

Land Use and Tenant Mix Considerations

Of course, commuting practices of suburban office employees are influenced by more than just the immediate built environment. What takes place both inside and around the physical confines of suburban office complexes—in

Photo 3.15.   A Bus Turnout, Shelter, and Sidewalk at the Hacienda Business Park in Pleasanton, California.
The transit terminus was built in advance of office construction. Long walking distances produced by the scale of the project, however, could discourage transit usage. (Photo by the author.)

Photo 3.16.   A Conveniently Sited Transit Stop at the Bishop Ranch Business Park in San Ramon, California.
(Photo by the author.)

terms of land use mixes as well as types of business enterprises—usually affects worker commuting preferences and traffic circulation even more.

Over the past several decades or so, city planners have begun to embrace the idea of land use integration as a way of both enriching working and living environments and cutting down on vehicular trip making. Some have called for the transformation of suburban workplaces into multifunction centers modeled after American and European cities of yesteryear when stores, shops, restaurants, offices, and residences stood side by side.[37] This marks a radical departure from the tradition of exclusive, segregated zoning found almost universally in America's suburbs. Although the idea of combining homes, shopping, and workplaces in a single neighborhood runs counter to what nearly every planner over 30 years of age was taught in school, there really is very little logic to buffering land uses in many suburban settings. Remarks one observer:

> Keep(ing) everything separate . . . may have made sense when people needed protection for a slaughterhouse or rendering plant next door. But in the age of "clean," white-collar industry, it makes little sense. It forces people into their cars, often for long trips on congested roads, just to get from home to work or to a grocery store.[38]

Indeed, the congregation of suburban activities into well-defined cores offers as much hope as any one area for arresting the swell of traffic along America's outskirts.

Balancing Jobs and Housing

It is obvious that the closer workers live to their jobs, average commuting distance will shrink and fewer miles will be logged onto areawide freeways and thoroughfares. And to the extent homes are built either within an office/mixed-use compound or close by, for employees who choose to live in these residences, the opportunities for walking, jogging, or cycling to work are greatly enhanced. Jobs-housing balancing, then, is a potentially potent means of safeguarding suburban mobility.

Presently, few suburban work centers in the United States have on-site housing. From the national survey, slightly less than 15 percent of suburban complexes with predominantly office functions had residential units for sale or lease on their premises. Over two-thirds of the survey respondents, however, indicated that new housing construction was expected nearby, and around 62 percent felt that a "large amount" of housing already existed within two miles of their work site.[39] Thus, many suburban office park settings could be characterized as having no on-site provisions for housing, yet ample supplies close by.

It was clear from interviews that most suburban office developers oppose intermixing housing and offices, partly over image concerns, but primarily because they see little profit potential in this kind of specialized housing market. The overwhelming majority of suburban office developers feel no direct responsibility for either building housing on-site or near-site, or for encouraging others to do so. The general attitude seems to be that the marketplace itself will respond to the housing needs of their tenants' workers, and any direct intervention by office developers could be counterproductive as well as foolhardy.

Nonetheless, there are a few outstanding examples of suburban office-housing intermixing, principally at high-rise megacenters. Table 3.2 identifies 11 of North America's largest suburban office complexes that plan to have at least 1,000 or more residential units on their premises at buildout. The vast majority of these developments currently offer owner-occupied condominiums and rental garden apartments (see Photo 3.17). Estimated price ranges for housing units are as low as $80,000 (1984 currency) in the case of suburban Philadelphia's Chesterbrook development to nearly $1 million at the Denver Technological Center, Playa Vista complex in western Los Angeles, and Houston's City Post Oak. Six of the developments, however, will price ten to 15 percent of all housing units in the affordable range, and several are planning low-cost housing exclusively for retirees. The Woodlands development, 27 miles north of downtown Houston, stands out among the 11 mixed-use projects for its emphasis on detached, single-family units (see Photo 3.18).

Some outlying communities have taken the integration of jobs and housing quite seriously. Costa Mesa, California, for instance, requires developments like the South Coast Metro (see Table 3.2) to build residential units, either on-site or within the city limits, to house at least 20 percent of their workers.[40] So far, 1,200 two- and three-story condominium units have been built within the South Coast Metro. Developers feel the inclusion of on-site housing has enhanced their project's marketability by creating a livelier and safer evening environment, and are contemplating adding more units in the future. In other areas, however, there has actually been a public backlash against commingling housing and jobs in suburbia. In the San Francisco Bay Area, for instance, developers of both the Hacienda and Bishop Ranch business parks were prohibited from constructing any housing on-site after areawide residents vehemently protested, fearing their community's image as a strictly zoned, upscale suburb would be tarnished.[41]

TABLE 3.2

**Characteristics of Major North American
Mixed-Use Office Developments at Buildout**

Project and Metropolitan Area	Total Project Housing Units		Percent of Total Project Floorspace Devoted to:				Total Project Floorspace in Millions of Square Feet	Total Land Acreage	Mileage to Regional CBD
	Undetached Multifamily	Detached Single-Family	Office[1]	Retail	Housing	Other[2]			
Las Colinas Urban Center:									
Dallas	4,000	1,000	55	10	10	25	11.7	960	15
Denver Tech. Center: Denver	4,750	250	85	5	5	5	40.0	850	10
City Post Oak: Houston	6,600	0	70	14	8	8	30.0	1,200	6
The Woodlands: Houston	2,500	4,500	58	5	16	21	4.1	2,000	27
Playa Vista: Los Angeles	8,000	0	25	40	12	23	8.2	926	20
South Coast Metro:									
Los Angeles/Orange County	1,200	0	72	17	4	7	21.0	2,240	36
Warner Center: Los Angeles	4,000	0	61	23	8	8	7.6	1,100	25
Opus 2: Minneapolis	1,000	0	80	3	10	7	6.0	560	20
Harmon Meadows:									
New York/Newark	2,600	0	72	5	18	5	7.5	550	10
Chesterbrook: Philadelphia	3,400	370	20	3	56	21	5.5	995	17
Scarborough Town Centre:									
Toronto	4,000	500	54	20	17	9	5.5	330	15

[1] Office category includes traditional office, light industrial, and R&D uses.

[2] Other category includes hotel, recreational, and institutional uses.

Source: 1984 survey of North American office developments.

Photo 3.17. Two Approaches To Housing Integration.
Top photo shows on-site, intermixing of townhouses with office uses at the Warner Center development in Los Angeles's San Fernando Valley. Lower photo shows medium-density, single-family housing congregating around the southern end of the 585-acre Bishop Ranch compound in San Ramon, California. (Photos by the author.)

Perhaps even more important than integrating homes and offices within a compound is the strategic balancing of jobs and housing at the subregional level—i.e., providing enough homes within approximately a five-mile radius of all major employment centers. It is not merely enough to achieve numerical parity in jobs and housing, however; importantly, there must also be a match between the housing preferences and purchasing capabilities of workers and the mix and cost of residential units provided. No real purpose would be served in siting, say, 5,000 expensive, large tract detached homes near a business park catering to back-office functions and staffed by secretaries, data processors, and billing agents. Successful jobs–housing balancing also requires demand–supply balancing.

In many suburban areas, jobs and housing are in an alarming state of disequilibrium. Imbalances are particularly glaring around some of the

Photo 3.18. **Aerial View of The Woodlands New-Town Development.**
The commercial and corporate center is surrounded by a lake, a nine-hole golf course, and single-family tract housing designed along a curvilinear road network. (Photo by Ted Washington, provided courtesy of The Woodlands Corporation.)

nation's fastest growing suburban work centers. Based on an approximate 15 square mile area, the ratio of employees to dwelling units stands at roughly 3:1 in Irvine and Santa Clara-Cupertino, California, 7:1 for City Post Oak, and 12:1 for the Westchester-El Segundo corridor in west Los Angeles, all of which have experienced phenomenal office growth over the past decade.

Many critics have indicted suburban municipalities themselves for the jobs-housing dilemma.[42] Local governments generally welcome the contributions commercial, industrial, and office developments make to their tax rolls, yet many turn a jaundiced eye toward housing developments that represent potential tax drains. Through exclusive, large-lot zoning and offering various enticements, many suburban communities have entered into head-to-head combat in the competition for corporate investors. Winners have become the homes of multinational corporations and high-tech firms while losers have ended up as repositories for track housing subdivisions. This laissez-faire approach has served to widen the rift between where people live and work, making nearly everyone a loser as far as traffic is concerned.

One of the more graphic examples of "exclusive zoning run amok" can be found in Santa Clara County, California, in the southern part of the Bay Area. There, enough land has been zoned to support 250,000 new jobs but only 70,000 new housing units.[43] Neighboring Alameda and Santa Cruz Counties have been saddled with housing many of Santa Clara County's displaced workers. As a consequence, one-way commutes of 50 miles to Santa Clara's Silicon Valley are not uncommon.

In those suburbs beginning to zone for mixed housing, newly constructed units have not always been targeted to local labor markets. While condominiums and luxury apartments are being accepted, most outlying jurisdictions still oppose construction of low- and even moderate-income housing.[44] Not even precedent-setting court rulings, such as the landmark Mount Laurel II decision in which the New Jersey Supreme Court ordered suburbs to provide affordable shelter, have made much of a dent in suburban attitudes. Notes one student of the suburbs: "On one level, there's a racial component to this opposition; but often, you find affluent suburban blacks joining with whites of the same class in opposing apartments."[45]

Clearly, the onus lies at the regional level for balancing jobs and affordable housing. Unless the right institutional apparatus exists for coordinating the introduction of office parks and residential tracks, an ad hoc, haphazard development pattern will likely continue along the nation's metropolitan fringes. One possible palliative would be to introduce regional tax-base sharing. This arrangement would force municipalities made up predominantly of industrial and commercial uses to reimburse bedroom communities for the enormous costs of housing their employees. By removing the incentive to attract only high tax-yielding companies, tax-base sharing could help to close the wedge between where suburbanites live and work. Although no place in the United States presently practices tax-base sharing in its pure form, Minneapolis-St. Paul has perhaps come the closest through extraterritorial sharing of selected regional income sources, such as sales tax receipts.

Some communities have also made conscientious efforts to stage the introduction of office developments in line with the availability of affordable worker housing. Both Costa Mesa and Santa Ana, California, for instance, index incremental increases in allowable office and industrial floorspace to housing availability. All building permits for industrial and office construction are conditioned on adequate housing also being provided for area workers. The suburban community of Walnut Creek, California, moreover, has passed an "office metering" ordinance that establishes triggers for imposing office building moratoria when jobs and housing get way out of kilter.[46] In all three California communities, public officials believe that phasing requirements will not only ensure that office construction coincides with increases in the areawide housing stock, but also that necessary roadway and transit improvements are put into place before the local infrastructure becomes overloaded.

Land use incentives, such as performance zoning, are likewise available for balancing subregional jobs and housing. For instance, municipalities could grant 20 percent increases in net employment densities whenever office parks are sited and staged in synch with affordable nearby housing. Floating zones[47] might also be established to provide builders some flexibility in where they locate offices and housing. Developers and their tenants can offer further incentives for employees who purchase homes close to their workplaces. At the Bishop Ranch business complex in San Ramon, California, for instance, several large corporations offer substantial relocation allowances to their employees, with higher bonuses given for those choosing to live close by. To date, over one hundred Bishop Ranch employees have taken advantage of relocation bonuses. In other areas of the country, however, employers have discontinued their programs after union officials began insisting that similar perquisites be offered to company workers nationwide. Not wishing to establish costly precedents, companies promptly scrapped their programs in these instances.

Regardless of how many carrots and sticks are used to achieve equanimity in jobs and housing, there certainly are no guarantees that either average commuting distances will shrink or workers will begin abandoning their automobiles as a consequence. For one, while a numerical balance in housing and jobs might be struck in a particular community, it will not necessarily be the case that those working in the municipality will occupy in-town residences. At the Warner Center compound in suburban Los Angeles, for instance, a recent survey conducted by project managers indicated that only around eight percent of all residents living on-site or within several blocks of the complex actually worked there.[48] Studies around several of Washington's suburban Metrorail transit stations have similarly found few incidences of office workers living in available nearby housing.[49] It might very well be the case that, subconsciously at least, some workers prefer a change of environment from where they spend stress-filled working hours and where they retire for the evening. Moreover, it is not clear that in cases where housing has been provided on-site or nearby, such as listed in Table 3.2, that workers can afford to purchase available units even if they wanted to. For instance, in the Bay Area suburb of Walnut Creek, a community that experienced explosive office growth over the past several years, the median home costs nearly $200,000, requiring roughly a $61,000 annual household income to qualify for, yet the median yearly income of its work force is just under $32,000. Clearly, it will take more than some numerical parity in jobs and housing to reduce suburban commuting; far more important will be the matching of residences with the earning levels and taste preferences of suburbia's work force.

Another possible impediment to shortening commuting distances by balancing homes and jobs is the configuration of regional thoroughfares. By a crow's flight, the average distance between workers' residences and offices might be fairly short; yet, the physical layout of roadways might force workers into roundabout journeys that only an automobile can realistically serve. As a hypothetical example,[50] consider the case of Houston, which has a classical spoke-and-wheel freeway network, as do many of the nation's fastest growing metropolises. As illustrated in Figure 3.2, if John Doe happens to reside at point A near a radial freeway link yet works at point B on a different radial connector, his journey to work is apt to be circuitous as well as compounded by several freeway-to-freeway interchange crossings. If, on the other hand, John's coworker, Jane Smith, lives at point C, her daily commute trip involves no radial-to-circumferential connections and is likely shorter, even though she resides farther away. Simply put, radial-loop roadway systems may be incapable of efficiently serving intrasuburban trips, regardless of how close residents are to their jobs or which travel modes they opt for.

Jobs-housing integration might also backfire by discouraging rideshar-ing and transit usage. Vanpooling, for instance, is most attractive to workers who live 20 miles or more from their offices since the time spent picking up other passengers en route becomes acceptable only over long distances. Building plentiful housing within, say, a 2- to 5-mile zone of suburban office parks might result in commuting distances that are too far to walk yet too

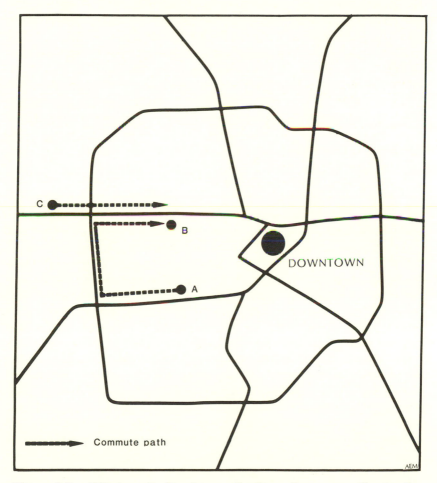

Figure 3.2. Effects of Roadway Configurations on Commuting Patterns.

Person A lives closer to workplace B than does person C, but ends up traveling farther.

close to efficiently carpool. Conceivably, the vehicular miles traversed each day by 1,000 workers who live within a five-mile radius of work and solo commute could exceed those of 1,000 coworkers who live 20 to 30 miles away and pool together in vans.

Finally, the trend toward multiple wage earner households could work against efforts to balance jobs and housing. Nationwide, the percent of households with two or more wage earners rose from 42.7 percent in 1960 to 68.5 percent in 1984, reflecting dramatic gains in the number of working American women.[51] For the majority of married households, then, a locational decision on where to buy or rent a home today must be made not only in light of closeness to a husband's job place, but in terms of proximity to a wife's as well. There is little doubt that more and more families today are choosing residential sites that minimize the average commute distance for both wage earners. Thus, unless a region has a large share of households where husbands and wives happen to work in the same vicinity, public policies aimed at jobs–housing balancing could prove fruitless.

Integrating Retail and Other Land Uses

The need for fusing together suburban land uses goes beyond a jobs–housing integration. Unless restaurants, banks, shops, recreational facilities, and the like are also sited close to employment centers, most suburban office workers will find it necessary to drive their own cars in order to access lunchtime destinations and run midday errands. While many of the nation's earliest office parks were sited near shopping centers and retail strips,[52] thus providing employees with myriad nearby luncheon and shopping options, today's developments tend to be far more isolated. From the national survey, the average distance from the geographic center of today's suburban office complexes to the nearest off-site retail establishment is approximately 1.5 miles, clearly too far to walk during the normal one-hour lunch break. Needless to say, a large share of the nation's suburban office workers must presently rely either on their own cars or efficient shuttle connections to take care of any midday business that is conducted off-premises, be it running to the bank or meeting a friend over lunch. Noon hour vehicular traffic itself usually poses few problems; cars driven to work during the A.M. peak, partly to assure midday mobility, usually do, however.

In recognition of the need to provide tenant support services and create viable village-like atmospheres, many suburban office developers have started integrating retail uses and ancillary facilities into their projects. The national survey revealed that around 42 percent of the largest American suburban office complexes currently have some supplementary retail or customer service activities, and another 7 percent plan to eventually include them. By far the most frequent type of on-site consumer function is eateries, ranging from formal restaurants to small delis. Around 40 percent of all office complexes sampled have some kind of on-site eating establishment, in many cases consisting primarily of company cafeterias. Other common on-site commercial activities include: convenience retail stores (17 percent of respondents); financial services, such as banks (13 percent of respondents); assorted customer services, such as gas stations and photocopy stores (12 percent of respondents); and consumer merchandise shops, such as clothiers and boutiques (11 percent of respondents).

Not surprisingly, the richest mixture of land uses and employee support services can be found at village-like megacomplexes. Table 3.1 previously presented land use statistics for some of the more substantial mixed-use suburban work centers in the U.S. and Canada. Several of these are described in more detail below.

DENVER TECHNOLOGICAL CENTER. After 15 years of a traditional office and industrial park form and character, over the past decade the Denver Technological Center has not only densified, but has also radically diversified. Throughout the 850-acre complex, the Tech Center's 12,000 employees currently enjoy a smorgasbord of daytime and evening activities including freestanding restaurants, cozy delis, outdoor cafes, small shopping clusters, banks, cinemas, gas stations, two prestigious hotels, and a health center. The center's current labor force is expected to more than quadruple in size by the turn of the century. Over 7.5 million square feet of additional retail and commercial floorspace is being scheduled to serve both new and existing tenants. The Tech Center's integration of mid- to high-rise structures, plazas, and pathways should prove attractive to the large volumes of foot traffic generated by all of these uses.

LAS COLINAS. The 12,000-acre Las Colinas development is a veritable new town situated midway between Dallas and Ft. Worth. A mix of commercial, industrial, and retail uses makes up the master-planned community, interspersed by waterways and open green belts. The heart of the new community is the 1,000-acre Urban Center where more than 600 businesses presently congregate in both large corporate office towers and small multitenant complexes (see Photo 3.19). The center's present daytime population of 50,000 is expected to balloon to between 150,000 and 200,000 by the turn of the century. Almost 100 retail establishments

Photo 3.19.   Las Colinas's Urban Village.
A people-oriented place, focused on Lake Carolyn and sur-
rounded by villa-style shops and high-rise office towers.
(Photo provided courtesy of Las Colinas Corporation.)

operate throughout the Las Colinas community, including nearly 40 restaurants, and homes for approximately 50,000 persons are being planned.

CITY POST OAK. With over 20 million square feet of development now and an additional ten million expected by buildout, City Park Oak is the largest concentration of office and commercial activity in the United States outside of a conventional downtown, and actually surpassed in size by only twelve CBDs in all North America (see Photo 3.20). While office uses dominate the development, an impressive 4 million square feet of assorted retail uses serve the daytime population of 85,000. The inclusion of numerous restaurants and 4,700 hotel rooms within the project has made Post Oak one of the more active, people-oriented night spots in the Houston area. Some establishments stay open as late as 2:00 A.M. for the late-night crowd.

PLAYA VISTA. One of the largest planned urban developments (PUDs) anywhere, Playa Vista is being designed as a self-sufficient com-

Photo 3.20. High-Rise Concentration at City Post Oak, Six Miles West of Downtown Houston off the I-610 Beltloop.
The current 107 office buildings in City Post Oak are punctuated by the 65-story Transco Tower, shown in the photo's foreground. (Photo provided courtesy of Rice Center.)

munity with a balanced mix of housing, employment, shopping, and recreational opportunities occupying a 926-acre tract some 20 miles west of downtown Los Angeles off the Pacific Ocean. When completed sometime around year 2000, nearly 9,000 new homes will be complemented by over eight million square feet of retail, office, and high-tech industrial space and 25,000 daytime workers. Also planned are a public marina, shoreline promenade, athletic fields, swimming pools, and a community-wide pedestrian and bicycle trail system.[53]

HARMON MEADOWS. Near the already successful Harmon Cove project in northeastern New Jersey's Meadowlands, Hartz Mountain Industries has begun construction of a 550-acre mixed-use development called Harmon Meadows. In addition to four million square feet of office space, Harmon Meadows will showcase two retail complexes containing over 50 stores and restaurants, an eightplex theater, a health club, and a flagship hotel. Around 2,600 townhouses will also dot the complex. Together with Harmon Cove's two million square feet of office space, 500 residential units, and hotel, New Jersey's Meadowlands is quickly taking on a viable urban/suburban identity that has enticed increasing numbers of Manhattan businesses to move west of the Hudson River.[54]

CHESTERBROOK. The 865-acre planned community of Chesterbrook, 17 miles west of downtown Philadelphia, will focus on a mid-rise corporate center housing 1.5 million square feet of office space and 3,000 employees when completed around 1990. The Chesterbrook development is being designed and marketed as a dynamic residential community sporting 3,770 dwelling units, several small shopping malls, and a first-rate hotel at buildout (see Photo 3.21).

SCARBOROUGH TOWN CENTRE. In coordination with the Toronto Metropolitan Council, the community of Scarborough has been building a new mini-downtown 17 miles northeast of the regional CBD since the early seventies. In reaction to increasing central city congestion and an overloaded infrastructure, Toronto's metropolitan government has sought to channel jobs that would have otherwise spilled over onto highway-oriented office and commercial strips toward several satellite subcenters. The Scarborough Town Centre is being designed as a focal point for new office construction, government services, retail functions, and cultural and entertainment activities. At buildout, 40,000 daytime workers and 8,000 permanent residents will co-occupy the 330-acre complex. A labyrinth of enclosed, temperature-controlled skybridges will eventually lace the compound, which along with several richly landscaped plazas, will create a strong pedestrian environment. A new advanced light rail transit line (ALRT) presently penetrates the Scarborough Town Centre, providing swift connections to Toronto's main core[55] (see Photo 3.22).

For nearly all these non-CBD developments, mixed land uses have not only created self-sustaining, village-like working environments, they have also markedly enhanced the marketability of projects. In the case of Denver's Tech Center, the executive director of marketing has estimated that land values are presently two to three times greater than those of competing projects in the Denver region, principally because of the Tech Center's mixed-use character.[56] Moreover, store owners and merchants are increasingly finding office parks and suburban work centers attractive places to locate, not only for aesthetic reasons, but also because they represent captive markets.

In sum, evidence is beginning to accumulate on the advantages of mixed-use suburban workplaces. To the extent office developers begin emulating some of these balanced projects, tremendous strides can be made toward safeguarding suburban mobility. The development industry should clearly pay close attention to the City Post Oaks, Denver Tech Centers, and Chesterbrooks of America when crafting suburban office master plans.

Photo 3.21. Aerial View of Chesterbrook Corporate Center, with Residential Communities in the Background.
(Photo provided courtesy of The Fox Companies.)

Photo 3.22. **Scarborough Town Centre, Present and Future.**
Top photo, the office/government complex and Y-shaped shopping mall are separated by the elevated advanced light rail transit line. Bottom photo, scale model of Town Centre at buildout, with buildings clustered around the rail line. (Photos by Peter Mykuz, provided courtesy of the city of Scarborough.)

Call for a New Suburban Design Template

Whether in low-density suburbs or compact central cores, good design and land use practices are absolutely essential if efficient access and unrestricted mobility are to be achieved. While rising gasoline prices, economic recessions, and other key determinants of commuting habits are clearly outside of developers' spheres of influence, equally important factors such as building designs, site layouts, and land-use mixing just as clearly are within their control. It is especially important for office developers to consider the mobility tradeoffs of certain site plans and land use choices at the very outset when the overall design, scale, and character of a project are being defined. Coordinating site planning and transportation can not only avert future access and mobility problems, it can produce a more functional and better quality working environment over the long haul as well.

Still, one cannot lose sight of the sober reality that, when it comes to designing suburban office complexes, transportation concerns have been usurped by overriding environmental quality and aesthetic objectives. While guaranteeing efficient on-site traffic circulation is essential toward creating an attractive work setting, issues such as the provision of transit amenities and efficient pedestrian connections generally fall toward the bottom of developers' priority lists. In the case of most campus-style office parks, the creation of a roomy, low-density built environment has unquestionably benefited *on-site* traffic circulation by spreading trips out. What these designs have done for *off-site* traffic circulation, however, is an altogether different matter. By discouraging, or in some cases precluding, transit and other ridesharing forms, many low-density designs contribute directly to downstream congestion by forcing employees to drive to work. The larger mobility problem, then, lies with the bottlenecks and traffic breakdowns along freeways and arterials leading to suburban workplaces that most office developments bear some responsibility for. It is clear that in a number of settings, free-flow on-site circulation is being achieved at the expense of off-site traffic jams.

This dilemma calls for a careful rethinking of our whole design approach toward suburban workplaces. It is important for both developers and municipal planners to recognize the communitywide implications of certain design schemes, not only in terms of traffic impacts but also with regard to the overall quality of suburban living. A stronger public–private partnership is needed to sculpture a suburban built environment that is tempered by the interests of the community at large, in addition to those of the developer. Certainly, any movement from sprawling office park designs to denser mixed-use, village-like projects would offer the greatest mobility payoff over the long run. Important precedents have already been established in this area, such as the remodelling of the Denver Technological Center, that could serve as paradigms for other suburban developments. Congregations of close-by offices, homes, restaurants, and shops offer the best hope for not only safeguarding mobility, but also for fostering viable suburban living and working environments.

Recently, there have been encouraging signs of public–private teamwork in coordinating design, land use, and transportation decisions on the urban fringes. In San Francisco's East Bay, for instance, the Alameda-Contra Costa Transit District has worked with several residential, shopping center, and office park developers on transit-related site planning matters. A report, titled "Guide for Including Public Transit and Land Use Planning," has emerged from these efforts and has been widely circulated within the East Bay's development community.[57] Similarly, the regional transit authority in highly suburbanized Orange County, California has sought to promote transit-sensitive design practices through an ambitious marketing effort. One in-house publication, "Consideration of Transit in Project Development," recommends design and land use strategies for integrating transit into new commercial and office complexes. The report concludes that "land use planning is where the private sector can contribute most towards solving transportation problems."[58] While these might appear like modest beginnings, they are exemplary of well-intentioned public initiatives that could spark private interest in designing suburban workplaces more with transportation in mind.

Possibilities for joint public–private initiatives in America's suburbs are discussed further in the following chapter. In addition to cooperative site and land use planning, there are numerous opportunities for collaborative efforts between both parties in containing suburban traffic and financing needed transportation improvements, both on and off site. Those traffic management strategies and joint financing programs that appear most promising for the urban fringes are concentrated on next.

Notes

1. J. Ross McKeever, *Business Parks* (Washington: The Urban Land Institute, Technical Bulletin 65, 1970), p. 45.
2. Ibid., p. 35.

3. See: Waldemar George, "A Plan for a Contemporary City," in *Le Corbusier in Perspective*, Peter Serenyi, ed. (Englewood Cliffs, N.J.: Prentice-Hall, 1975).

4. See: Christopher B. Leinberger, "New Shape of Cities Will Impact Corporate Location," *National Real Estate Investor*, Vol. 26, No. 14 (1984), p. 40; and C. Kenneth Orski, "Suburban Mobility: The Coming Transportation Crisis?" *Transportation Quarterly*, Vol. 39, No. 2 (1985), pp. 285–86.

5. Orski, "Suburban Mobility," p. 285.

6. Floor area ratio (FAR) equals the total floorspace of a building divided by the size of the lot on which it sits.

7. Orski, "Suburban Mobility," p. 286.

8. Ibid.

9. Boris Pushkarev and Jeffrey Zupan, *Public Transportation and Land Use Policy* (Bloomington: Indiana University Press, 1977).

10. Richard F. Galehouse, "Mixed-Use Centers in Suburban Office Parks," *Urban Land*, Vol. 43, No. 8 (1984), p. 13.

11. McKeever, *Business Parks*, pp. 15–16. The average size of research parks in the 1970s was estimated to be considerably higher than this average—around 650 acres. For discussions on R&D parks, see: Douglas R. Porter, "Research Parks: An Emerging Phenomenon," *Urban Land*, Vol. 43, No. 9 (1984), p. 8. Some of the nation's recently constructed R&D parks dwarf even the very largest office complexes. Among the largest built to date are: Sterling Forest in New York, with more than 20,000 acres; the Research Triangle in Central North Carolina, with 5,000 acres; the Huntsville Research Park in Alabama, spanning over 2,000 acres; and the University Research Park in Charlotte, North Carolina, with almost 1,400 total acres.

12. This estimate is based on results of the national survey and inventories obtained from local government agencies.

13. See discussion of the Hacienda Business Park's design concept in Chapter Six, for instance.

14. Paul Reimer, "Future High-Tech Parks," *Urban Land*, Vol. 42, No. 11 (1983), pp. 21.

15. Institute of Real Estate Management, *Office Buildings: Income/Expense Analysis, Downtown and Suburban* (Chicago: Institute of Real Estate Management, 1984).

16. McKeever, *Business Parks*, p. 34.

17. Robert Campbell, "Cities for Cars and Towers vs. Cities for People," *Boston Globe* (May 6, 1984). Quoted in: Galehouse, "Mixed-Use Centers in Suburban Office Parks," p. 13.

18. Quoted in: Harre W. Demoro, "Bay Sprawl Alarms Architects," *San Francisco Chronicle* (February 15, 1985), p. 24.

19. Galehouse, "Mixed-Use Centers in Suburban Office Parks," p. 12.

20. Ibid.

21. Kevin Lynch and Gary Hack, *Site Planning* (Cambridge: MIT Press, 1984), p. 197.

22. Ibid., pp. 197, 313.

23. Urban Land Institute, "Opus 2," *Project Reference File*, Vol. 13, No. 2 (1983).

24. Based on national survey results, an estimated five percent of office developers nationwide have reconfigured their roadway systems to better accommodate buses and wide-axle vehicles on-site.

25. McKeever, *Business Parks*, p. 28.

26. These estimates are based on national survey results. The ranges were from 2 to 6.5 spaces per 1,000 gross square feet of floorspace and from .33 to 3 spaces per employee. Most zoning ordinances require around 3.5 spaces per 1,000 square feet for suburban office projects.

27. W. Paul O'Mara and John A. Casaza, *Office Development Handbook* (Washington: Urban Land Institute, Community Builder's Handbook Series, 1982), p. 56.

28. Ann Lenny, "Canyon Corporate Center—From RVs to R&D: Transition to a Higher Use," *Urban Land*, Vol. 43, No. 4 (1984), p. 24.

29. This is based on a land cost of $3 to $7 per square foot. The construction costs for surface parking range from $1.50 to $2 per square foot (1982 currency), including surfacing, striping, draining, illuminating, and landscaping. See O'Mara and Casaza, *Office Development Handbook*, p. 58.

30. O'Mara and Casaza, *Office Development Handbook*, pp. 54–55.

31. R. Gauldin, "Developing a Suburban Office Park," *Mortgage Banker*, Vol. 40, No. 2 (1979), p. 44.

32. O'Mara and Casaza, *Office Development Handbook*, p. 57.

33. Gauldin, "Developing a Suburban Office Park," p. 44.

34. Kit Dailey, "Aliso Viejo: A Transit Planner's Ultimate Dream," *Mass Transit* (August, 1980), p. 55.

35. Government Code 66475.2, State of California.

36. The range in average walking distances between on-site bus stops and main building entrances is 50 feet to nearly one-half mile. By comparison, the estimated mean distance from the center of parking lots to main building entrances is 116 feet.

37. Campbell, "Cities for Cars and Towers vs. Cities for People," p. 13; Demoro, "Bay Sprawl Alarms Architects," p. 24.

38. Neal Peirce, "Fort Collins: How to Grow Fast, with Class," *The Denver Post* (September 8, 1985).

39. Other survey responses to the availability of nearby housing were as follows: "moderate but growing amount"—23 percent; "modest amount"—9 percent; and "little or none"—6 percent.

40. See Chapter Five for further discussions on the South Coast Metro Center's housing program.

41. See Chapter Six for additional discussions of community resistance to office-housing integration in the East Bay of the San Francisco area.

42. See: David E. Dowall, *The Suburban Squeeze* (Berkeley: University of California Press, 1984).

43. Ibid.
44. Lawrence D. Maloney, "America's Suburbs Still Alive and Doing Fine," *U.S. News & World Report* (March 12, 1984), p. 61.
45. Ibid.
46. The Walnut Creek ordinance rations building permits until adequate road capacity and public transit facilities are in place. Once a roadway reaches level of service D, what traffic engineers consider unstable flow, no new building or occupancy permits will be issued. Walnut Creek officials hope that such an ordinance will prod the development community into self-policing its office building activities and sponsoring wide-ranging programs aimed at reducing traffic, such as vanpooling. While other communities, like Petaluma, California, and Boca Raton, Florida, legislated strict growth controls during the environmentally conscious 1970s, the Walnut Creek ordinance is the first to limit growth specifically on the basis of traffic conditions.
47. A floating zone describes a zoning district adopted in a zoning ordinance but not fixed or mapped to any location in the community. Fixation of the floating zone is often expressly invited by application of the landowner.
48. See Chapter Five for additional discussion on the Warner Center housing program.
49. Washington Metropolitan Area Transit Authority, "Metro Joint Development Projects" (Washington: WMATA, 1983, unpublished agency report); Alinda C. Burke, "Summary of WMATA's Land Development Transactions" (paper presented at the Seventh Annual Lincoln Institute/USC Law Center Land Policy Conference on Transportation and Land Development," Los Angeles, February 1984); and Carole Baker, "Tracking Washington's Metro," *American Demographics,* Vol. 5, No. 11 (1983), p. 35.
50. See: Rice Center, "Mobility and Congestion: Office Location Issues in Houston," *Research Brief* No. 1 (April 1979), p. 6, for additional discussions on the relationship between housing location and suburban commuting patterns in the Houston area.
51. U.S. Department of Commerce, Bureau of the Census, *Statistical Abstract of the United States: 1985* (Washington: U.S. Government Printing Office, 1984), p. 399.
52. McKeever, *Business Parks*, p. 14. In this 1970 study, a survey of 41 American office parks found that ten were close to regional shopping centers. In 1984 a national survey of 120 developments indicated only 19 (16.5%) were within five miles of a regional shopping complex.
53. See Chapter Five for further case study discussion of the Playa Vista project.
54. See: Kelley Roark, "Development in the Meadowlands: Correcting Past Mistakes," *Urban Land*, Vol. 44, No. 3 (1985), pp. 12–13.
55. Advanced Light Rail Transit is considered an intermediate technology between conventional heavy rail rapid transit and light rail/streetcar types of systems. ALRT systems are being constructed in the Toronto metropolitan area, Vancouver, British Columbia, and Detroit. They are generally characterized by

fully automated, intermediate-capacity trains propelled by linear induction motors and operating on elevated tracks that connect modest, sometimes simple side platform stations.

56. Galehouse, "Mixed-Use Centers in Suburban Office Parks," p. 12.
57. Alameda-Contra Costa Transit District, "Guide for Including Public Transit in Land Use Planning" (Oakland, Calif.: AC Transit, 1983, unpublished agency report).
58. Orange County Transit District, "Consideration of Transit in Project Development" (Santa Ana, Calif.: OCTD, 1982, unpublished agency report).

4

Suburban Traffic Management

APPROACHES AND PROSPECTS

Transportation Management

A mixed bag of both public and private initiatives is today being pursued in the battle to head off suburban gridlock. At the forefront has been the emergence of employer associations, typically groups of developers, business executives, and other private interests who have banned together to deal with common transportation concerns. Sometimes referred to as Transportation Management Associations (TMAs), these private sector forums have become particularly active around suburban mixed-use centers, sponsoring employee ridesharing and shuttle services, lobbying for state highway funding assistance, and promoting other assorted programs aimed at reducing peak trips, such as flexible work schedules.

Another recent development has been the passage of municipal ordinances in a number of suburban communities across the country that either seek to regulate the volume of peak hour auto traffic or pass on the costs of necessary roadway improvements to private developers and employers. To date, trip reduction ordinances have been enacted in the suburbs of Los Angeles, San Francisco, and Sacramento, California. Legislation that exacts fees from suburban developers for building new highways can be found in Fairfax County, Virginia; Orange County, California; and several other rapidly developing areas.

Not all efforts to enlist private sector support in suburban road financing have been coercive. Most private interests fully recognize that the marketability and long-term success of their projects depend crucially upon guaranteeing their tenants, employees, and customers good access as well as promoting orderly growth on the urban fringe. Most also appreciate that

95

public funds for new roadway construction are scarce. Not surprisingly, then, a sizable share of recent suburban interchange, road widening, and related infrastructure improvements have been privately financed. Some have been negotiated during the permit approval process while others have been conceived, designed, and marshalled through to implementation by developers themselves.

This chapter explores the current and potential roles of these and other emerging traffic managment strategies in the struggle against suburban gridlock. Some efforts, such as ridesharing and flex-time, aim principally to make more efficient use of existing roadspace and available automobile seats by encouraging coworkers to double-up into carpools or commute outside of the traditional rush hours. These, known widely as "transportation system management" (TSM) strategies,[1] rely almost entirely on voluntarism, namely the willingness of workers to alter their usual commuting habits. Programs such as trip reduction ordinances, on the other hand, represent formal legislative mandates to curb congestion; just the same, however, the intent of such ordinances is to prod employers into initiating TSM actions such as vanpooling. Other strategies, like public/private cofinancing of freeway expansions, involve informal bargaining over site-specific improvements, with private contributions sometimes totalling into the millions of dollars. Despite their differences in approach, these strategies have overlapping purposes as well as the same ultimate objective of safeguarding suburban mobility.

Transportation Management Associations (TMAs)

TMAs have proven to be effective coalitions for dealing with the knotty access problems found at many suburban work centers, especially ones with poor public transit connections. Most associations, anywhere from five to 75 employer members, engage in a wide range of activities, such as promoting ridesharing through computerized matching services, purchasing fleets of vans for employee pooling, assisting members in meeting government trip reduction mandates, underwriting internal shuttle services and park-and-ride circulators, financing areawide street improvements such as signal upgrading, lobbying for suburban political interests, and even planning for long-range transportation projects like future rail transit extensions. These organizations are not solely dedicated to "management" as their titles suggest, but rather a panoply of transportation-related activities, some involving sizable cash disbursements.

Most TMAs are supported through membership fees, sometimes voluntary, although most often mandatory. Among the larger TMAs, formal rules and bylaws usually govern the actions of policy boards, and full-time staffs carry out day-to-day functions and policy directives. Smaller associations typically operate less formally, using roundtable meetings to thrash out solutions to site-specific problems, like manning a particular intersection with a traffic officer. While some TMAs have been initiated by land developers themselves, in most cases they have been formed by employers within an office complex or defined geographic area. Where they have been spearheaded by developers, landholder and tenant participation in the TMAs is almost always required in covenants and leasing agreements.[2]

Despite the wide press TMAs have received in the transportation literature in recent years,[3] to date only two dozen or so have emerged nationwide.[4] One of the first was formed by a group of businessmen and developers associated with the Tysons Corner mall and office complex in Fairfax County, Virginia, which presently boasts a labor force of 70,000 and more than 400 retail establishments.[5] Only 40 years ago a sleepy intersection with a gas station and small grocery store, Tysons Corner is expected to double its 12.5 million square feet of office space within a decade, becoming the largest "downtown" in Virginia.[6] In response to choking rush-hour traffic, the Tysons Corner Association has launched an areawide vanpool program for employees and a free shuttle circulator for shoppers and workers. These services have been credited with removing some 5,000 cars from overburdened local streets, although rush-hour traffic still often moves at a snail's pace and the group readily admits far more needs to be done.[7]

Comparable TMAs can be found in El Segundo, Pleasanton, and Orange County, California; City Post Oak and The Woodlands, Texas; and outside of downtown Denver, Hartford, Cleveland, and Boston. In all of these settings, large concentrations of white-collar employees working in non-CBD locations with meager or insufficient transit services have spawned the formation of TMAs. The City Post Oak Association, responsible for managing the trips generated by 65,000 employees at the mixed-use supercomplex six miles west of downtown Houston, has helped underwrite the cost of operating 100 vans serving 1,200 workers. And at the 850-acre Denver Technological Center, a fee levied on all employers has gone toward financing a successful ridesharing program, private bus services, several off-site freeway interchanges, and the resignalization of local surface streets.[8]

Many large employer associations have additional agendas beyond just transportation, such as working with city planners on regional housing policy and environmental issues. The Santa Clara County Manufacturing Group, for instance, has not only coordinated ridesharing programs throughout the Silicon Valley,[9] but has also actively promoted residential development on San Jose's job-rich, but housing-poor, northside. The group has likewise worked closely with local transit officials in coordinating the development of several new high-tech office parks with the construction of San Jose's new Guadalupe Corridor light rail transit (LRT) line. Opportunities for joint development of LRT station areas have also been discussed, with the association serving as a sounding board for public-private dialogue.

Not all TMAs have been success stories, however. The Newport Center Association in Southern California, set up in the late seventies to promote ridesharing among 10,000 employees of Newport Beach's expanding office and retail hub, folded after one year, largely due to the lack of top-level executive commitment and interest.[10] Other TMAs have curtailed their activities as they have matured. Most notably, the El Segundo Employer's Association (ESEA), representing the massive aerospace and electronics industrial complex near Los Angeles's International Airport, has recently cut its staff in half and abandoned its in-house ridematching program, concentrating instead almost exclusively on lobbying for state funding assistance.[11] This abrupt about-face has come as a mild shock to some observers, as ESEA has over the past several years been hailed as the archetype of employer involvement in ridesharing. The group has been credited with luring 24 percent of El Segundo's employees to carpools and vanpools, earning it one of the American Planning Association's "Outstanding Contribution to Planning" awards in 1982.[12] The belief among ESEA's Board of Directors that the employee vanpooling market had already been saturated, along with some participants' concerns over spending too much money on "soft" programs like ridematching, led to this retrenchment.

Additionally, while TMAs have blossomed in large suburban megacenters and areas with critical masses of workers, they have had a difficult time getting off the ground where multiple small-scale office parks exist, oftentimes where they are needed the most. And there has been little in the way of intercompany or intercomplex coordination of TMA-types of activities. In places like west Los Angeles, west Houston, the north Dallas parkway area, and Orange County, opportunities abound for coordination among different independent TMAs. To date, however, most large suburban office developers and employers have shied away from cooperative efforts with neighbors, preferring not to drum up any new administrative responsibilities or deal with possible logistical headaches.

The absence of a united voice for confronting common transportation problems along corridors dotted with office developments could have grave consequences in some rapidly growing settings. Indeed, the cumulative traffic impacts of numerous loosely organized office and retail centers can be every bit as troublesome as large-scale megacomplexes. One prime example of this is the Highway 101 peninsula corridor linking San Francisco and San Jose, where 25 million square feet of mixed office, commercial, and hotel development spread over 55 separate projects was approved between 1982 and 1984. While different municipalities stretched along the 35-mile corridor have awarded assorted projects negative declarations in their environmental reviews of traffic impacts, regional planners estimate that the cumulative effects of these developments will quickly oversaturate the existing six-lane freeway.[13] In fact, a doubling of the normal one and one-quarter rush-hour commuting time between San Jose and San Francisco has been projected within the next 15 years because of this building frenzy.

All and all, TMAs appear to have a promising future in America's suburbs. From interviews, the overwhelming majority of developers currently involved with TMAs believe that their projects are more marketable as a result, giving them a winning edge over their competitors. TMAs offer a free-wheeling, entrepreneurial framework for attacking suburban mobility problems. They have also responded to a common institutional void, taking charge in the absence of a public authority directly responsible for suburban or interjurisdictional mobility issues. More and more, TMAs are replacing the public manning process, carrying out planning functions, for instance, that have historically been the sole province of councils of government and regional planning organizations. Unencumbered by usual bureaucratic distractions, TMAs have been able to respond more promptly and imaginatively to their clients' unique mobility needs than local governments ever could. Indeed, they are apt to become indispensable vehicles for launching successful suburban transportation campaigns in the future.

Ridesharing

One valuable policy lesson transportation planners have learned over the past decade is that ridesharing programs are only successful when employers get directly involved. Self-matching boards placed in prominent public places, radio jingles, and other promotional efforts that do not involve employers have usually been abysmal failures at getting people to commute together.[14] To no great surprise, the emergence of TMAs has proven a tremendous boon to suburban ridesharing. Additionally, a number of

large individual corporations and regional nonprofit organizations, such as
Los Angeles's Commuter Computer, Inc., have inaugurated successful carpooling and vanpooling programs in outlying areas.

Employer sponsorship of ridesharing in suburbia is still in its infancy,
however. The national survey of suburban office complexes revealed that
only 16 percent currently have formal carpooling/vanpooling programs,
although another 5 percent plan to mount future rideshare campaigns (see
Photo 4.1). Most efforts have been sponsored by individual companies,
usually located in large, mixed-use developments, rather than by TMAs.
The majority of suburban businesses backing rideshare programs designate
a staff member as "program coordinator." Most coordinators work only
part-time, however, spending fewer than ten hours per week on ridesharing
matters. Only two of the 120 surveyed complexes have full-time coordinators. The job chores of coordinators usually involve some combination of
maintaining computerized matching lists of existing and potential poolers,
administering van purchases and leases, arranging group insurance policies,
program marketing, and monitoring ridesharing progress. Statistically, the

**Photo 4.1. Vanpool Connection at the Hacienda Business Park in
Pleasanton, California.**
(Photo by the author.)

presence of a coordinator seems to be making a difference. The estimated share of employees pooling to work among all surveyed office parks was just under 5 percent. Among those with coordinators, admittedly a small subsample, the share was 11 percent.

Several successful ridesharing programs presently flourish in the suburbs. Particularly impressive have been the vanpool programs sponsored by Rockwell International in Golden, Colorado and Lawrence Livermore Laboratory in Alameda County, California, with over 60 percent of all employees pooling to work in both places.[15] Other suburban rideshare programs with employee participation rates of over 40 percent currently thrive at the Fluor Corporation and the nearby regional headquarters of the Auto Club in central Orange County, California,[16] Tektronix, Inc. of Beaverton, Oregon, and the Transnational Motor, Inc. in Grand Rapids, Michigan. In the case of the two Orange County programs, assorted "carrots" such as 25 percent travel allowances and free lunches for participants have proven to be effective lures. Transnational Motor, Inc. of Grand Rapids, moreover, pays one-half of the total premium for employees' group auto insurance as an incentive to rideshare.[17]

TMA-backed suburban ridesharing programs have not been quite as prosperous as those sponsored by individual companies. Among the most successful have been programs initiated by TMAs from Bishop Ranch (San Ramon, California), City Post Oak (Houston), and The Meadowlands (northeast New Jersey), with each area enjoying a 25 to 35 percent employee rideshare participation rate. However, in other settings, such as the Denver Technological Center and The Woodlands, Texas, only around 5 percent of all employees have signed up so far for subsidized vanpools.[18]

As discussed in Chapter Three, the detached layout and sheer enormity of many suburban office parks have had a lot to do with some of these poor showings. In the case of megaprojects, the dispersal of 10,000 or more employees over several square miles, coupled with the usual absence of internal circulators and the provision of ample free parking, stack the odds heavily against ridesharing programs. Moreover, employees' residences are often widely scattered so as to make ridesharing impractical. At places like the Denver Technological Center, where more than 400 tenants account for the 12,000 workers, the preponderance of small employers has also greatly complicated ridematching.

Where few on-site consumer services, such as restaurants and banks, are available, ridesharing's chances for success are even slimmer. The fear of being stranded without a car is indeed one of the biggest deterrents to ridesharing in suburban work settings. A preponderance of suburban employees drive to work because they rely so heavily upon their personal vehicles during the course of a workday. A recent survey of 2,500 employees at the mixed-use South Coast Plaza in Costa Mesa, California, for instance, found that 45 percent needed their cars for personal reasons and 83 percent needed them to conduct business at least once a week.[19] In the case of the mammoth Bishop Ranch project on the Bay Area's fringe, over one-third of all surveyed employees needed their cars during the workday at least twice a week. One way around this dilemma would be to make company cars and idle vans available to rideshare participants during the midday. To date, no TMA has sponsored such a floating vehicle program, however the idea has been broached at Bishop Ranch and several other office complexes as well. Although this arrangement could inflate company insurance premiums and overhead expenses, the resulting inducement to ridesharing might well justify any additional outlays. Alternately, a vehicle leasing and rental service could be explored. This service might resemble a conventional automobile rental agency, with the added dimension of short-term day use rentals and overnight leasing to anyone missing their pool due to overtime work or inadvertency.[20] A short-term car rental experiment is currently underway in a San Francisco neighborhood of 5,000 apartment dwellers, however so far the concept has only been discussed in suburban work settings.

Finally, several "intangibles" have hampered ridesharing in the suburbs. At executive and R&D parks, for instance, a certain amount of prestige is usually attached to driving alone and parking in a reserved space. Quirks can also be found at the employer level. In the case of some corporate tenants at a handful of large high-tech complexes, employees have been directed by their superiors not to comingle or share rides with workers from other firms to prevent any "trade secrets" from being divulged. Indeed, the social mores and behavioral norms of many upscale suburban work centers seem to be at odds with ridesharing and other TSM initiatives.

Making ridesharing work in suburban office settings remains a lofty challenge, although recent successes give some cause for optimism. Where one-quarter or so of all employees participate, ridesharing can spell the difference between bumper-to-bumper traffic and free-flow conditions. To company backers, it can also return high dividends by reducing parking construction costs as well as worker absenteeism and tardiness.[21] A 1982 survey of 100 facilities managers working for major high-tech firms in California's Silicon Valley emphasized the high premium many employers are beginning to place on suburban ridesharing. Among a list of 13 potential facility services and improvements managers would most like to see in suburban office complexes, ridesharing ranked second, surpassed only by the wiring of telecommunication lines within buildings.[22]

Transit and Paratransit

Transit's Suburban Dilemma

Conventional fixed-route bus services are even less competitive with the private automobile in suburban office settings than vanpools. Densities on the residential as well as employment ends of suburban transit routes are often too low to make even a slight dent in areawide traffic conditions. When Fairfax County ran a cross-county bus service in the early eighties to the burgeoning Tysons Corner complex, for instance, it attracted only six riders per trip. The run was quickly scrubbed due to the paucity of interest.[23]

In most outlying office settings, public buses usually skirt the perimeters rather than penetrate directly into complexes. Only 38 percent of the developments surveyed nationally had public or private buses operating on-site. Some developers are reluctant to invite buses into their compounds, partly for concerns over safety liability and partly for image reasons. Diesel vehicles weaving throughout a complex, after all, are probably the last things amenity-minded architects and image-conscious developers have in mind when designing a business park. Moreover, some transit authorities have been known to frown on requests for on-premise services, fearing that headways will lengthen and schedule maintenance will suffer by doing so. Transit managers are particularly gunshy of establishing such precedents, fearing that a floodgate of similar requests will be opened if they begin detouring routes too freely.

Given transit's limited presence in office complexes, not surprisingly, only an estimated 2 percent of all suburban employees nationwide bus to work.[24] Even at larger mixed-use complexes that have on-site transit services, like the Denver Technological Center and Orange County's South Coast Plaza, as noted previously, fewer than 5 percent of all employees and shoppers commute by bus. This is despite the fact that both places are major transit transfer points, with, in the case of the South Coast Plaza, as many as 12 bus routes converging into the premises at any one time. According to Orange County's transit chief, excessive walking distances, at residential rather than employment terminuses, have been the bane of his operations.[25] Surveys show, for instance, only 21 percent of all South Coast

Plaza employees live within a five-minute trek of a bus route, generally considered the maximum time people will spend walking to a stop.[26]

America's transit industry has failed to respond to the needs of suburbia. To date, it has served the suburbs using conventional approaches. It should come as no surprise, then, that ridership is plummeting faster in suburbia than in any other setting of most U.S. metropolitan areas and that disaffected suburban jurisdictions are beginning to withdraw their financial support of transit in places like the Twin Cities, Washington, D.C., Kansas City, St. Louis, and Detroit.[27]

Although the odds seem to be stacked heavily against transit on America's urban fringes, within any looming crisis often lies the seeds of reform. Fundamentally what is called for are revolutionary changes in how transit is deployed in the suburbs. Traditional fixed-route, set-schedule services are in dire need of radical surgery. In most cases, radial systems should be replaced by grids offering high degrees of route interconnectivity so as to better serve the continuing dispersal of regional trips. Perhaps even more importantly, highly flexible forms of mass transportation that span the usual limited commuting choices of either riding a bus or driving oneself—often lumped together as paratransit—need to be fully exploited. A rich mix of suburban service options, such as private buspools, shared-ride taxis, and even for-profit jitney vans, would probably do as much to cut into the solo driving market as any single traffic managment program or technological fix.

Current Suburban Transit Practices

Before exploring these possibilities further, what kinds of transit incentives are currently being offered in the suburbs? Besides designing amenities like bus shelters and pullouts into office parks, a number of suburban developers and employers have begun distributing bus schedules and fare information and selling transit passes on-site. In several areas, businesses subsidize their employees' bus fares. In Westchester County, New York, for instance, many of the larger corporations buy unlimited monthly bus commutation tickets and either give them to their workers or sell them at reduced prices through payroll deductions.

In addition, while some dozen or so suburban office complexes nationwide have privately funded internal shuttle circulators, a few have bought full-size buses for off-site operations as well. Thirty-five miles east of San Francisco, developers of Bishop Ranch and the nearby Hacienda Business Park have recently purchased a combined total of six premium-type coaches that run to and from nearby BART stations[28] (see Photo 4.2). In both places, private contractors operate the buses, which are free of charge to Bishop Ranch's employees and presently cost Hacienda's workers 90 cents a trip. Far more substantial transit investments are either being considered or are under construction in several other suburban areas. In Las Colinas, Texas, the master-planned new town midway between Dallas and Ft. Worth, a privately financed fixed-guideway system is scheduled to begin full operations in late 1987[29] (see Photos 4.3a and b). The people-mover—which is being modelled around the driverless tram at the nearby Dallas International Airport—will interconnect major office and retail centers in Las Colinas's core. Just to the east, a group of leading Dallas developers have offered to donate land and contribute to the financing of a 23-mile light rail line traversing their commercially and industrially zoned landholdings.[30] Light rail connections are also being explored between BART and the Bishop Ranch and Hacienda Business Park complexes. Developers in both places have already purchased and set aside an abandoned railroad right-of-way for a possible future LRT linkage to the regional rapid transit system. Given the emphasis placed on aesthetics and healthy working environments by many high-tech firms, quiet and nonpolluting electrified light rail systems could prove to be compatible additions to large office parks where they can be economically justified.

Reforming Traditional Suburban Transit

While these anecdotes certainly deserve recognition, the greatest opportunities for reversing transit's eroding presence in suburbia lie with radically redesigning traditional services. Calls for major reform within the transit industry in the wake of suburbanization are nothing new:

> Can we not pause long enough in this headlong decentralization process to see where we are going. The mass transportation industry is caught in a strong tide which is sweeping this and many other businesses toward disaster. . . . [The] situation calls for strong expression and vigorous leadership.[31]

Delivered at the 1940 annual meeting of the American Transit Association, this forewarning indeed holds as much relevance today as it did nearly half a century ago.

Among the major facelifts most fixed-route suburban bus services should undergo is the conversion of spoke-and-hub systems into integrated cobweb-like networks that use office parks, shopping malls, and other

**Photo 4.2.   Private Bus Services for Office Employees at the Bishop
Ranch Business Park (above) and Hacienda Business Park
(below) in Alameda County, California.**
(Photos by the author.)

Photo 4.3a. Completed Phase of Las Colinas's Personal Transit System.
24-passenger vehicles weave between office towers in the Urban Center. (Photo provided courtesy of the Las Colinas Corporation.)

Photo 4.3b.   Completed Phase of Las Colinas's Personal Transit System.
Aerial view of the elevated guideway that skirts around Lake Carolyn and the connecting Canal Plaza. (Photo provided courtesy of the Las Colinas Corporation.)

activity nodes as timed-transfer points. Only this kind of network eases the hassle of making connections, an unfortunate but necessary part of transit trip making in an environment of dispersed origins and destinations.[32]

Outlying office and retail subcenters form natural building blocks for multifocal, timed-transfer networks. They offer both the ridership base and the physical space necessary for a coordinated system of synchronized buses to work. Recent experiences in Edmonton, Alberta; Portland, Oregon; Denver, and several other primarily western cities provide useful precedents for designing such multidestinational networks.[33] In Edmonton, the regional bus system was completely overhauled in the mid-seventies. All services were reorganized around 17 outlying transit centers, in addition to the main downtown terminus, with routes blanketing the city in a combined criss-cross and radial fashion (see Figure 4.1). Presently, anywhere from five to ten bus routes converge simultaneously on one of Edmonton's outlying transit centers precisely five minutes and thirty-five minutes after the hour. Transit patrons scramble from one bus to another to make their connections, and almost like clockwork, buses depart three to five minutes later. (This practice is known as "pulse-scheduling" since the convergence and departure of buses at regular intervals is akin to a pulse beat.) The majority of Edmonton's connection-transfer centers are located in shopping mall parking lots or in the heart of mixed-use office and retail districts. Roughly half of the centers themselves are fully enclosed, temperature-controlled structures with comfortable passenger staging areas (see Photo 4.4).

By radically altering its route structure and scheduling practices, the city of Edmonton has successfully adapted transit to mimic the area's emerging cross-town and lateral commuting pattern. Today, Edmontonians can reach nearly 90 percent of a 130-square mile area within 50 minutes or less via public transit.[34] In addition to Edmonton, several other areas (Portland, Denver, and Vancouver, British Columbia) have recorded anywhere from 50 percent to 200 percent increases in ridership over the past five to ten years—a period of stagnant or declining ridership in most other parts of the United States and Canada—after converting over to timed-transfer operations.

Flexible Mass Transportation

Studies show that timed-transfer systems do not necessarily work well everywhere. Residential densities of anywhere between 3,000 and 6,000 persons per square mile seem best suited for operationalizing these networks.[35] In suburban areas with densities far below the 3,000 persons per

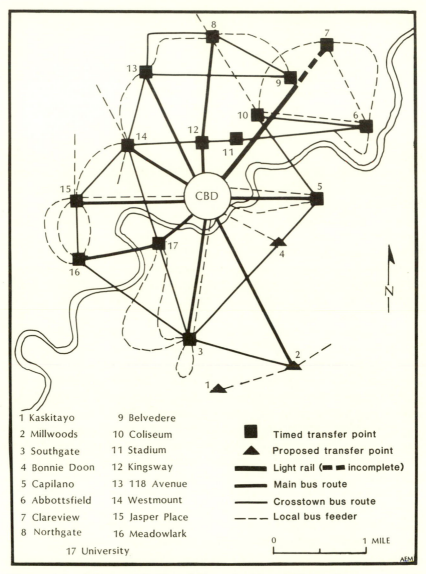

1 Kaskitayo   9 Belvedere

2 Millwoods   10 Coliseum

3 Southgate   11 Stadium

4 Bonnie Doon   12 Kingsway

5 Capilano   13 118 Avenue

6 Abbottsfield   14 Westmount

7 Clareview   15 Jasper Place

8 Northgate   16 Meadowlark

        17 University

■ Timed transfer point

▲ Proposed transfer point

━━ Light rail (━ ━ incomplete)

━━ Main bus route

── Crosstown bus route

─ ─ ─ Local bus feeder

0   1 MILE

Figure 4.1.   **Edmonton's Timed-Transfer Transit Network.**
(Sources: Edmonton Transportation Department, "Timed-Transfer System Planning in the City of Edmonton," agency report, 1984; and Debra A. Newman, Marlies Bebendorf, and Juliet McNally, "Timed-Transfer: An Evaluation of Its Structure, Performance and Cost," Washington: U.S. Department of Transportation, Urban Mass Transportation Administration, research report, 1983, pp. 2–10.)

Photo 4.4. Transit Connection at Edmonton's Southgate Transit Center.
Upper photo, buses converge all at once on the Southgate Center located on the fringe of Edmonton's Southgate Shopping Mall. Lower photo, precisely three minutes after they arrive, all buses platoon out of the center to provide both local and regional services. (Photos by the author.)

square mile minimum threshold, more flexible modes of mass transportation are needed, either as feeders into timed-transfer centers or else as direct connectors into outlying workplaces themselves. While synchronized, multi-focal bus systems like Edmonton's are clearly preferable to noncoordinated, radial ones, any contribution they make toward easing suburban congestion will be only marginal at best as long as any transferring is involved.

Perhaps as important as any one policy lesson learned by transportation planners over the past two decades has been that Americans simply abhor transferring. Rather than driving to a commuter station, switching modes, and waiting for a connection, more often than not they will stay in their vehicles and continue on to their ultimate destination, particularly when there is a free parking spot awaiting them. Idly waiting at a busy curbside for a connecting bus is an even bigger irritant. In fact, studies show that most commuters perceive the "dead time" of waiting for a connecting bus or train to be upwards of three times as long as it actually is by a watch's dial.[36]

Paratransit modes, such as shared-ride taxis and private commuter buses, are the best answers devised yet to the dreaded transfer problem. They alone offer some of the flexibility and convenience of the private auto-mobile combined with the mass-carrying features of buses.

If paratransit services such as shared-ride taxis, jitneys, buspools, and dial-a-vans are so attractive, then why aren't they more prevalent today? The primary culprit has been excessive government regulation on entry and pricing. To protect the public from the threats of unscrupulous taxi wars, price gouging, and unfit carriers as well as to shield public transit operators from head-to-head competition, most municipalities, suburban ones included, strictly regulate the number and quality of paratransit offerings. By squelch-ing free enterprise and competition, however, regulations have brought about a highly centralized, monolithic form of mass transportation—namely, fixed-route, set-schedule, downtown-destined, 48-passenger bus connections. Thus, the overwhelming majority of metropolitan commuters are left with two fairly limited choices: either drive or pool with someone, or take a bus. Deregulation could markedly widen the number of service options available to commuters heading for suburban work sites.

Places where restrictions on shared-ride taxis, bus pools, and other paratransit options have been lifted or eased offer valuable lessons for suburban traffic planners. Currently, private taxicabs provide shared-ride services in Phoenix, Norfolk, and some 20 other cities across the country where population densities do not warrant extensive fixed-route services, but where alternatives to the private car are sought.[37] In southeast Virginia's Tidewater area, for instance, taxi companies circulate sedans, mini- and maxi-vans, and small buses throughout suburban Chesapeake and Virginia Beach, taking pools of residents to their workplaces, regional shopping malls, and other scattered destinations.[38] In the city of Chesapeake, where two lightly used bus routes were replaced by shared-ride taxis in 1979, ridership immediately increased along the corridor, while operating costs per passenger dropped by 43 percent within one year. In Phoenix, Marin County, California, and several other places, premium shared-ride services contracted out to private taxi companies have been used to keep a lid on the scale of the public transit system in an attempt to hold costs constant. A growing list of municipal transit agencies are discovering that paratransit providers are not competitors who "skim the cream" off their business, but rather "they are friends who actually skim the deficit."[39] Recent experiences with citywide decontrol of taxis in Seattle, San Diego, and Portland, moreover, have resulted in noticeable service improvements, such as an average 20 percent reduction in wait times.[40]

Another promising development has been the emergence of private commuter bus services and bus clubs on the urban fringes (Photo 4.5). In the Los Angeles area, hundreds of subscription buses provide comfortable connections to employment centers scattered throughout the region for over 5,000 daily customers.[41] One program is sponsored by Hughes Aircraft, a major aerospace company headquartered near Los Angeles's international airport. Hughes has contracted with a private operator to run buses on ten routes, each about 12 to 15 miles in length, which serve residential areas with fairly high concentrations of company employees.[42] Employees subscribe to the service monthly through Hughes, with the company underwriting a share of their commuting expenses. Several other private bus operators are providing intrametropolitan services in the Los Angeles area to ten or so different employment districts. One, Commuter Bus Lines, Inc. operates intercounty routes of 30 to 50 miles in length, connecting several large work sites.[43] Comparable regionwide commuter bus lines can be found in Virginia's Tidewater area, although unlike in Los Angeles, services there generally concentrate on blue-collar markets. The fact that willing entrepreneurs are making profits in all these settings indicates that there is a ready market of workers who will patronize suburban bus transportation and pay fares of as much as $4 per trip given good quality service. Indeed, premium service features—from the provision of roomy, guaranteed seats with padded headrests to the convenience of front-door drop-offs at customers' offices—have been the hallmark of all successful suburban bus operations to date.

As with shared-ride taxis and other forms of paratransit, commuter

buses have also been stymied by tight regulatory controls in many areas of
the country. In the case of Los Angeles's buspools, they are treated as inter-
city carriers, subject to state Public Utility Commission (PUC) oversight.
California's buspool operators must obtain route authority and have their
fare schedules periodically approved by the PUC. In cases where public
transit agencies file protests against requests to initiate new private bus
routes, often with labor pressure to do so, new service requests are almost
routinely denied.

In sum, there is a growing market for intersuburban commuting to outlying employment centers. Because of protective legislation, much of this
demand has gone unfulfilled, however. Loosening the noose of regulatory
controls will be an important step toward combating suburban congestion in
coming years.

**Photo 4.5.   Private Commuter Bus Service in Suburban Contra Costa
County, California.**
(Photo by the author.)

Modified Work Schedules and Cycling Programs

Increasingly, suburban employers and TMAs are looking to tactics even cheaper and simpler than ridesharing and paratransit programs to ease chronic traffic headaches. Among the lower budget strategies currently being pursued are flexible work schedules and cycling incentives.

Allowing workers to arrive and depart at different times of the workday has proven to be an effective way of spreading out the maddening rush-hour crunch experienced along many suburban corridors. Transportation planners have long argued that modifying work schedules, if only marginally, can relieve congestion by shaving those 15 to 30 minute "subpeaks" that cause many roadways to break down. The congestion-easing ability of rearranged work schedules was clearly demonstrated in Los Angeles during the 1984 Summer Olympics. There, the switch from an 8-to-5 to a 6-to-3 workday by roughly one-third of the Los Angeles area's employers during the two weeks of the Olympics helped to unclog normally congested freeways, even though 11 percent more daily trips were being made.[44] Although staggered work hours shaved only a small number of vehicles off the peak hour in absolute terms, reductions were enough to slash the region's "delay minutes"—time spent going less than 35 m.p.h.—by 86 percent.[45]

Nationally, survey results indicate that nearly 40 percent of all large suburban office developments have some form of modified work schedules—be it flex-time, staggered work hours, or multiple work shifts. Several of the larger suburban employers surveyed were averse to flex-time because they feared it would lead to an overly lax working environment. Staggering shifts within a one- to two-hour period around the A.M. and P.M. peaks was generally considered a preferred alternative. Other suburban employers have never seriously considered flex-time or staggered work schedules because either their office functions are highly interdependent or because exogenous circumstances require everyone to be on-board at certain hours, such as in the case of brokerage houses that set their clocks according to the trading hours of the eastern stock exchanges.

Flex-time and staggered work schedules are becoming increasingly common in California's suburbs. At the massive Warner Center complex, for example, some 3,000 employees of two large insurance companies presently enjoy flex-time privileges. At both places, shifts begin and end every 15 minutes, from 6:00 to 9:00 A.M. and from 3:00 to 6:00 P.M. Surveys show, given the chance, many workers have opted to arrive before the usual rush hours, take shorter lunch breaks, and leave work early—thus, accruing extra "prime-time" daylight hours in the afternoon for themselves. And contrary to popular opinion, flexible work hours have encouraged, rather than deterred, the formation of carpools, including intercompany ones. Given some latitude as to when they commute, employees of both insurance headquarters find it easier to match up with people who live and work near them, and who drive to work at roughly the same time. Past research has also found that companies adopting flex-time generally enjoy lower absenteeism and turnover rates in addition to higher productivity.[46]

Another trend that could serve to reinforce both flexible work hour and ridesharing programs has been the growing interest in on-site child-care facilities at several suburban work centers. The nation's first freestanding child-care center within a suburban office complex is now going up at Pleasanton, California's Hacienda Business Park. Planners hope the center will allow more working parents to join carpools since they will no longer be burdened with making a side trip each morning and evening to drop off and pick up their children. By providing a common terminus for both the parent's and the child's trip each morning, on-site child care facilities can eliminate the need for trip-chaining, thus allowing more point-to-point rather than roundabout commuting.

Another low-cost strategy introduced by several suburban companies has been to reward employees who use their own muscle power to get to work. Done as much to encourage employee fitness as to discourage auto travel, several large employers in California's Silicon Valley have promoted cycling by financing areawide trail improvements, distributing cycling route information, and offering discounts on all bicycle purchases through local vendors. Some programs have paid off handsomely. In the case of one large R&D firm in Palo Alto, for instance, an estimated 25 percent of the 2,200 company employees currently cycle to work, reducing parking demand by at least 500 spaces. With their relatively flat terrains and inviting weather, many fast-developing sunbelt and west coast metropolises have proven to be particularly ideal for cycling and walking.

Based on the national survey, only about 1 percent of all suburban office employees presently either bike or walk to work. Where office parks have bike paths integrated with a communitywide trail system in addition to on-site amenities such as showers, lockers, and rack facilities, as many as 3 to 5 percent of all employees are pedalling to and from work. Although the impacts of cycling incentive programs on suburban traffic conditions are apt to be minute at best, along with ridesharing and other TSM programs they can certainly make a meaningful contribution, particularly where appreciable numbers of employees live within one to three miles of a suburban employment center.

Traffic Impact Ordinances and Legislation

The threat of a traffic deluge has prompted an expanding list of suburban municipalities and county governments to introduce wide-ranging legislation aimed at either reducing vehicular trips or off-loading some of the responsibility for financing necessary roadway improvements to the private sector. Three major fronts of activity have been: (1) *Trip Reduction Ordinances*—whereby developers and employers are held to a stipulated phasedown in the percentage of solo auto trips made to their establishments; (2) *Impact Fee Ordinances*—whereupon developers must pay for areawide transportation improvements based on the estimated amount of traffic their projects will generate; and (3) *Incentive Ordinances*—whereby assorted waivers of zoning code requirements, such as minimum off-street parking levels, are granted in return for instituting traffic mitigation programs like ridesharing.

The emergence of such ordinances has reflected the growing recognition that the private sector holds the wherewithal and purse strings for effectively dealing with local problems like traffic buildup. Indeed, "public/ private partnerships" has become one of the more popular catchphrases of the eighties, a reference to the growing willingness of both sides to "scratch each other's back" in the pursuit of common objectives. In urban settings, most attention has focused on "benefit sharing" whereby local governments seek financial returns for major transportation investments, like a new rapid transit system, that confer benefits to those owning property adjacent to rail stations. Transit station connection fees and benefit assessment districts, for example, have been employed extensively to help cover capital expenses associated with building modern rail projects in Washington, Miami, and Baltimore. In more suburban settings, the trend has been toward "cost sharing" where local governments shift a portion of the expense in building a new freeway ramp and similar improvements necessitated by new growth to private developers and nearby landowners.

Enlisting the support of the private sector in paying for highway improvements is nothing new. For years, municipalities have required developers to provide streets, sidewalks, lighting, and other fixtures within subdivisions. Over time, the geographic boundaries of these infrastructural improvements have gradually expanded outward. Increasingly, developers are being asked to finance highway improvements adjacent to their properties to accommodate the passage of their employees and customers as well as areawide residents. Moreover, they are being called upon not only to provide additional roadway capacity both on- and off-site, but also to actually reduce their employees' vehicular commuting below that which would normally be expected. These widening spheres of responsibility have reflected both the recognition that private sector involvement must extend beyond individual property lines and that building more freeway lanes and off-ramps, by themselves, will not be enough to handle the onslaught of traffic descending upon America's suburbs.

Trip Reduction Requirements

Landmark ordinances that mandate reductions in peak-hour traffic can be found in several areas of the country. The first was enacted in Placer County, California, west of Sacramento. In 1981, county supervisors passed legislation requiring developers to reduce vehicular traffic produced by their projects 20 percent below the volume that would normally be expected based on Institute of Transportation Engineer's (ITE) trip generation rates. As a precondition to subdivision and permit approval, developers must enter into a legally binding agreement to implement assorted TSM programs, such as vanpools and preferential carpool parking, which will bring about the 20 percent reduction target. Most local observers maintain that the ordinance has been directly responsible for holding traffic congestion at bay along the fast-growing U.S. 50 corridor west of Sacramento.

Several other suburban jurisdictions have recently followed Placer County's lead, including Costa Mesa and Pleasanton, California, and Fairfax County, Virginia, while nearly two dozen or so others are seriously considering similar ordinances.[47] In response to worsening congestion spawned by the opening of several large office-retail megacomplexes, the city of Costa Mesa currently requires all new developers to implement TSM programs prior to the issuance of building permits and to submit status reports prior to receiving certificates of occupancy. Fairfax County's approach to traffic regulation has been more occasional. There, subdivision and building permit approvals are conditional on developer commitments to introduce transportation management programs whenever traffic counts exceed certain agreed-upon levels.[48]

To date, the most comprehensive, far-reaching trip reduction ordinance introduced anywhere is Pleasanton's. In 1980, when a large consortium announced plans for the 860-acre Hacienda Business Park on Pleasanton's north end, community leaders became alarmed over the threat of increasing traffic impinging on the area's easygoing, small-town character. A 300-member citizens' committee was formed to discuss ways to bate the traffic menace posed by Hacienda and other proposed office parks. The overwhelming consensus was that all companies moving into new complexes, as well as those already in Pleasanton, would be required to adopt strictly enforced policies that would lower peak-hour auto trips. With the support of many of the area's employers and developers, an ordinance was drafted, debated, and subsequently adopted in late 1984.

Pleasanton's ordinance stipulates that all employers with 50 or more persons, in addition to all employers located in business complexes like Hacienda, must institute various TSM programs to reduce peak trips by 45 percent, assuming that all workers would normally drive alone. The ordinance allows reductions to be staged over four years. (For many employers, since 15 to 20 percent of all workers already commute some alternative way, the actual decrease in solo commuting they will be held to is 25 to 30 percent.) Moreover, all participating employers are required to appoint a "workplace coordinator," post information on ridesharing and other commute alternatives, and conduct annual surveys to monitor progress. To assist employers as well as oversee the ordinance's enforcement, a task force of businessmen, transit managers, city officials, and citizens has been formed. The group is by no means a figurehead. Not only can it require adoption of specific TSM measures, it can also increase trip reduction goals on a case-by-case basis. Companies failing to comply with any part of the Pleasanton ordinance are subject to fines of $250 per day.

It should be noted that prior to the trip reduction ordinance, the city of Pleasanton already had established a strong precedent for controlling growth. A 2 percent annual ceiling was placed on all new residential construction in 1976, largely over concern for the community's fragile natural environment, in particular a low water table and unstable topsoils. Like many other suburban communities, Pleasanton has shied away from closing its doors to incoming businesses and industry because of the high tax returns they produce. The decision to reduce peak-hour vehicles rather than rely solely on cash contributions for building new roads unquestionably evolved out of the larger community objective of preserving the local ecology and promoting orderly growth.

Surveys of travel trends during the first year of Pleasanton's ordinance have been encouraging. At the Hacienda Business Park, by far the community's largest single workplace, a mid-1985 survey of nearly all employees indicated that 31 percent chose not to drive alone to work—up from around 20 percent only a year earlier. One-quarter of the Business Park's employees now rideshare, and 6 percent either patronize transit, walk, or cycle to work. The ordinance also seems to have prodded a growing number of employers to implement flexible working arrangements.

At Hacienda, for instance, the widespread introduction of flex-time has allowed 28 percent of all workers to miss Pleasanton's 7:30 to 8:30 morning peak and 51 percent to avoid its 4:30 to 5:30 evening peak. One firm with over 2,500 employees (AT&T, Inc.) was able to reduce its employees' peak-hour trips by one-half within just seven months of the ordinance's passage through a combination of encouraging both alternative modes of commuting and off-peak travel. Another firm with 176 workers achieved a remarkable first-year peak trip reduction of 86 percent almost entirely by flexing work hours.

Advantages of Trip Reduction Approaches. Notwithstanding Pleasanton's first year experiences, because of their recency, it is difficult to draw a verdict on just how successful trip reduction mandates have been or will be. Compared to assessment district financing and various forms of exactions, trip reduction ordinances grant employers and developers a fair degree of latitude and autonomy in dealing with their own specific mobility problems. In Pleasanton, the newly enacted ordinance applies to almost all employers, not just the tenants of new developments. Since everyone is generally "in the same boat," the ordinance promotes intercompany coordination of ridesharing and other TSM programs. Without question, the biggest plus of the trip reduction approach is its demand-side orientation—it responds to the suburban mobility crisis by modifying travel behavior rather than increasing the vehicle-carrying capacity of freeways and arterials. Its emphasis on ridesharing and other commute alternatives has placed it in particularly good standing with conservationists and environmentalists.

Potential Problem Areas. The true litmus test of a trip reduction ordinance is whether it can actually be enforced. In Costa Mesa, even though several large office projects have been approved over the past five years with specific TSM conditions attached, to date there has been very little monitoring of progress toward meeting conditions.[49] During Pleasanton's first year of enforcing its ordinance, moreover, only 32 percent of all firms conducted a required travel survey, although the threat of fines subsequently upped the compliance figure to 90 percent. Another concern is whether public officials will be able to accurately gauge the actual amount of solo driving-to-carpool conversion going on. In Pleasanton's case, surveys are required once a year, leaving open the possibility of unrepresentative sampling when workers know their bosses are closely watching their commuting habits for a particular week. Some critics have also pointed to the arbitrariness of adopting a rigid criterion like 45 percent—why not 42 percent or 47 percent? Others have expressed contempt over the peremptory tone of these ordinances, preferring instead programs based more on voluntarism. Still others fear that community transportation coordinators might turn into "traffic czars," with authority to order Draconian changes in company work hours and other internal corporate policies. These charges, however, may be a bit excessive. In Pleasanton, only one firm was actually fined for failing to meet the 15 percent first-year reduction target among the 36 companies that fell under the ordinance's control, and this was largely because the firm failed to demonstrate a good faith effort and cooperate with city officials. Several other firms fell short of the 15 percent trip reduction mark, but were spared fines because reasonable progress was being made.

Another downside of trip reduction ordinances is their emphasis on individual companies rather than congested settings. By focusing primarily on in-house efforts to cope with traffic, almost literally on a building-by-building basis, these ordinances could have the perverse effect of turning attention away from cumulative and citywide mobility problems. Additionally, their concentration on only peak-hour travel does little to discourage auto usage, and thus energy consumption and pollutant emissions, during other periods of the day.

Traffic Impact Fees

A more common legislative approach to suburban traffic management has been the exaction of impact fees from developers for financing areawide roadway improvements. Rather than assessing individual landowners based on their real property valuations, these ordinances collect monies according to how much traffic a future development will likely generate. Two key features of traffic impact ordinances—the collection of fees only from *future* developers and the emphasis on *off-site* improvements—have been the most controversial. Unlike trip reduction ordinances, moreover, impact fees are usually imposed before any project is actually built. In most instances, payment of exactions is a precondition to receiving various discretionary permits, such as site plan approval, conditional negative declarations, certificates of occupancy, special use privileges, and building permits.

By far, the largest number of traffic impact ordinances have been enacted in Southern California, although they can be found in Florida, New Jersey, Colorado, and around the Washington metropolitan area as well. Among the more significant programs established to date have been the following.

WASHINGTON METROPOLITAN AREA. Fairfax County plans to

impose a $2.65 per square foot fee on new developments to finance sorely needed highway improvements at the intersection of Route 50 and Interstate 66, the location of a future county government center and a 620-acre office-hotel complex.[50] Requests for rezoning and subdivision approval within the county must also include proffers from the developer that list infrastructural improvements he or she intends to make.[51] One Fairfax County developer has agreed to pay $20 million toward construction of a cross-county highway and new interchange. Across the Potomac in Montgomery County, Maryland, the impetus for creating an "Impact Fee District" has come from the business community itself. Private developers have proposed a program that would raise nearly $40 million over a 20-year period to match the terms of bonds for financing necessary transportation improvements in a rapidly growing portion of the county.[52] In return, builders would have a green light for constructing offices and apartments.

STATE OF FLORIDA.   Florida has pioneered the development of impact fee legislation at the state level. In May 1985, Florida's legislature passed a breakthrough state plan and growth management bill that mandates up-front, earmarked funding for requisite new roads in addition to expanded sewer and water facilities before new developments are approved. Given Florida's intense growth pressures, state officials found it necessary to legislate impact fees not only to help cover a $30 million backlog in infrastructure bills, but also to make it exceedingly costly to pursue leapfrog development or to overbuild the state's fragile coastline and barrier islands.[53] At the local level, moreover, Palm Beach and Broward Counties, both part of greater Miami, have been assessing road impact fees since 1981, although funds in both places are limited to improving existing roads rather than expanding networks or filling in missing links.[54]

SAN DIEGO COUNTY.   The county requires developers to pay fees as a precondition to subdivision approval, with a portion of all proceeds going to the local road improvement funds in the subregional planning area surrounding the subdivision.[55] The city of San Diego requires additional fees for street landscaping and traffic signal installation. Immediately to the north of San Diego, the city of Carlsbad has passed an ordinance that collects an earmarked fee of 3 percent of a project's construction valuation for street and traffic engineering improvements.[56]

ORANGE COUNTY.   Landowners along three proposed freeway corridors dissecting the central part of Orange County will be assessed "corridor fees" that are expected to yield over $600 million, about 60 percent of the total project construction costs. Developers will contribute to the fund based on the projected amount of traffic their projects are expected to generate. In the city of Costa Mesa, a one-time fee of $30 per projected daily trip generated by a development is currently collected, and in nearby Santa Ana, a dedicated highway fund is maintained through a 1 percent assessment levied on all businesses (based on gross building square footage). And in the city of Irvine, a unique "point system" has been devised that collects traffic improvement fees to reflect the intensity, not just the type, of land use. A square foot of industrial space is assigned one point whereas the same chunk of mid-rise office space is assessed three points, with each point costing a developer anywhere from $0.84 to $1.88, the higher charge being for longer range projects that exceed general plan development goals.[57] Fees for high-density office space can be substantial, reaching $5.64 per square foot. A particularly inventive feature of the Irvine ordinance is the granting of fee offsets not only for introducing TSM programs, but also for providing mixed-use functions, such as on-site restaurants and retail shops.

LOS ANGELES COUNTY.[58]   The most ambitious impact fee programs anywhere are today found in Los Angeles County. In Century City,[59] developers pay a one-time fee of $800 for each afternoon peak trip generated on an average weekday, while in nearby Westwood Village, the same per trip exaction has recently been set at a staggering $5,600. Farther to the west in Los Angeles's Westchester District, where new office construction remains brisk, an ordinance calling for a one-time fee of $2,010 per trip to cover an estimated $235 million in needed roadway improvements was recently approved by the Los Angeles City Council. In all three outlying districts, covenants affixed to land parcels bind all tenants, current and future, to participate in TSM programs. Developers can receive credits against their fee obligations by introducing vanpooling, dedicating land for transit centers, building pedestrian bridges, and pursuing similar initiatives. In the case of the Westchester ordinance, TSM programs that promise to reduce peak trips by 15 percent are also required prior to the issuance of a building permit. A particularly novel feature of the Westchester ordinance is the provision for "Transfer of TSM Rights"—enabling a developer or lessee to receive fee credits by introducing TSM programs aimed at reducing solo auto trips at *adjacent* employment sites. Credits for providing on-site corporate housing and tenant support services are also granted.

Advantages of Impact Fee Programs. The major advantage of impact fee ordinances is that they are based on proven principles of welfare economics—those who impose the cost on society of increased congestion, noxious air, and other disbenefits should pay for whatever public improvements are necessary to correct them. By forcing developers to fully internalize the marginal (or extra) costs of their projects, economists argue, not only will necessary public infrastructure be provided, but more orderly growth will also be mediated through the marketplace. In particular, a fee structure produces an incentive for desirable infill development in settings for which road capacity is readily available. However, should a developer overbuild or erect a project prematurely, he pays the consequences. Impact fees likewise appeal to many suburbanites' sense of equity—those benefiting most directly from the construction of freeway interchanges and arterial widenings should pick up the tab.

Another major selling point for communities interested in the impact fee approach is that it generates a pool of funds for financing areawide, rather than just near-site, transportation improvements. In most areas of the country, developers finance either on-site or near-site infrastructure improvements and dedicate land as a prerequisite to subdivision approval; however, the downstream effects of a new office or residential project are often overlooked in the process. By establishing a trust fund for financing areawide transportation improvements, fee ordinances ensure that developers are responsible for more than just their own "front doorstep" problems.

Finally, in that most traffic impact ordinances are targeted at developers of office and industrial complexes, they remove some of the current inequities associated with local roadway tax financing. On both a square footage and per employee basis, office developments pay far less in property taxes than retail establishments, yet they contribute far more to congestion. Suburban shopping trips generally take place during the midday, in the evening, and on weekends when traffic levels are relatively low whereas office trips are almost wholly concentrated during rush hours. Traffic impact fees directed at office developers, then, serve to redress present day biases in the tax financing of local road improvements.

Current and Potential Problem Areas. A number of stumbling blocks still stand in the way of widescale adoption of traffic impact legislation, however. Some are political, others are logistical. Among the stickiest unresolved problems are the following.

EQUITY AND FAIRSHAREMANSHIP. Some grumbling over the fairness of traffic impact fee requirements has been aired in places that have introduced such ordinances. In almost all cases, fees are only passed on to new, yet-to-be-completed projects. Ambient levels of congestion—i.e., traffic problems created by developments built prior to the passage of an ordinance—are largely overlooked. Developers charge that they are being forced to foot the bill for costly infrastructural improvements while previously existing establishments whose businesses contribute equally to traffic snarls get off scot-free. Moreover, in some cases developers of new residential and sometimes even retail projects are exempted from impact fee requirements, compelling some office builders to file formal complaints charging blatant discrimination for being singled out as roadway financiers. Many suburban investors are not only concerned over others getting a "free ride," but also about possibly having to pay for past traffic planning mistakes and oversights. Broward County, Florida's impact-free program initially came under attack on the grounds that it sought "to correct the sins of the past."[60]

The difficult question remains, then, whether communities should be concentrating on just incremental versus cumulative traffic impacts. Proponents of current ordinances argue that municipalities are simply invoking the time-honored principle of marginal cost pricing—namely, only those whose projects necessitate additional roadway investments to accommodate traffic beyond current "stable" levels should be forced to pay. Critics counter that more of an assessment district approach should be followed— that is, all property owners within a certain boundary should be charged the "average cost" for making necessary infrastructural improvements. Fashioning a fee program that distributes traffic impact charges equitably among existing and new developments remains a formidable challenge for all parties involved.

MEASURING COSTS AND BENEFITS. Compounding matters even more has been our inability to accurately measure the true marginal cost of each additional rush-hour trip generated by a new suburban project. Figures ranging anywhere from $800 to $5,600 per peak hour auto trip have been arrived at for outlying settings that are not tremendously different from one another in size or local traffic conditions. The most common approach has been to estimate total peak auto trips generated by all new developments slated for a specific area using ITE (Institute of Transportation Engineers) trip generation rates, project the cost of all roadway improvements needed to accommodate these volumes, and divide the latter by the former. Thus, average vis-à-vis marginal costs are actually being measured, even though these ordinances have been sold to the public as dealing specifically with incremental impacts.

Trip generation rates themselves are subject to criticism since most have been empirically derived from more urban-like settings and do not necessarily reflect current or future suburban travel behavior. Moreover, it is extremely difficult to gauge the spatial extent of suburban traffic impacts. It is hard enough to estimate the transportation costs imposed by a well-defined cluster of buildings much less a loosely knit corridor of offices, shops, factories, and other mixed uses. The successful implant of traffic impact ordinances in other areas will undoubtedly hinge on our ability to design more accurate yardsticks for gauging the dollar amount new land developments are responsible for as well as the geographic boundaries of those assessments.

TEMPO PROBLEMS. Just as there are spatial difficulties in determining traffic impacts, temporal problems abound as well. In particular, under most ordinances there is a mismatch between when impact fees are collected and when actual improvements are made. Usually, fees are assessed and collected prior to the issuance of building permits and occupancy certificates, and funds are accumulated in a reserve account for financing future projects. In a number of cases, this cash flow problem has been to the consternation of developers who have paid large sums of money to trust accounts only to see few if any actual roadway improvements implemented. In Costa Mesa, California, for instance, over $3 million in fees were collected from developers between 1978 and 1984, yet during that period all funds accumulated in a bank account and no new construction was financed.

LEGAL AND JUDICIAL CHALLENGES. The tempo problem has led to charges that such fees are confiscatory and discriminating taxes—i.e., developers are being taxed without receiving any tangible benefits, at least within a reasonable time period. Some critics have gone one step farther, challenging the legal authority of municipalities and county governments to exact cash contributions from private developers to finance off-site highway and transit improvements. Still-pending litigation in Broward County, Florida, over the legality of road-impact fees has frozen over $20 million in revenues that have been collected to date.[61] Courts in California and Florida have recently ruled that any fee levied against a new development must be earmarked for capital expansion necessitated by that development—i.e., it must be used for purposes that only benefit those individuals who pay it.[62] San Francisco's recent attempt to impose a "transit impact development fee" on all new downtown construction was initially struck down on the grounds that it was a tax in disguise, thus a violation of California's Proposition 13.[63] Some California cities have challenged this strict legal interpretation, citing State Government Code, Section 66484, which states that "fees imposed by a local agency to defray the cost of construction of major thoroughfares as a condition of approval of a final subdivision map or a building permit do not constitute a 'special tax.' " Still, the legal future of areawide traffic impact fees remains clouded even in California. Narrow legal rulings on how traffic fees can be spent could give rise to "band-aid" planning solutions, with funds targeted solely toward the frontdoor access problems of specific office developments at the expense of neglecting the larger regional mobility implications of these projects.

JURISDICTIONAL GAPS. Inconsistencies in how adjoining and neighboring municipalities approach traffic mitigation could also undermine the effectiveness of traffic impact ordinances. For instance, a city's roadway improvements might depend crucially on corresponding improvements being made by an adjacent jurisdiction. It could only take a single municipality's abstention from a subregional fee assessment program to leave crippling gaps in a thoroughfare system. The intense competition for new businesses in many rapidly growing areas could impede efforts to build a united front in tackling interjurisdictional mobility problems. In a booming area like Orange County, California, where 26 separate suburban jurisdictions and their respective Chambers of Commerce are actively vying for choice developments, there is a pervasive fear that impact fees and restrictive controls could drive investors across city lines. According to some local observers, several Orange County developers have already "voted with their radials," choosing to locate in municipalities that have no impact ordinances over those that do.

SUPPLY SIDE BIAS. In contrast to trip reduction ordinances, impact fee programs aim to deal with mounting congestion problems by expanding roadway capacity rather than modifying commuters' traveling habits. By providing more lanes of suburban freeways and arterials, these ordinances could perpetuate the exodus of jobs and residents from downtowns presently well served by transit. The distinctive "concrete and pavement" bias of these ordinances could ultimately deal a death blow to transit and paratransit modes in many outlying settings. Moreover, history has taught us that supply-side responses all too often exacerbate the very problem they attempt to solve—additional road capacity often generates new traffic, which in turn necessitates further expansion, which induces more traffic, and so on and so on. The threat posed by such a vicious circle is even more serious in suburbia where unprotected open space and farmland often lie on the horizon, vulnerable to the sprawl-inducing effects of increased traffic. Some transportation planners argue that congestion levels should actually be allowed to worsen so as to force more and more suburban commuters to seek alternatives to solo driving.

PREEMPTION OF TRANSIT. By collecting higher fees from large, dense developments, traffic impact ordinances could induce some investors to downscale their projects below their original planned levels. Over the long run, this could dilute the customer base needed to make transit and ridesharing viable suburban commute alternatives. Fee credits for mixed-use activities, such as allowed in Irvine and west Los Angeles, could be used to counterbalance this unintended effect.

EXCESSIVE DISCRETION. Most impact fee ordinances grant municipal departments considerable discretion in determining the exact amount of traffic a development will likely generate, where and when roadway improvements will be made, what types of TSM programs qualify as fee credits, and at what point building permits will be issued. In Los Angeles, where city staffers wield considerable discretionary control over who pays what, a number of developers have criticized the open-ended, discretionary nature of existing traffic impact ordinances. A common fear seems to be that the "rules of the game" will change over time as new political leaders take office and set new internal policy directives.

Incentive Ordinances: Parking Reductions

Several communities around the country have enacted ordinances that use "carrots" rather than "sticks" to elicit private sector involvement in solving suburban traffic problems. Usually, ordinances allow developers to reduce code-required parking as a *quid pro quo* for commitments to initiate ridesharing programs. For example, in both Los Angeles and Palo Alto, California, developers can introduce "effective alternatives to auto access," such as vanpool leasing and cash payments to local transit agencies, in return for less stringent parking requirements. Moreover, builders in Orlando and St. Petersburg, Florida, have the option of contributing to a TSM fund in lieu of providing the usual four parking spaces per 1,000 square feet of office space.[64] Similar ordinances can be found in

Montgomery County, Maryland; Hartford, Connecticut; and Bellevue, Washington.

A major appeal of parking reduction ordinances is that they offer something for everybody. For municipalities, they can be a tremendous boon to communitywide ridesharing. The availability of bountiful, free parking is widely recognized as the biggest deterrent to ridesharing and transit usage in suburban America today.[65] Only through programs that trade off code-required parking for sponsorship of vanpool and carpools can any gainful strides be made in curbing the spread of solo suburban commuting. For developers, these ordinances can likewise prove remunerative. As discussed in the previous chapter, there is a growing recognition that parking gobbles up valuable real estate that could otherwise be used for more productive purposes. More and more, escalating land prices are forcing developers to seriously consider downscaling their on-site parking facilities.

Resistance to Parking Reductions. To date, parking reduction ordinances have unfortunately had little success in inducing developers to purchase employee vans instead of paving over parking lots. In Los Angeles, for instance, the local ordinance permitting up to a 40 percent reduction in code-required parking has failed to attract a single taker during its inaugural two years.[66] Other parking ordinances have likewise stimulated very little interest from the development community.

The impediments to widespread adoption of parking reduction ordinances are manyfold. Foremost, most developers consider the trade-off of specifying parking for vanpools simply too risky. Given the enormous costs of building suburban office complexes, developers tend to be conservative with their portfolios, preferring to invest cautiously and prudently. Parking is widely perceived as a one-time, up-front investment with a proven track record. Moreover, it is a permanent fixture to the land. In contrast, suburban ridesharing programs are largely untested and require ongoing funding support. Nor are they permanent. A ridesharing program can fold at any time, whether due to a sudden plunge in gasoline prices or an economic recession. Historically, carpooling and transit usage have proven to be far more sensitive to exogenous events, such as OPEC oil policies, than to factors within a developer's control. Investors rely heavily on assurances that their transportation programs will be there to serve them at all times. Parking provides that.

Perhaps just as important, a number of banks and lenders have frowned on past attempts to introduce below-standard parking facilities in suburbia. Some have refused investment loans unless more universally accepted levels of parking are provided. Many lending institutions have taken the position that parking restrictions detract from a project's marketability and thus threaten its long-term potential for success.

Administrative foot-dragging and logistical obstacles have also plagued parking reduction ordinances enacted to date. Developers have avoided Los Angeles's program because of the lengthy delays in processing and approving requests (up to nine months long), as well as the absence of explicit criteria for evaluating the success of ridesharing substitution.[67] Enforceability concerns, moreover, have impelled some municipalities to scuttle their proposed parking reduction ordinances. Unless there are specific covenants attached to a parcel of land, once an original developer leaves the scene, a city can lose considerable leverage over enforcement of the conditions attached to a use permit. Subsequent property owners could legally challenge whether they are bound by parking reduction agreements to which they were not a party. Covenants mandating ridesharing participation are virtually untested waters and would likely be resisted by many developers as a cloud on titles.

To date, the stiffest opposition to parking reductions has come from large executive and business park complexes on the urban fringes. The common perception in these settings is that regardless of how many ridesharing incentives are introduced, professional, white-collar employees will remain wedded to their personal automobiles and thus will insist upon hassle-free parking.

Alternative Parking Control Strategies.   In response to all these concerns, a number of developers in California and Texas have begun staging the phasedown of parking using a "trial-and-error" approach. Since most large-scale office projects are built over multiple phases, developers can initially reduce parking below industry standards, making adjustments in subsequent phases depending upon how successful ridesharing programs become. Thus, if vanpools fail to lure many customers, parking can be increased above usual standards during the second phase of a project. If, on the other hand, vanpools prove successful, parking standards might be lowered even further over the second and ensuing stages. By indexing parking stalls to the formation of vanpools over time, developers of multiphased projects in San Ramon and Westchester, California, hope to strike the right balance between parking reduction and TSM programs.

Another promising approach to suburban parking controls is shared-use arrangements where parking spaces serve two or more adjacent landowners without conflict or encroachment. Shared parking could work particularly

well around many suburban megacomplexes. For example, a parking facility might be used by office employees during the day and serve patrons of a
nearby theater at night. A recent study estimated that nearly one-quarter of
all employees of suburban work sites nationwide patronize nearby developments during the course of a day, suggesting that the opportunities for
shared-used parking are substantial.[68] Some precedents have already been
established in this area. At the South Coast Plaza multipurpose complex in
Costa Mesa, for instance, a shared-use parking agreement between office
and retail uses has been in existence since 1978. Similar arrangements have
been negotiated between office and commercial developers in Las Colinas,
Texas and Calgary, Alberta. Still, most municipal zoning codes today prohib-
it shared-use parking, either in central cities or the suburbs.

An alternative approach to rationing parking is to collect a user's fee.
The South Coast Plaza and Warner Center complexes in Southern California
do charge customers and employees going commercial rates for parking in
their multilevel garages, although in both places over two-thirds of all
employees receive reimbursements from their employers for all monthly
parking expenses as an in-kind fringe benefit. In the vast majority of suburban office settings, moreover, parking fees would be impractical. Notes one
suburban office manager: "Parking charges would be impossible to adminis-
ter here because of our campus environment; we'd literally have to put
gates, with guards, all over the place."[69]

Cooperative Agreements and Financing

Not all private developers have been pressured into financing off-site transportation improvements, nor have all municipalities chosen the ordinance
route in battling suburban congestion. Increasingly, both parties are entering
into cooperative agreements that spell out mutual funding responsibilities
for off-site roadway improvements. In recognition of today's constrained
municipal budgets, growing numbers of suburban developers have proceeded to negotiate cost-sharing deals with public authorities. Proclaims one
large California developer: "In the post-Proposition 13 era, government isn't
going to pay for it all . . . and never will again."[70]

In contrast to impact fee programs, negotiated financing of off-site
roadway improvements involves notching out ad hoc, case-by-case agreements among public and private interests. The real advantage to a
developer is that, unlike trust fund programs, he has some direct control
over how his contributions are spent. Through the process of negotiations,

developers can usually secure guarantees that certain "pet projects" will be funded. This is not necessarily so with traffic impact ordinances where funds are pooled together for areawide projects.

The major drawback of the negotiated approach seems to be that, so far at least, almost all funding has gone toward near-site, rather than subregional, roadway improvements. The emphasis seems to be more on resolving front-entrance access problems rather than relieving the downstream effects of, say, 50,000 new peak trips generated by a colossal employment center that just opened. Near-site investments can contribute little to the vehicular capacity of an area if other regional improvements are not built in tandem. This lesson was brought to light in the case of a $9 million developer-financed four-lane highway expansion in McLean, Virginia, that abruptly changes into a narrow two-lane road at the owner's property line.[71] Additionally, negotiations rest on promises that cannot always be delivered. Because of the current glut in office space in many areas of the country, some developers may be forced to renege on commitments to build areawide road improvements as they face bankruptcy.

Nationally, cooperative financing of subregional highway improvements has become fairly commonplace. Based on the national survey, an estimated two-thirds of all suburban office developers have helped pay for off-site roadway construction in some form. Well over half of these public/private coventures have involved joint financing of areawide traffic control improvements, such as installing computer-controlled signal networks. Only four of the surveyed developers had financed any off-site transit improvements.

Some of the largest private sector contributions for off-site suburban roadway improvements recorded to date are listed in Table 4.1. Over $300 million has already been spent or pledged toward new infrastructure in the vicinity of 13 rapidly expanding office corridors in nine major U.S. metropolitan areas (see Photo 4.6). The three largest private contributions have come from developers of monumental office/industrial projects along California's urban fringes. The Irvine Company has agreed to spend at least $65 million on constructing three freeway off-ramps, several parkways, and a host of traffic control improvements in close proximity to the massive Spectrum development.[72] Just to the south in San Diego, developers of Rancho Carmel, a 1,500-acre mixed-use development, have pledged nearly $58 million worth of freeway improvements, park-and-ride facilities, bike trails, and a computerized traffic control system.[73] The most generous contribution to date has come from the developers of the Hacienda Business Park in Pleasanton where over $80 million has been committed toward major free-

TABLE 4.1
Major Private Sector Contributions to
Roadway Improvements Outside of Metropolitan CBDs

Metropolitan Area	Contributor	Amount Contributed	Location and Types of Improvements
Denver	Joint Southeast Public Improvement Authority	$23 million*	Highway upgrading in southeast Denver area.
Houston	West Houston Association	$8.5 million	New four-lane arterial in west Houston.
	Several Private Developers	$2.3 million	New interchanges and ramps on Katy Freeway.
Los Angeles	Private Developer	$4.0 million	Assorted roadway improvements in Universal City area.
	Private Developer	$30 million*	Interchange ramps and signal upgrading in Westchester District.
New York/ Newark	Private Developer	$11 million	Highway, bridge, and freeway off-ramp improvements in the Meadowlands.
Orange County, Calif.	Private Developer	$65 million*	Freeway, parkway, ramps, and signal improvements for Irvine Spectrum.
	Private Developer	$1.3 million	Traffic control in Newport Beach Area.
Philadelphia	Private Developer	$2.0 million	Freeway interchange near the Chesterbrook Corporate Center.
San Diego	Private Developer	$57.5 million	New arterials, freeway overpasses, and signal upgrades for north county area.
San Francisco	Private Developer	$14 million	Freeway interchange, signal upgrade, and road widening in San Ramon.
	Private Developers	$85 million	Freeway interchanges, computerized signaling, soundwalls, and landscaping in Pleasanton.
Washington, D.C.	Private Developers	$22 million	New highway and overpass in Fairfax County and Tysons Corner area.

*Proposed Private Contribution.

Sources: K. Orski, *The Private Challenge to Public Transportation, Urban Transit*, C. Lave, ed. (San Francisco: Pacific Institute for Public Policy Research, 1985), pp. 311–31; T. Hazlet, *They Built Their Own Highway, Reason* (November 1983), pp. 23–30; *Transportation Partnerships*, L. Keefer, ed. (Washington: Newsletter No. 16, 1984); and survey and field interview results.

**Photo 4.6.   Privately Financed Freeway Interchanges at the Chester-
brook Corporate Center Outside of Philadelphia (above)
and the Bishop Ranch Business Park on the Fringes of the
Bay Area (below).**
(Top photo provided courtesy of The Fox Companies; bottom
photo by the author.)

way and arterial investments as well as the construction of areawide pedestrian and cycling trails, residential sound barriers, and flood control canals.

Additionally, in Texas, Colorado, and Maryland landowners have joined forces to create new taxing districts for financing areawide roadway construction. The largest privately initiated taxing district to date has been formed by the Joint Southeast Public Improvement Authority in Denver. There, over $23 million is being collected among landholders to finance arterial and interchange improvements along the I-25 corridor.[74] The West Houston Association, moreover, privately planned and financed ten miles of Park Row, a four-lane arterial, by persuading property owners to create an assessment district that divvies up costs according to the portion of highway fronting on their property.[75] Similar group financing projects are underway in Dallas, San Antonio, and Montgomery County, Maryland.

It is important for local officials to recognize the cash flow liabilities at stake in sinking millions of dollars into public infrastructure. For most investors, the financing of both on-site and off-site transportation improvements can involve substantial initial cash outlays. In the case of one California suburban megacomplex, the annual cost of all transportation programs (e.g., freeway interchanges, shuttle buses, transit shelters, etc.) has averaged around one-eighth of the project's gross yearly rental income during its first few years of operation. At buildout around the year 2000, transportation costs are expected to fall to only about 2 percent of gross annual rent.[76] Thus, the owner has been absorbing fairly high front-end costs during the project's buildup stage; when rental revenues reach their peak, transport outlays will plummet to a small fraction of total annual receipts. Clearly, the pro forma risks and financial commitments associated with off-site road building can be enormous.

It should be pointed out that at least one community has taken formal steps to institutionalize up-front, public negotiations with developers. Fort Collins, Colorado, 60 miles north of Denver and one of the fast-growing metropolitan areas during the 1970s, passed a "Land Development Guidance System" in 1981 that gives developers considerable latitude in negotiating their projects. They can either "buy into" the infrastructure by paying exactions and financing new projects, or design their developments in such a way that the community's overall quality of life is preserved. In effect, developers are challenged to accommodate Fort Collins's goals: mixed land uses, pedestrian and bicycle circulation, and no public costs for private developments.[77] The land-guidance system also removes all minimum parking requirements under the rationale that business "won't cut its own throat." Fort Collins has for all intents and purposes replaced zoning by a more informal process of deal-making that is conducted in the spirit of protecting the larger community interest.

In closing, public-private cofinancing of areawide transportation improvements will work as long as cost burdens are distributed fairly. Recent events testify to the private and public sectors' abilities to transcend traditional spheres of responsibility and create effective coalitions for solving suburban congestion dilemmas. Still, the role of private interests in roadway financing is not based on benevolence and philanthropy. Rather, an essential ingredient for any successful cost-sharing program must be corporate reward. As Kenneth Orski puts it:

> The most solid and enduring basis for private sector involvement lies in the concept of enlightened self-interest. Business executives must be convinced that their participation in local transportation activities will result in positive gain. This is not to say that corporate leaders will weigh the benefits of their participation in narrow dollars-and-cents. On the contrary, their motivations often may be quite diffuse. It may be a desire to attract and retain a workforce, to improve employee productivity and morale, . . . or even to improve the general business climate in the community. But, however indirect, the element of self-interest must be there in order to sustain long-term support.[78]

Future Prospects

America's suburbs certainly are not lacking in technical know-how for dealing with traffic predicaments. A rich mix of programs—some operational and managerial, others institutional and financial—are currently available for safeguarding the nation's suburbs from looming traffic tie-ups. Still, the effects of any one or two efforts are apt to be marginal, at best, over the long run. In tandem, however, the right cluster of transportation management tools could prove decisive in forestalling suburban gridlock. In many outlying corridors, all it takes is a three to five percent reduction in peak-hour traffic volumes to free clogged arteries and restore circulation. What is called for, then, is a more strategic, visionary planning approach whereby both public and private interests work together in crafting the right balance of transportation management programs tailored to specific suburban needs.

Of course, any viable and lasting effort must go beyond simply implementing a checklist of TSM and roadway improvements. Major legal, political, and behavioral impediments have to be dealt with as well. Indeed, overcoming regulatory barriers to for-profit vanpools, longstanding political jealousies between neighboring jurisdictions, or the distrust some corporate leaders have toward mass transportation pose far greater challenges than physically designing timed-transfer bus systems or generating computerized carpool matchlists. Closer institutional coordination is particularly essential if cross-boundary problems, such as intersuburban congestion, are to be satisfactorily resolved.

One common denominator of nearly all successful suburban traffic mitigation programs to date has been the expanding role of the private sector. Whether through forming employer associations, launching in-house ridesharing programs, or bankrolling off-site roadway projects, businesses and private developers are emerging as lead players in the war against suburban congestion. Most are more than willing to pay their fair share simply because they realize that the long-term profitability of their investments hinges crucially on good access and livable suburbs. The popular image of private developers and public agencies as long-feuding adversaries on suburban issues is being debunked through the course of the 1980s. Joint public-private partnerships in the finance of areawide freeway interchanges, roadway expansions, and even transit improvements are becoming more and more common. One guarantee most developers insist upon, however, is that the "rules of the game" remain the same over time. If a $2,000 per peak trip exaction is to be levied on all new office developments, for instance, investors need to be assured that the dollar amount is firm. Market feasibility calculations and tough business decisions ride crucially on investors knowing their exact dollar commitments. A closer understanding of the rules and constraints both sides operate under will only come with experience.

Among the demand-side strategies examined in this chapter, TSM measures such as ridesharing and bus transit will likely play somewhat limited roles as long as jobs and housing remain out of balance in suburbia. Certainly employer sponsorship of vanpools and the institution of timed-transfer networks would help, however, given today's low densities and fragmented land uses in most suburban settings, any form of mass-commuting will have a difficult time competing with the private automobile. Based on Pleasanton's experiences, however, flex-time and staggered work arrangements could make major inroads toward unlocking suburban gridlock if given the chance. Programs such as flex-time are effective because they are relatively cheap, can be implemented quickly, and provide immediate traffic relief. Employers, left to their own initiative, however, are unlikely to alter work schedules simply because there is usually no pressing corporate reason to do so. When the employer is faced with the prospect of having to pay as much as $250 per day for failing to reduce employees' peak hour trips, the idea of staggering when employees come to and leave work becomes much more attractive. At least in the short run, then, trip reduction ordinances probably offer the best hope for unclogging suburban streets. For this reason, suburban communities that are feeling the pains of rapid growth would be wise to take a serious look at trip reduction programs under way in places such as Pleasanton.

While supply-side responses can relieve suburban congestion in the near term, they are rarely lasting solutions. The inherent weakness of building new capacity to serve suburban trips is that once traffic is relieved, the forces behind sprawl once again are set into motion. One even might argue that suburban congestion should be left to run its own course so that communities are forced to pass trip reduction ordinances and commuters are pressured into carpools. Obviously some new road facilities will be needed along the urban fringes to handle the growth in lateral commuting, though by themselves, they are clearly not the answer. Even if there were ample funds to expand road capacity at will, politically potent suburban constituents probably would not allow many new expressways to be built in their own back yards. Since funds are so scarce, however, the private sector no doubt will have to foot the bill for the bulk of new road improvements. While private dollars are needed for constructing new interchanges and overpasses to serve large work centers, developers also must be held accountable for the upstream and downstream effects of their projects. For this reason, programs that pool funds for areawide improvements, such as benefit assessment districts and impact fee arrangements, seem preferable to negotiated financing of site-specific projects.

Overall, recent progress toward safeguarding suburban mobility has been encouraging, providing useful lessons to developers, employers, and community planners. Still, much remains to be done. The multitude of sticky issues as well as the opportunities for inventiveness become even more apparent, however, when one looks closely at specific case study settings. The following two chapters build upon this and the previous ones by examining assorted design, management, and financial topics bearing on suburban mobility in two areas experiencing some of the most intense development pressures on their perimeters anywhere—Los Angeles and Orange Counties in Southern California, and the San Francisco Bay Area of Northern California. Both areas have been leaders in launching effective transportation management programs and also offer contrasting perspectives toward site and land use planning on the urban fringe.

Notes

1. TSM actions represent low-cost, quick-response approaches to improving the management of transportation resources, usually involving such programs as ridesharing, flexible work hours, one-waying streets, metering freeway ramps, and the like.

2. See the Irvine Spectrum and Hacienda Business Park case studies in Chapters Five and Six respectively for further discussions of mandatory TSM involvement.

3. See: C. Kenneth Orski, "Changing Directions of Public Transportation in the United States," *Built Environment*, Vol. 8, No. 3 (1982), pp. 157–66; Eric Schreffler and Michael D. Meyer, "Evolving Institutional Arrangements for Employer Involvement in Transportation: The Case of Employer Associations," *Transportation Research Record*, No. 914 (1983), pp. 42–49; and D. Torluemke, "Employer's Perspective: Transportation," *West Plan* (Fall 1983), pp. 14–15.

4. This estimate was the consensus among participants of the conference on "Mobility for Major Metropolitan Growth Centers" sponsored by the Urban Mass Transportation Administration, U.S. Department of Transportation, held in Los Angeles in November 1984. This estimate is also in line with the national survey finding of four formal TMAs among the 120 suburban office park respondents.

5. P.R. Valente, "Public Transportation in the 1980's: An Era of Change," *Public Management*, Vol. 64, No. 7 (1982), pp. 6–8.

6. Christopher Conte, "The Explosive Growth of Suburbia Leads to Bumper-to-Bumper Blues," *Wall Street Journal* (April 16, 1985), p. 37.

7. Ibid.

8. William R. Eager, "Innovative Approaches to Transportation for Growing Areas," *Urban Land*, Vol. 43, No. 7 (1984), pp. 6–11.

9. See Chapter Six for additional discussions on the Santa Clara Manufacturing Group.

10. Scheffler and Meyer, "Evolving Institutional Arrangements," pp. 46–47.

11. See Chapter Five for more detailed discussion on the El Segundo Employer's Association.

12. Torluemke, "Employer's Perspective: Transportation," p. 14.

13. Metropolitan Transportation Commission, "Potential Traffic Impacts of Recent Development Along Route 101" (Oakland, Calif.: unpublished agency report, 1983).

14. See: Alan Altshuler, *The Urban Transportation System: Politics and Policy Innovation* (Cambridge, Mass.: MIT Press, 1979); and John R. Meyer and Jose A. Gomez-Ibanez, *Autos, Transit and Cities* (Cambridge, Mass.: Harvard University Press, 1981).

15. Dingle Associates, Inc., *Ridesharing Programs of Business and Industry*

(Washington: Federal Highway Administration, U.S. Department of Transportation, 1982).

16. See Chapter Five for further discussions on the vanpool programs sponsored by the Fluor Corporation and Automobile Club of Southern California.

17. Milton Pikarsky and Christine M. Johnson, "American Transportation in Transition," *Built Environment*, Vol. 8, No. 3. (1982), pp. 167–171.

18. Eager, "Innovative Approaches to Transportation for Growing Areas," pp. 6–8.

19. See Chapter Five for additional discussions on ridesharing activities at Orange County's South Coast Plaza.

20. For further discussions on the short-term auto leasing concept, see: Ekistic Transportation Systems, "A Transportation Management Plan for Bishop Ranch Business Park" (Redondo Beach, Calif.: unpublished consulting report, 1983).

21. Valente, "Public Transportation in the 1980's," pp. 6–7.

22. Paul Reimer, "Future High-Tech Parks," *Urban Land*, Vol. 42, No. 11 (1983), pp. 22–23.

23. Conte, "The Explosive Growth of Suburbia Leads to Bumper-to-Bumper Blues," p. 37.

24. According to the national survey, the average percent of employees who commute by bus was around 1.6 percent for the smaller (under one-half million square feet) developments and 2.8 percent for the larger ones. These figures are consistent with the 1980 journey-to-work census results whereby only 1.6 percent of all commute trips with both ends in the suburbs were via mass transit. See: Philip M. Fulton, "Changing Journey-To-Work Patterns: The Increasing Prevalence of Commuting Within the Suburbs in Metropolitan Areas," *Transportation Research Record* (1986, forthcoming).

25. James P. Reichert, "Wanted: National Policy on Suburban Transit," *Transit Journal*, Vol. 5, No. 3 (1979), pp. 37–42.

26. Ruth and Going, Inc., "South Coast Metro Area Pilot Transportation System Management Program" (San Jose, Calif.: Consulting Report prepared for the Orange County Transportation Commission, 1983), pp. III.11–III.15.

27. Task Force on Public-Private Cooperation in Urban Transportation, "Competition and Urban Mobility" (Washington, D.C.: Transportation Research Board, unpublished paper, 1985).

28. See Chapter Six for a more detailed description of the Bishop Ranch and Hacienda Business Park contracted bus services.

29. Eager, "Innovative Approaches to Transportation for Growing Areas," p. 11.

30. C. Kenneth Orski, "Suburban Mobility: The Coming Transportation Crisis?" *Transportation Quarterly*, Vol. 39, No. 2 (1985), p. 292.

31. Harland Bartholomew, "Effect of Urban Decentralization Upon Transit Operation and Policies," *Proceedings of the American Transit Association Fifty-Ninth Annual Convention* (New York: American Transit Association, 1940), p. 486.

32. For further discussions of the timed-transfer concept, see: Robert R. Piper, "Transit Strategies for Suburban Communities," *American Institute of Planners Journal*, Vol. 43, No. 1 (1977), pp. 380–85.

33. See: Vukan Vuchic, Richard Clarke, and Angel Molinero, *Timed Transfer System Planning, Design and Operation* (Washington: Technology Sharing Program, Office of the Secretary of Transportation); and Debra A. Newman, Marlies Bebendorf, and Juliet McNally, *Timed Transfer: An Evaluation of Its Structure, Performance and Cost* (Washington: Urban Mass Transportation Administration, U.S. Department of Transportation, 1983).

34. J.J. Bakker, "Advantages and Experiences with Timed Transfers" (Washington: Paper presented at the Transportation Research Board Annual Meeting, January 1981).

35. Newman et al., *Timed Transfer: An Evaluation of Its Structure, Performance and Cost*, p. 2.27.

36. Martin Wachs, "Consumer Attitudes Towards Urban Transit Services: An Interpretative Review," *Journal of the American Institute of Planning*, Vol. 42, No. 1 (1976), p. 98.

37. Roger F. Teal and Genevieve Giuliano, "Increasing the Role of the Private Sector in Commuter Bus Service Provision," *Built Environment*, Vol. 8, No. 3 (1982), pp. 172–83.

38. James C. Echols, "Use of Private Companies to Provide Public Transportation Services in Tidewater Virginia," *Urban Transit: The Private Challenge to Public Transportation*, Charles A. Lave, ed. (San Francisco: Pacific Institute for Public Policy Research, 1985), pp. 79–100.

39. Charles A. Lave, "The Private Challenge to Public Transportation—An Overview," *Urban Transit: The Private Challenge to Public Transportation*, Charles A. Lave, ed. (San Francisco: Pacific Institute for Public Policy Research, 1985), p. 2.

40. See: Pat Gelb, *Effects of Taxi Regulatory Revision in Seattle, Washington, San Diego, California, and Portland, Oregon* (Washington: Urban Mass Transportation Administration, U.S. Department of Transportation, 1983); and Robert Cervero, "Revitalizing Urban Transit—More Money or Less Regulation?" *Regulation*, Vol. 8, No. 3 (1984), pp. 36–42.

41. This program operates independently of the El Segundo Employer's Association vanpool program discussed previously.

42. Genevieve Giuliano and Roger F. Teal, "Privately Provided Commuter Bus Services: Experiences, Problems, and Prospects," *Urban Transit: Private Challenge to Public Transportation*, Charles A. Lave, ed. (San Francisco: Pacific Institute for Public Policy Research, 1985), p. 169.

43. Ibid., pp. 158–59.

44. Conte, "The Explosive Growth of Suburbia Leads to Bumper-to-Bumper Blues," p. 37.

45. Mark A. Stein, "Freeways: Victory Lies in Flexibility," *Los Angeles Times* (September 2, 1984), pp. 1, 32, and 33; and Genevieve Giuliano, "The Los Angeles Summer Olympics: Lessons in TSM," *ITS Review*, Vol. 8, No. 4 (1985), pp. 4–6.

46. David W. Jones, Jr. and Francis Harrison, "Off Work Early: The Final Report

of the San Francisco Flex-Time Demonstration Project" (Berkeley: Institute of Transportation Studies, University of California, 1983).

47. Joann S. Lublin, "The Suburban Life: Trees, Grass Plus Noise, Traffic and Pollution," *The Wall Street Journal* (June 18, 1985), p. 35.

48. Orski, "Suburban Mobility," p. 293.

49. Ruth and Going, Inc., "South Coast Metro Area Pilot Transportation Management Program," p. 2.19.

50. C. Kenneth Orski, "The Private Challenge to Public Transportation," *Urban Transit: The Private Challenge to Public Transportation*, Charles A. Lave, ed. (San Francisco: Pacific Institute for Public Policy Research, 1985), p. 316.

51. D.W. Schoppert and W.S. Herald, "Private Funds for Highway Improvements," *Transportation Research Record*, Vol. 914 (1983), pp. 42–43.

52. Orski, "Suburban Mobility," p. 289.

53. Neal Peirce, "Problems of Growth Spark Willingness to Change," *The Charlotte Observer* (September 3, 1985).

54. Ruth Knack, "How Road Impact Fees are Working in Broward County," *Planning*, Vol. 50, No. 6 (1984), pp. 24–26.

55. Orski, "Changing Directions of Public Transportation in the United States," p. 159.

56. Transportation Partnerships, "Conference on Transportation Partnerships" (Washington: Metropolitan Washington Council of Governments, newsletter publication), p. 4.

57. Victor Carniglia, "Updating Industrial Zoning: The Irvine Business Complex," *Urban Land*, Vol. 44, No. 3 (1985), pp. 15–19.

58. See the case studies in Chapter Five for more in-depth discussions on Los Angeles's traffic impact fee programs.

59. Century City in west Los Angeles has close to seven million square feet of office space, 35,000 employees, 1,100 hotel rooms, 240 shops and restaurants, a repertory theater, and 1,200 dwelling units. Nearby Westwood Village, adjacent to the UCLA campus, has around 2.5 million square feet of office space, 20,000 employees, 600 hotel rooms, and 560 shops and restaurants.

60. Knack, "How Road Fees Are Working in Broward County," p. 25.

61. Ibid., p. 25.

62. Orski, "Suburban Mobility: The Coming Transportation Crisis?" p. 291; and Harry Stewart, "The Legal Path," *Planning*, Vol. 50, No. 6 (1984), p. 27.

63. As of this writing, San Francisco's transit impact fee program remains in litigation. Monies are being collected and held in an interest-earning escrow account pending the outcome of current lawsuits.

64. Orski, "Suburban Mobility," p. 291.

65. Donald Shoup, "Cashing Out Free Parking," *Transportation Quarterly*, Vol. 36, No. 3 (1982), pp. 351–64.

66. David Curry and Anne Martin, "City of Los Angeles Parking Management Ordinance" (Washington: Paper presented at the Annual Meeting of the Transportation Research Board, January 1985). Also, see Chapter Five for further discussions of the Los Angeles parking reduction ordinance.

67. Ibid., p. 16.

68. Barton Aschman, Inc., "Shared Parking Demand for Selected Land Uses," *Urban Land*, Vol. 42, No. 9 (1983) pp. 12–17.

69. William Trombley, "Suburbs Gear Up to Beat Traffic," *Los Angeles Times* (December 28, 1984), p. 24.

70. Ibid., pp. 22–23.

71. Schoppert and Herald, "Private Funds for Highway Improvements," p. 42.

72. See Chapter Five for additional discussions on the Irvine Spectrum project.

73. Orski, "The Private Challenge to Public Transportation," p. 317.

74. See: Eager, "Innovative Approaches to Transportation in Growing Areas," pp. 6–7; and Joint Southeast Public Improvement Association, *Update*, Vol. 2, No. 2 (1983), agency newsletter.

75. Thomas Hazlett, "They Built Their Own Highway . . . and Other Tales of Private Land-Use Planning," *Reason* (November 1983), p. 27.

76. Capital cost estimates are based on a 30-year amortization period and a 10 percent discount rate. All transportation cost information was supplied by the project developer.

77. Neal Peirce, "Fort Collins: How to Grow Fast, with Class," *The Denver Post* (September 8, 1985).

78. Orski, "The Private Challenge to Public Transportation," pp. 330–31.

5

Southern California Case Study

SAFEGUARDING MOBILITY
IN LOS ANGELES AND ORANGE COUNTIES

Contextual Setting

Southern California is often hailed as the "automobile capital of the world." It, perhaps more than anywhere, symbolizes Americans' growing dependency on the motor vehicle and offers the most graphic testament to how freeways can irrevocably shape the overall scale, living environment, and social character of a metropolis. Laced by over 4,000 miles of freeways, expressways, and superhighways, the greater Los Angeles region has witnessed urban sprawl over the past 30 years unmatched anywhere in the world.

This case study focuses on mobility issues posed by intensive office development in several rapidly growing sections of Los Angeles County and Orange County. In 1984, the two counties had a combined population of just over ten million and a workforce of roughly 5.3 million.[1] Like many other southern and western boom areas of the country, the fastest growing sectors of Southern California's regional economy have been in service and information-related industries, particularly those associated with the high-tech and entertainment fields. The high-tech sector itself, including electronics and aerospace industries, presently makes up 20 percent of the two counties' economic base and accounted for 40 percent of all new jobs created during the seventies.[2] Regional forecasts call for continued healthy population and employment growth in both counties over the next 15 years, on the order of 3 to 4 percent annually.[3]

The lion's share of Southern California's recent high-tech and office growth has been concentrated around the airport area of west Los Angeles and in central Orange County. Although neither setting could be character-

144

ized as "suburban" in the pure sense of the word, both nonetheless constitute substantial non-CBD growth nodes, lying 20 and 40 miles respectively from downtown Los Angeles. Another burgeoning employment center is taking form in the far outreaches of the San Fernando Valley some 25 miles northeast of downtown Los Angeles. Combined, these three case corridors offer a rich context for examining suburban mobility issues in America's largest conurbation west of the Appalachians.

In both Los Angeles and Orange County, the recent sprouting of numerous satellite growth centers has gained political favor for reinforcing regional planning goals. Over the past decade, elected officials in both places have formally endorsed the "centers concept" as part of their respective General County Plans whereby hierarchical networks of high-density growth nodes are called for, each interspersed by low-density, mainly residential, suburban-style neighborhoods. In Los Angeles, over 50 "urban centers" encompassing three distinct density hierarchies have been officially designated, with downtown Los Angeles continuing in its role as the preeminent retail and employment district. By comparison, Orange County has designated 11 fairly equal-sized major activity centers, no one of which is being targeted as the future downtown focus.

All the case study settings explored in this chapter represent Southern California's most rapidly expanding "urban center" and stand out as impressive showpieces of mixed office-commercial development. Three case areas, shown in Map 5.1 in relation to Los Angeles's CBD, are examined throughout this chapter:

WEST SAN FERNANDO VALLEY. A focal point of growth in Los Angeles's sprawling San Fernando Valley has been *Warner Center*—a 1,100-acre, master-planned, mixed-use complex off the Ventura Freeway (I-101). Warner Center includes a 32-building business park, 250 acres of diversified light industrial uses, an emerging center of office towers, an indoor shopping mall, several large corporate headquarters, and on-site housing. Only roughly one-half developed, future growth will concentrate primarily around the Warner Center Plaza, a core area slated for six new mid- to high-rise office towers and a new prestigious hotel.

WEST LOS ANGELES. The 16-square mile area of western Los Angeles lying immediately north and south of the international airport complex (LAX) today contains over 40 million square feet of office, light industrial, and hotel space, more than in all of downtown Los Angeles. Another 40 million square feet in investments are planned for this corridor over the next 15 years. Currently, many of the 186,000 employees in this area work for large aerospace corporations and dense contractors, including Rockwell International, Hughes Aircraft, and McDonald Douglas. Over 20 new large-scale office, R&D, and mixed-use projects flanking LAX are either under construction or in the advanced planning stages. Two specific projects examined in this chapter are: *Howard Hughes Center*—a planned 5.1 million square feet mid-rise office development with an on-site hotel and retail uses in the Westchester District; and *Playa Vista*—a massive 926-acre planned urban development (PUD) near the Marina del Rey district, scheduled for 8,800 new attached housing units, 2,400 hotel rooms, and 6.5 million square feet of retail, office, and high-tech industrial space.

CENTRAL ORANGE COUNTY.   The golden triangle of Newport Beach, Irvine, and Santa Ana in Central Orange County has become a hotbed of office and commercial activity over the past decade. Since the mid-seventies, over six million square feet of nonresidential floorspace have been added annually, and today one out of nine Fortune 500 firms maintains an office within the triangle area. Two major nuclei of the

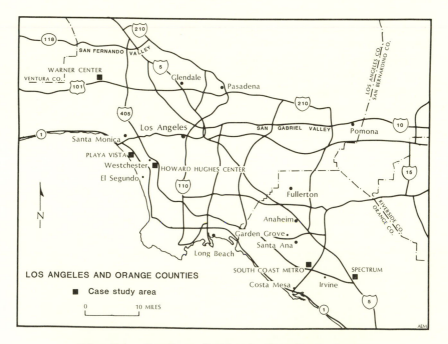

Map 5.1. Southern California Case Study Setting

building boom have been: *South Coast Metro*—straddling the Costa Mesa-Santa Ana border and bounded by two freeways, this mixed-use 3.5 square mile megacomplex is expected to have 45,000 workers at buildout in 1995. Most of the 15.5 million square feet of office and R&D growth is slated for the South Coast Plaza area, a moderately high-density town center with several office towers, a 400-seat repertory theater, several prestigious hotels, a regional shopping mall and garden-style townhouses. *Irvine Spectrum*—a master-planned bioscience and high-technology park that will be spread over 2,900 acres in four distinct parcels of land owned by the Irvine Company in the eastern corner of the Irvine Ranch. The four individual projects will feature an industrial center, a high-tech center, a bioscience and medical research and teaching center, and mid- to high-rise core of offices, theaters, restaurants, and ancillary uses.

Table 5.1 presents comparative background information on the types of land uses, physical dimensions, and locational characteristics of these study sites.

Each of the three settings is distinct in its own right, and differs markedly from the more traditional campus-style office developments sprouting elsewhere in the United States. Most of the projects lie in fairly built-up areas, and are surrounded by a sea of urban uses, with low-to-moderate density residences dominating the surrounding cityscape. In addition, many of Southern California's emerging satellite work centers are bordered by a hodgepodge of freestanding office and retail complexes of varying sizes and tenant mixes. Despite some of their idiosyncrasies, the Southern California case sites offer particularly intriguing insights into up-and-coming suburban mobility issues if for no other reason than they are among the most imposing large-scale developments mushrooming up outside of CBDs anywhere in the United States.

Key Mobility Issues in Southern California

Although Los Angeles and Orange Counties have among the highest per capita lane miles of freeway in the United States, stop-and-go conditions are generally the rule along virtually all stretches during rush hours. Most of the region's thoroughfares were built in the 1950s and 1960s for an area with about half the current population. Consequently, average rush-hour freeway speeds are today below 35 mph, and in some corridors, under 10 mph.

TABLE 5.1
Background Summaries of Southern California Case Study Sites

Area and Project	Type of Development	Total Acreage	Total Building Square Footage (in millions, nonresidential) Current[a]	Buildout[b]	Project Status	Expected Completion	Total Employment Current[a]	Buildout[b]	Mileage From Downtown Los Angeles
West San Fernando Valley, Los Angeles: *Warner Center*	Mixed-use – office, retail, R&D, light industrial, hotel, residential	1,100	4.5	7.6	First several phases completed	1989	25,000	55,000	25
West Los Angeles (Westchester, LAX & El Segundo Areas): *Howard Hughes Center*	Primarily office; hotel and retail	67	0	5.1	Under construction	1990	0	13,000	20
Playa Vista	Mixed-use – retail, R&D, office, hotel, residential	926	0	8.2	Under construction	2000	0	25,000	20
Total Western Los Angeles	Mixed-use – office, R&D, retail, hotel	21,760	41	83	Over 20 major projects in varying stages of completion	2000	186,000	359,000	20-25
Central Orange Co.: *South Coast Metro*	Mixed-use – office, retail, hotel, residential	2,240	12	21	Several phases completed	1995	15,000	45,000	36
Irvine Spectrum	Primarily bioscience and high-technology part; some retail and office	2,900	0	41	Under construction	2000	0	100,000	40

a As of 1985.

b When project is completed.

Source: All data were obtained from field interviews.

148

Despite both deteriorating roadway conditions and the presence of the world's largest all-bus transit system, the vast majority of Southern Californians still rely on their private automobiles for commuting. In 1980, only 6.4 percent of Los Angeles's workers commuted via public transit, while in Orange County the share was below 2 percent. Within the specific case study areas discussed in this chapter, transit's mode split is even lower. All three do, however, enjoy relatively high rates of carpool and vanpool patronage. In 1980, ridesharing constituted 18.5 percent, 20 percent, and 23 percent of all commute trips in central Orange County, west Los Angeles, and west San Fernando Valley respectively.

Among the case sites, traffic congestion is most acute in the airport area of west Los Angeles. Vehicular volumes exceed capacity during peak periods on over half of the major arteries serving this area, including the eight-lane San Diego Freeway (I-405), where one-hour volumes exceeding 20,000 vehicles have been recorded. Much of central Orange County operates at more tolerable congestion levels, generally in the range of 85 to 95 percent of capacity. Spot congestion and traffic pileups plague several critical intersections around the South Coast Metro Center, however. On the other hand, peak traffic conditions have been more favorable around the Warner Center in west San Fernando Valley, partly due to the reverse direction of many commute trips destined to this area.

Regional planners largely attribute clogged roadways as well as high levels of auto-dependency along these growth corridors to gross mismatches in where jobs and housing are sited. Southern California's sprawling, somewhat fractured settlement pattern is principally responsible for this imbalance. In the burgeoning west Los Angeles area, nearly 60 percent of all work trips are presently external (i.e., made from outside the subregion).[4] As shown in Figure 5.1, external trips made to and from the LAX-Westchester area are multidirectional, radiating along several dozen different axes to the north, east, and south. The Southern California Association of Governments (SCAG) projects that work trips to the LAX district will increase 71 percent over 1980 volumes by 1992, presaging an even more diffuse pattern of commuting by the century's close.

Cross-town commuting has also become quite prominent throughout Los Angeles's San Fernando Valley. A 1984 survey of trip origins-destinations among Warner Center employees revealed that most arrived from all corners of the 180 square mile San Fernando Valley. One-third were found to live within five miles of the Center, while another one-third commuted more than 40 miles round-trip to work. Over 90 percent of the Center's 25,000 employees drove to work by themselves.

Recent journey-to-work statistics reveal a similar geographic dispersal of commute trips to and from employment centers in central Orange County. Only 18 percent of all South Coast Plaza employees, for instance, live in either Costa Mesa or Santa Ana; on the other hand, over twice as many reside in one of several affluent surrounding coastal communities, on average commuting 25 to 30 miles to work each day. Presently, over 90 percent of South Coast Plaza employees solo commute, and despite the convergence of a dozen regional bus routes near the center, virtually none patronize transit.[5] Part of the reason for transit's dismal showing has to do with the home-end of the commute trip—only 21 percent of South Coast Plaza employees live within a five-minute walking distance of a bus route. High rates of auto-dependency can also be attributed to the fact that peaking tends to be far less pronounced than at most business centers. Fewer than

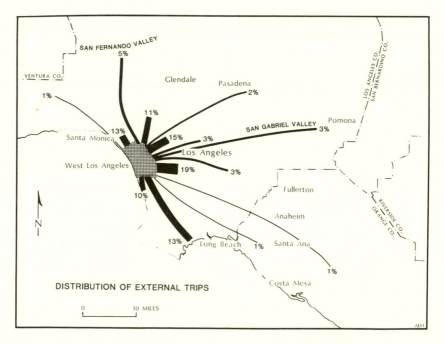

Figure 5.1. Place of Residence of All Work Trips Made to and from the West Los Angeles Area.
(Source: City of Los Angeles, *Los Angeles Coastal Transportation Corridor Specific Plan*, Los Angeles: Departments of City Planning and Transportation, 1985.)

two-thirds of all South Coast Plaza employees, for instance, arrive to work during the traditional 7:00–8:00 A.M. due to the large number of financial tenants who time their work hours to coincide with East Coast stock exchange activities.

South Coast Plaza's experiences are by no means endemic to all of Orange County, however. At other nearby business centers, ridesharing has become extremely popular. Nearly one-quarter of all workers at the two million square foot Irvine Business Center, for instance, have joined either a carpool or vanpool. As mentioned in the previous chapter, one of the most successful employer-based ridesharing programs in the nation thrives at the nearby Fluor Corporation headquarters in Irvine, where around 40 percent of the company's 6,000 workers pool to work.

Design and Land Use Issues in Southern California

Project Scale and Site Characteristics

Compared to many other suburban workplaces around the country, most office complexes in Los Angeles and Orange Counties are being built at moderately high densities. At the Warner Center, Howard Hughes Center, South Coast Metro, and a host of other mini-downtowns, clusters of mid- to high-rise office towers, interconnected by pedways and skywalks, are being built and sited to form viable urban/suburban cores. The intent in all these areas is to create a pedestrian-oriented town center environment, complete with retail, recreational, cultural, and other tenant-support services. An equally important impetus for verticalizing office buildings has been the rapidly escalating cost of real estate in choice suburban locales such as Westchester and Costa Mesa.

Both developers and public officials hope the trend toward mid-rise and high-profile office construction in suburban Los Angeles and Orange County will prove conducive to carpooling and other commute alternatives over the long run. As a further inducement to share rides, developers of the Warner Center, South Coast Metro, and several other Southern California megacomplexes have pared down on-site parking to the 3.0–3.5 spaces per 1,000 square foot range. Several Southern California developers are counting on the catalytic effects of more intensive site designs and reduced parking to push carpooling, vanpooling, and transit's combined share of intersuburban commuting eventually up to the 25 percent mark.

Several Southern California site designs deserve particular recognition for their attention to pressing access and mobility concerns. *Warner Center*

Plaza, the centerpiece of the massive multipurpose Warner Center compound, is being built as a people-oriented project, complete with ornately landscaped plazas, open concourses, and other pedestrian conveniences. In recognition of its architectural theme, the Plaza has been cited by the Los Angeles City Planning Department as the "single most outstanding example of urban center development in Los Angeles today."[6] The project's master plan calls for the Plaza to become the main downtown focus of the entire San Fernando Valley when it is fully completed sometime around 1990 (see Photo 5.1). Six office and commercial towers, ranging from 12 to 28 stories, along with a luxury 470-room hotel, are either already standing or planned over the next five years. An integrated network of partially enclosed skywalks, pressed for by the city of Los Angeles when the Center's land parcels were initially zoned,[7] will interconnect the six towers. Warner Center designers hope the pedway system will help coalesce the Plaza's built environment in view of the project's fairly spacious FAR of 2:1. Four peripherally sited parking garages, each built with four or five levels, will also be fed by pedestrianways. Project planners have opted to stack vehicles into multilevel structures rather than spread them along acres of asphalt to help reinforce the "people place" design focus of the core.

Encircling Warner Center's high-profile core is a mix of low- to midrise retail, R&D, and light industrial buildings. Immediately east of the Plaza lies the Warner Business Park, with 1.1 million square feet of office/R&D space spread over 44 one- to three-story buildings. Flanking both the Plaza and Business Park are two large corporate headquarters, each employing over 6,000 workers. The perimeter of the project is occupied primarily by light industrial and retail uses. Along most radiants, densities at the Warner Center complex taper off sharply as one leaves the high-rise office core. Thus, even though the central Plaza area strongly emphasizes pedestrianization, an extensive grid of four-lane collectors and arterials, along with abundant surface parking, envelops most of the project to ensure easy auto access and unencumbered circulation. In recognition of the long-term risks an auto-dominated park poses, Warner Center developers are looking into transferable development rights (TDRs) and the construction of secondary land uses over surface parking lots as means of intensifying perimeter areas of the complex.

In the west Los Angeles corridor, the planned three million square foot *Howard Hughes Center* office complex similarly stands out for its proposed pedestrian and transit-oriented design. The entire 67-acre project is being built around an architecturally integrated high-rise office and mixed-use center that will serve as the focal point for all carpool, vanpool, and com-

Photo 5.1. New Office Towers at the Warner Center Plaza in Los Angeles's San Fernando Valley.
All buildings and peripheral parking garages will be interconnected by a grade-separated pedestrian skybridge. (Photos by the author.)

muter bus connections (see Photos 5.2 and 5.3). Surrounding smaller-scale buildings are being configured so that the maximum pedestrian walking distance will be one-quarter of a mile. All parking structures are being relegated to perimeter locations, and a grade-separated enclosed pedestrian pathway will interconnect buildings as well as parking facilities.

As in the case of the Warner Center in Los Angeles's San Fernando Valley, the *South Coast Metro* is similarly striving to become the dominant urban/suburban focus of sprawling Orange County (see Photo 5.4). Heretofore, Orange County's growth has followed almost a textbook polynucleated pattern, clustering around ten or so comparably sized nodes (e.g., central Anaheim, Santa Ana, Garden Grove, Newport Beach, and Costa Mesa). By adopting a high-rise versus campus-style profile, South Coast Metro developers hope to eventually win out over their competition to become Orange County's dominant downtown core.

The flagship of the entire 2,200-acre Metro complex is the largely completed South Coast Plaza, featuring one of the nation's largest shopping malls, a performing arts center, a hotel, a condominium village, and several high-rise office towers catering mainly to financial, accounting, legal, and other "upscale" professions (see Map 5.2 and Photo 5.5). Because of its mixed-use, high-rise character, the Plaza has been designated by the county's transit authority as one of two countywide major connection and transfer locations. Twelve different bus routes converge on the Plaza, offering front-door access at both the shopping mall and high-rise town center complexes. Despite transit's high profile, as mentioned earlier, only 4 percent of Plaza employees use it to get to work. Charging workers going commercial rates for parking at the Plaza's two 3,300 space garages has also failed to sway their allegiances away from auto-commuting. Local observers attribute transit's poor showing largely to the tenant composition of the Plaza—primarily professional firms with fairly high-salaried staffs.

Two other case sites—Playa Vista and Irvine Spectrum—are likewise being planned around high-rise, mixed-use, office-oriented centers, however the bulk of employee floorspace in both of these complexes will be laid out more along the lines of traditional two- to three-story campus-style developments. *Playa Vista*—one of few settings where nearly 1,000 acres of prime buildable land have gone untouched some 50 years after surrounding urban uses have been fully developed—is being designed as a hybrid between a massive "new-town/in-town" and a suburban office park/PUD (see Map 5.3). Low- to mid-rise office towers separated by open plazas will grace the mixed-use project where 25,000 white-collar and high-tech employees are expected. Recreation is a key element of the Playa Vista plan, with gen-

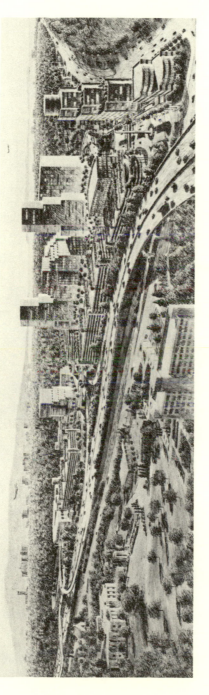

Photo 5.2. Artist's Rendering of the Three Million Square Foot Howard Hughes Center Business Complex. It fronts on the San Diego Freeway (I–405), with the LAX International Airport and Santa Monica Bay in the background. (Rendering by Carlos Diniz and photography by Annette Del Zoppo, provided by courtesy of Howard Hughes Center.)

erous amounts of land to be devoted to a linear park system and a shoreline promenade along the marina.

The awesome, 2,900-acre *Irvine Spectrum*—a planned bioscience, high-tech, and commercial supercomplex—is to be the newest addition to the city of Irvine, the nation's largest master-planned community. Photos 5.6 and Map 5.4 show the physical layout and access routes of the four key phases of the park:

Irvine Center: seven million square feet of mid-rise and high-rise construction, including offices, restaurants, theaters, and retail shops;
Irvine Industrial Center: 16 million square feet of light industrial and manufacturing uses serving 160 companies;

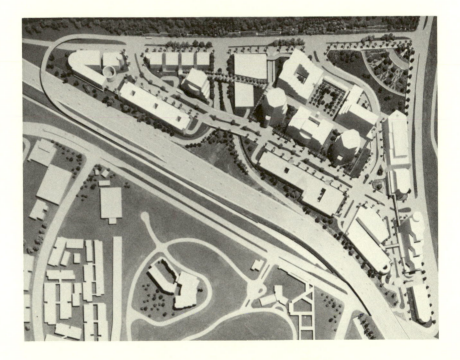

Photo 5.3.   Overhead View of Model of the Howard Hughes Center Master Plan.
Central pedestrian spine will interconnect office towers and fringe parking garages throughout the triangular site. (Photo by Wayne Thom, provided courtesy of Howard Hughes Center.)

Irvine Technology Center: 5.5 million square feet of low-rise clustered space housing electronics, aeronautics, and other high-tech oriented firms; and

Irvine Bioscience Center: seven million square feet of low- to mid-rise building space for medically and biologically-oriented firms and a new teaching hospital.

Map 5.4 reveals the extensive network of parkways and boulevards that will embroider the complex, feeding into multiple interchanges of the converging Santa Ana (I-5), San Diego (I-405), and Laguna (State Route-133) freeways. Despite the project's seemingly strong automobile/freeway orientation, Map 5.4 also pinpoints the location of a proposed on-site multimodal station that would be served by bus, taxi, and commuter rail and possibly even light rail transit and high-speed "bullet train" services, both of which are being considered for this corridor.

In general, the design guidelines drawn for the Spectrum follow the low-density, high-amenity character of a classical suburban office park more closely than any of the Southern California case settings. Although the

Photo 5.4.   Artist's Rendering of the South Coast Metro Complex at Buildout.
Metro is bordered by the San Diego Freeway (I-405) and the Newport/Costa Mesa Freeway (SR-55). (Rendering by Thomas Tomonga and photography by Larsens Photography, Inc., provided courtesy of the South Coast Metro Alliance.)

Irvine Center, dubbed the "Golden Triangle" because of the three-way confluence of bordering freeways, will function as a vigorous urban center, it is apt to be overshadowed somewhat by the massive campus-style profile of the remaining complex. Outside of the Center, the project's overall FAR will be .35-to-1, roughly the national average for office parks. According to the Spectrum's design guidelines, all structures must meet minimum setback requirements and height limits of 40 feet, and are to be oriented toward roadway entrances to facilitate auto access[8] (see Photo 5.7). Thus, with the

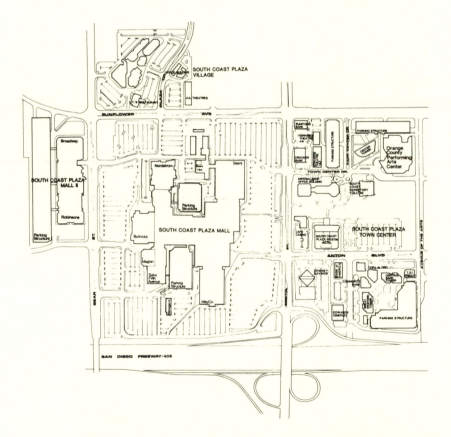

Map 5.2.   Land Uses at the South Coast Plaza in Central Orange County, Combining Retail, Office, Hotel, Residential, and Performing Arts Activities.
(Map provided courtesy of the South Coast Metro Alliance.)

Photo 5.5. Outdoor Arcade at the South Coast Plaza, Featuring Water Fountains, Desert Plantings, and Stone Sculptures. (Photo by Larsens Photography, Inc., provided courtesy of the South Coast Metro Alliance.)

exception of the high-density core, the Irvine Spectrum will likely take on the distinctive auto-oriented form of most office parks being built along America's urban fringes.

Land Use and Tenant Mix Characteristics

In addition to being unique for their high-rise, clustered profiles, several Southern California case sites stand out for their unusually strong mixed-use characters. All five case study projects include or plan to include a wide array of on-site consumer services, such as restaurants, shops, theaters, hotels, and, in several cases, in-door health and recreational facilities. These village-like, self-sufficient environments are expected to do more to promote ridesharing, transit usage, and foot travel over the long run than any single factor.

Additionally, three of the case projects—Warner Center, Playa Vista, and South Coast Metro—either currently have or are planning on-site hous-

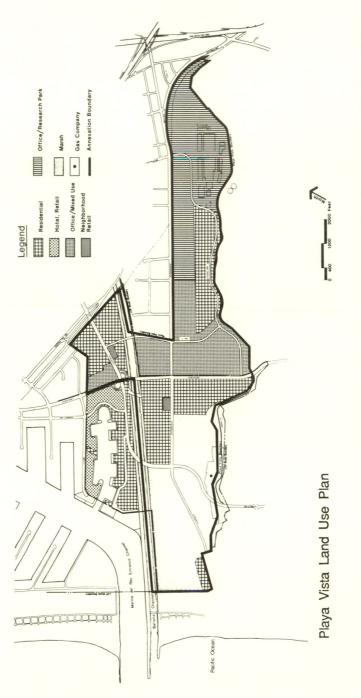

Playa Vista Land Use Plan

Map 5.3. **Land Use Plan for the 1,000-Acre Playa Vista New-Town/In-Town Development near Marina del Rey and Playa del Rey in Western Los Angeles.** (Map provided courtesy of the Howard Hughes Development Corporation.)

160

Photo 5.6.   Aerial View Looking West at the Four Segments of the Evolving Irvine Spectrum Development. Site 1 will be the commercial Irvine Center. Site 2 is the partially developed Irvine Industrial Center. Site 3 is to be transformed into the Irvine Technology Center. Site 4 is being planned for the Irvine Bioscience Center. (Photo by Aerial Eye, provided courtesy of the Irvine Company.)

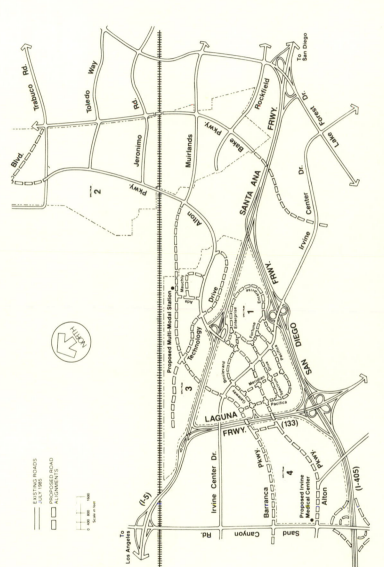

Map 5.4. **Proposed System of Access Routes for the Irvine Spectrum, Including a Proposed Multimodal Rail Transit Station.** (Map provided courtesy of the Irvine Company.)

Photo 5.7. Artist's Rendering of Building Profile at the Irvine Spectrum.
All structures subject to 40-foot height limits and direct roadway access requirements. (Rendering by Thomas Tomonga, provided courtesy of the Irvine Company.)

163

ing aimed at tenants' employees. This is particularly significant in view of the lopsided ratio in jobs-to-housing around most of the study sites. Table 5.2, drawn largely from municipal and subregional census data, reveals the severity of the housing shortage situation in 1980. For each of the subregions, job slots in all instances exceed housing units by at least 50 percent and in several cases by far more. The situation is most acute in the rapidly expanding Westchester/LAX area of western Los Angeles where jobs outnumber dwelling units four to one. The table also reveals that regional planners expect these imbalances to widen when many areas begin reaching their planned buildout stage. The ultimate jobs-to-housing ratio projected for the Westchester/airport area, for instance, is over 12-to-1. All of this suggests, of course, that the continued displacement of employees from their workplaces by critical housing shortages will force more and more to commute over long distances, and overwhelmingly in their own vehicles.

TABLE 5.2

Ratios of Total Employment to Total Dwelling Units
for Selected Southern California Case Study Settings

Area	Actual 1980	Year 2000 Projection[a]
West San Fernando Valley Area	1.82:1	1.90:1 [b]
West Los Angeles Area	1.80:1	10.48:1 [b]
Westchester/LAX Area	4.01:1	12.35:1 [b]
Playa Vista	NA	2.83:1 [c]
Central Orange County		
Irvine Spectrum Area	1.80:1	1.98:1 [c]
City of Irvine	2.91:1	3.29:1 [b]
Cities of Costa Mesa and		
Santa Ana	1.60:1 [d]	1.94:1 [b]

[a] For SCAG designated subregions most closely approximating study areas.

[b] Estimated at Community Plan buildout.

[c] Estimates by private developer.

[d] 1984 estimates by the cities of Costa Mesa and Santa Ana.

NA = Not Applicable.

Sources: Southern California Association of Governments, "SCAG-82 Modified Forecast: Population, Housing, Employment" (Los Angeles: SCAG, agency report, 1985); Summa Corporation, "Playa Vista: The Plan" (Los Angeles: unpublished report, 1982); Austin and Associates, "Continuing Study of the California Economy" (Irvine: unpublished consulting report, 1984).

Perhaps the most outstanding example of integrated housing and employment development being proposed in Southern California is the Playa Vista project. At buildout, some 8,800 attached single family dwelling units will be interspersed over 325 acres of the total 926-acre compound situated on the unincorporated strip of land wedge between Marina del Rey to the north and the LAX district to the south. A broad spectrum of housing is being proposed, with 15 percent of all homes to be priced in the "affordable" range and 7.5 percent reserved for low-income rental. With the continuing trend toward multiple-worker households, Playa Vista developers anticipate that the 6,800 upper-middle income units will be purchased by a significant portion of the 25,000 permanent employees who work on the site. Developers also expect that the project's medium densities, in combination with the strategic siting of housing, employment, shopping, and recreational facilities, will create a village milieu supportive of transit. Ten or more privately operated shuttle buses will circulate through the development in a continuous figure-eight pattern to serve Playa Vista residents and workers. Numerous transit amenities, such as bus shelters and turn-out lanes, in addition to an extensive trail system, are also being planned.

The Playa Vista type of project, however, still represents more of the exception than the rule in Southern California. Very few of the region's office and commercial developers have chosen to integrate any kind of housing into their projects so far. And there has been little conscious effort to stage the phase-in of jobs to match housing availability. Where there has been coordinated housing and office development, it has generally been at the insistence of local municipalities. As mentioned in Chapter Three, the city of Costa Mesa recently passed an ordinance requiring large office developments like the South Coast Metro to provide housing, either on-site or within the city limits, to serve at least 20 percent of their tenants' employees. Metro's developers have proceeded to build 1,200 condominium units throughout the 3.5 square mile complex. Although there was initially some hesitancy to do so, any skepticism over on-site housing quickly waned as units began to sell as soon as they were listed. Metro's developers maintain that mixed-use activities in general, and on-site housing specifically, have contributed appreciably to the marketability of the overall project. Although they admit that mixed land uses themselves have not coaxed any firms to locate at the Metro complex who were not otherwise inclined to do so, they nonetheless feel that the availability of consumer and on-site housing services has tipped the scales in their favor over other competitors.

Again, there can be no guarantees that by simply building housing either on-site or nearby, future traffic snarls will be avoided. Although few large land developers have done more to promote housing than the Irvine Company, it has been conservatively estimated that only around 25 percent of Irvine residents actually work in the community.[9] Thus, despite the fact that there are almost three times as many jobs in Irvine as there are homes, only one quarter of the population that lives there have local jobs. Similarly, for the Warner Center development in the San Fernando Valley, project managers estimate that only around 8 percent of the residents living either at townhouses and apartments located on-site or at nearby condominiums actually work in the office/light industrial park. Although only estimates, these figures do suggest that job-housing integration, by itself, will never likely be a panacea toward commandeering traffic congestion, and that perhaps what is more important is the balancing of jobs and residences at the subregional versus site-specific level.

Transportation-Related Design Features

Several Southern California office centers have built-in design features that could spur employee ridesharing and transit usage. All the case sites either presently or will eventually provide preferential parking for carpoolers. The Warner Plaza, for instance, plans to have loading and drop-off zones for vanpools and carpools at all building entrances. A recent survey of the Plaza's current employees found that 22 percent would likely carpool given free, preferential parking privileges. Showers, lockers, and racks are also being provided at the six Warner Center Plaza office towers as an inducement to cycling. At the Playa Vista and Irvine Spectrum developments, moreover, bus turnout and turnaround areas, along with attractive, well-lit bus shelters, will be strategically sited. Another case project, the Howard Hughes Center in Westchester, does not plan to operate transit on-site, although various near-site transit amenities (e.g., covered shelters) are being provided and a core complex is being built to allow the possible addition of a transit center sometime in the future. Developers of the Howard Hughes Center have placed a higher premium on designing the entire complex for convenient vanpool access. All peripheral parking garages, for example, will have three extra feet of elevation on each floor to accommodate vanpools. Project developers expect the added cost of this airspace to be minimal over the long run. Additionally, the most convenient stalls in all garages will be reserved for vanpools and carpools. Attractive pedestrian skybridges will feed directly into all preferential parking areas. An overriding design theme of the Howard Hughes complex is to segregate foot traffic from vehicular traffic through the liberal use of pedways.

Transportation Management

Transportation Management Associations

As in other parts of the country, the major institutional response to the congestion threats posed by large-scale suburban developments in Southern California has been the creation of transportation management associations (TMAs). More private sector alliances have sprouted in Southern California over the past few years to deal with local area access and mobility problems than perhaps anywhere in the country.

One of the nation's first TMAs was the El Segundo Employer's Association (ESEA). Formed in 1981 by 24 large corporations with a combined labor force of over 100,000, ESEA's principal charge has been to improve "the total transportation system in and around the aerospace, electronics and defense employment area near Los Angeles International Airport."[10] Financed by a voluntary fee (currently $1.75 per employee or per 200 square feet of leasable space), ESEA's programs during its first two years were wide ranging, including: promotion of company-based carpool and vanpool services; etching out the conceptual plans for a possible light rail transit line in the area; jointly funding, along with the city of El Segundo, ten part-time traffic officers to control rush-hour flows at vital intersections; and financing assorted intersection and signalization improvements. Over the past several years, the Association's ridesharing efforts have been particularly successful—almost 25 percent of all workers in the city of El Segundo commute some way other than by a single occupant auto, despite the area's modest level of public transit services. Recently, however, ESEA has curtailed its activities, reducing the size of its paid staff, and abandoning in-house ridematching and transportation planning. The Association's new focus has been on lobbying for state and federal funds to finance local street, highway, and transit improvements.

Among the case study sites, the only project-level TMA formed to date has been the Warner Center Association (WCA). The Center's fourteen largest employers make up the WCA, paying annual dues based on the size of their respective work forces. The association advocates "complementary land use and transportation policies as a priority," and has spearheaded programs to "improve access to and circulation within Warner Center."[11] Specific actions taken to date include: ridesharing promotion, implementation of surface street and signalization improvements, funding assistance for widening the Ventura Freeway (U.S. 101), and lobbying for extending the proposed regional metrorail project to the west San Fernando Valley. Each of WCA's fourteen participating companies has appointed an Employee Transportation Coordinator, most of whom spend around five to 10 percent of their time on transportation matters. Coordinators meet on a monthly basis as a network to further organize carpooling and vanpooling among their companies. In addition, the Association has hired a full-time ridesharing program manager to implement a centerwide ridesharing demonstration program. The full-time manager heads up the Warner Center Commuter Connection Office, a partnership of the Warner Center Association, the city of Los Angeles, and the regional ridesharing agency, Commuter Computer. The Commuter Connection is funded jointly by the city, WCA, and a countywide dedicated sales tax. Municipal support has been in the form of a pass-through federal grant, provided in the hope that WCA will serve as a role model for other regional employment centers to emulate.

Southern California's biggest TMA, on a par with the nation's very largest, is the Orange County Transportation Coalition (OCTC). Formed in 1979 by six of the county's leading business executives, the group currently boasts 52 member-companies representing around 130,000 employees.[12] To date, OCTC has functioned principally as a lobbyist for securing state highway funds for the county. Third-party consultants are hired to carry out all transportation planning functions and lobbying chores. A minimum fee of $1,000 per member finances these activities.

At least two of the yet to be completed case study developments—the Irvine Spectrum and the Howard Hughes Center—anticipate future TMAs. Perhaps the most impressive groundwork anywhere is being laid for the Spectrum's Association. There, covenants require all land purchasers and building lessees with 30 or more employees to actively participate in the TMA. The Irvine Company, developer of the project, has set an ambitious target of reducing future peak-hour traffic by 50 percent, to be brought about through TMA-sponsored programs. The Association will be supported by an assessment levied on all participating companies, and is expected to operate with an annual budget approaching $500,000. Project developers and Orange County officials alike hope the Spectrum's TMA will become a bellwether of future private sector initiatives in the county.

Although TMAs have enjoyed enviable popularity in Southern California recently, as mentioned in the previous chapter, there nonetheless have been some disappointments. Notably, the Newport Center Association, formed by local business interests representing some 10,000 workers in the densest cluster of offices in Newport Beach, folded after only one year of existence. The Association, which sought to promote and finance various traffic mitigation programs in the beach community, floundered because top-level corporate executives were unwilling to embrace it.[13] There has also been little progress toward inaugurating a formal TMA at the South Coast Metro complex in central Orange County. Although several consulting studies strongly recommend the formation of such a group, nothing has been done so far due to both a lack of interest and concern over duplicating the umbrella functions of the Orange County Transportation Coalition.

Ridesharing and Commute Alternatives Programs

By far, the most common traffic management strategy being pursued in Southern California's suburbs is rideshare promotion. At the regional level, Commuter Computer holds the spotlight as the largest nonprofit ridesharing organization in the country. Since the mid-seventies, Commuter Computer has registered over 40 percent of the employees of 1,700 large firms in a five-county area, and has been credited with creating over 50,000 separate carpools and vanpools since the mid-seventies. The organization concentrates primarily on large employers (over 1,000 workers), providing not only matching services, but performing insurance brokerage and rideshare coordination training as well. Besides carpool activities, Commuter Computer has been instrumental in the formation of approximately 500 third-party vanpools, 500 company-sponsored vanpools, and 100 private commuter bus services throughout Southern California.[14]

Other important regional ridesharing actors are the Orange County Transit District (OCTD) and the South Coast Air Quality Management District (SCAQMD). OCTD, Orange County's chief public transit operator, performs free computer matching services and has helped consummate over 4,000 carpool pairings over the past five years. In contrast to Commuter Computer, OCTD has focused primarily on smaller firms and businesses in hopes of becoming a wholesale broker of matching, training, and marketing services. OCTD's continued involvement in ridematching is not as much a philanthrophic gesture as it is a realization that carpools can help control soaring costs by relieving the agency of running near-empty buses to low-density neighborhoods. SCAQMD has entered Southern California's ridesharing picture by recently proposing regulations that would require all regional employers of 700 or more workers to hire a full-time coordinator and sponsor pooling programs where public transit is unavailable. The requirements, which many local observers expect to be adopted in some form over the next several years, aim to reduce solo commuting, and thus mobile sources of pollutants, to meet stringent state and federal air quality standards.

At the subregional level, several noteworthy ridesharing programs have been sponsored by employers in the El Segundo/LAX and Irvine areas. Hughes Aircraft Company, for instance, has contracted out ten commuter buses to serve both its employees' work trips and circulate between the numerous company buildings scattered around the LAX area. Over 30 vans are also leased to Hughes' employees at subsidized rates. As mentioned earlier, the Fluor Corporation of Irvine likewise provides vans for its workers. So far, over 100 8- to 16-passenger coaches have been leased at 75 percent of cost. The company also offers various bonuses (e.g., free lunches and Disneyland tickets) to employees who rideshare. Nearby at the Auto Club of Southern California's regional headquarters, similar incentives have been adopted, resulting in a 47 percent carpool mode split among its employees.

Among the specific case study projects, the most ambitious ridesharing efforts are currently under way at the Warner Center complex. There, over 7,000 of the total 25,000 employees have registered with Commuter Computer. One of the largest companies, Prudential Insurance, has purchased 40 vans for employee commuting and maintains a full-time staff position to coordinate all phases of the pooling program. With the recent addition of a full-time rideshare coordinator for the entire complex, the Warner Center Association hopes eventually to meet its lofty vehicle occupancy goal of 1.5 persons per vehicle (compared to a citywide average of 1.1). By comparison, the other largely completed case study project—South Coast Metro— has experienced little in the way of formal or informal ridesharing interest so far, despite the fact that "major buildings in the Metro Area were approved with specific TSM plan development conditions attached."[15]

Perhaps the biggest obstacle to ridesharing in the South Coast Metro and surely other Southern California workplaces as well has been office workers' heavy reliance on their private automobiles for conducting midday business. Following up on the discussions of the previous chapter, a recent survey of 2,500 South Coast Metro employees found that 44 percent and 19 percent respectively used their cars for personal business and work purposes at least three times per week.[16] One-third of the respondents indicated that they would consider joining a hassle-free carpool, however the overwhelming majority of workers noted they were quite satisfied with their current commuting mode. Similarly, a 1984 survey of Warner Center employees revealed that 77 percent needed their cars before and after work, while 53 percent relied on their cars during normal working hours. Neither development, nor any of their tenants, has established a formal program for making company cars available to rideshare participants during the midday, although such an arrangement has been discussed by the Warner Center Association, possibly using idle company-owned vans.

Traffic Impact Ordinances and Legislation

Perhaps the most progressive action being taken in Southern California toward financing new infrastructure has been the passage of various traffic impact ordinances. Several novel ordinances, briefly outlined in Chapter Four, were recently approved in western Los Angeles. Notably, in Westwood Village, a large office, retail, and theater district near the UCLA campus, an impact ordinance was enacted in early 1985 that exacts a one-time $5,800 fee for each afternoon peak-hour trip generated, on an average weekday, by new land uses. The Westwood Regional Center Transportation Fund has been set up from the proceeds of the ordinance to finance necessary areawide roadway and transit improvements. The ordinance also attaches covenants to all land parcels that require tenants to participate in TSM programs. An in-lieu-of provision allows developers in the Westwood area to credit against the fee levy any off-site transportation improvements they pay for. A similar program has recently been approved in the nearby high-rise office village of Century City, where all new developments are being assessed a one-time fee of $800 per rush-hour trip they are expected to generate.

What appears to be the most far-reaching impact fee program (in terms of potential revenue yield, at least) recently has been approved for the Westchester and LAX areas of western Los Angeles. The ordinance exacts a one-time fee of $2,010 for each P.M. rush-hour trip produced on an average weekday by new land developments.[17] The fee program aims to equitably distribute the cost of building as much as $235 million in transportation improvements throughout the Westchester/LAX area to future land developers.[18] As in Westwood, all collected monies are to be placed in a reserve account for future subregional transportation projects, and an in-lieu-of credit provision is honored. Moreover, developers of any new project generating 42 or more P.M. peak-hour trips are required to enter into a legally binding agreement to create a TSM program that reduces normally expected traffic volumes by at least 15 percent prior to receiving a building permit. To ensure compliance, an annual "TSM Status Report" is also required. Nonconformance assessment fees are imposed against all violators. A particularly creative provision is a "Transfer of TSM Rights"—allowing a developer or lessee to create a TSM program that removes automobiles from adjacent employment sites, crediting these reductions against his or her own requirements. Other innovative features include credits for on-site corporate housing and staging requirements to index the introduction of project phases to the availability of suitable areawide transportation infrastructure.

Similar ordinances and exaction requirements have been put into place or are being considered in central Orange County. As mentioned in the previous chapter, Costa Mesa presently exacts $30 per projected daily trip generated by all new developments while Santa Ana levies a 1 percent assessment based on gross building area, with all revenues earmarked for municipal transportation improvements. In addition, the city of Irvine currently collects impact fees from all new developers once their projects use up allotted "points"—that is, generate traffic volumes that exceed General Plan thresholds.[19] Local officials feel the point system has yielded a vital revenue stream for financing large-scale transportation improvements, though some critics argue that it has encouraged gargantuan projects since only large landholders can afford the fees.

With regard to specific Orange County case projects, the city of Costa Mesa passed an ordinance in 1981 requiring developers of the South Coast Metro to implement TSM programs prior to the issuance of building permits and to submit a status report prior to any building occupancy; to date, however, there has been little enforcement of this mandate.[20] Moreover, the city of Irvine, in addition to imposing the point system requirement, plans to hold developers of the Irvine Spectrum to a 30 percent reduction in estimated traffic volumes through TSM programs before issuing any building permits. Finally, a countywide ordinance was recently passed that requires all landholders along three corridors scheduled for the next wave of development to pay impact fees for constructing three new freeways.[21] The fees will be pro-rated among all currently planned and future developments on the basis of their projected contributions to congestion. The levies are expected to generate $630 million, more than 60 percent of the total project cost.

Although Southern California developers have generally been supportive of recent ordinances, from interviews it was apparent that many are concerned about the fairness of these requirements. In particular, representatives of several developments believe a contentious "free-rider" situation is brewing—i.e., a select few are being forced to foot the bill for costly infrastructure improvements while existing businesses that contribute equally to congestion pay nothing. Some have also challenged the open-ended, discretionary nature of these ordinances, fearing that future policy changes in how fees are assessed or requirements enforced could backfire on them. Notwithstanding these and other concerns, many Southern California observers remain optimistic that these ordinances will generate sorely needed revenues to finance both local and regional transportation improvements. As long as pressure to develop land in highly desirable suburban locations continues to mount, most investors indicate they will support exaction programs as long as money is spent prudently and fairly.

Negotiated Private Financing of Transportation Improvements

Besides enacting traffic impact ordinances, several municipalities in Southern California have struck behind-the-scene deals with private developers to help finance new areawide infrastructure. Of particular note has been the Irvine Company's offer to contribute approximately $65 million toward local transportation improvements in support of the Spectrum complex. Dedicated funds will go toward constructing three freeway off-ramps, two parkways, and 14 projects related to traffic control, including a new interchange.[22]

Interviews with other private developers suggested that negotiated financing of off-site roadbuilding will proliferate throughout Southern California in coming years. Developers of the Howard Hughes complex expect to contribute over $20 million toward off-site improvements, including arterial widening, rechannelization of intersections, signal upgradings, and the construction of a new freeway off-ramp. Improvements will be credited against the project's fee obligation imposed by the recently passed Westchester/LAX traffic impact ordinance. In anticipation of these outlays, investors expect the square footage cost of the Howard Hughes Center complex to increase on the order of $7 to $10, adding nearly $1.00 to $1.25 per square foot to annual office rents. Overall, negotiated financing of off-site improvements has a bright future in Southern California as long as developers can credit payments against exaction fees. In particular, private financing provides developers guarantees that specific roadway improvements will be built nearby, whereas there can be no such assurances under a subregional trust fund. Of course, Southern California's impact fee revenues are equally, if not more, important to ensure that all developers remain accountable for the upstream and downstream traffic impacts of their projects as well.

Parking Management Programs

In addition to the various parking features being designed into Southern California's suburban office complexes, several exemplary parking management programs recently initiated also deserve notice. The city of Los Angeles has been particularly aggressive in encouraging developers to substitute ridesharing, transit, and other TSM programs for parking stalls. A citywide ordinance, passed in 1983, permits developers to take up to a 40 percent reduction in code-required parking by launching commute-alternative programs. To date, however, Los Angeles's parking ordinance has failed to attract many takers, with only one serious inquiry having been made since its inception. This lukewarm reception has been attributed to a number of factors, including: a general unawareness of the program's existence, an unwillingness of some developers to tolerate an estimated three- to nine-month delay in processing and approving the request, a lack of clearly defined criteria for evaluating the success of ridesharing substitution, diffusion of administrative responsibilities among three municipal departments, and the reticence of some lenders to finance any projects with below-standard parking capacity.[23] Furthermore, because most office projects have square footage limitations on individual land parcels as well as minimum setback and open-space requirements, some developers claim there is little incentive to reduce parking. The rationale seems to be that as long as certain sections of land cannot be built upon, they might as well be used for parking. In the words of one developer, "It's cheaper to pave land with asphalt than to groom grass."

This general reluctance to reduce parking seems to be most pervasive in Southern California's suburban extremities. In west Los Angeles, however, there is growing interest in trimming parking levels, largely because of the prohibitively high cost of land. At the Howard Hughes Center, developers estimate that each stall will cost around $12,000, which when capitalized comes to around $120 a month per space. Accordingly, investors feel a strong economic incentive to shave parking from the current standard of four spaces per 1,000 square feet of office space to three spaces per 1,000 square feet (with an option to go even lower, to 2.5 spaces per 1,000 square feet). In addition to the obvious cost savings, project developers believe that substitute TSM programs will help stem congestion so as to give the project a decisive marketing advantage over its nearby competitors.

A particularly inventive feature of the Howard Hughes Center's parking reduction scheme is its allowance for adjustments over time. Developers plan to use a "test and see" approach. Since the entire project will be built over five distinct stages, they intend to build below-standard parking on the first phase, adjusting the actual number of spaces built in subsequent phases depending upon the success of ridesharing and TSM programs. Thus, through a gradual phasedown/phase-in approach, project developers hope to strike the proper balance between parking stalls and TSM programs. Moreover, as an incentive for its occupants to reduce parking, the developers will include a clause in all leases to buy back parking spaces that are not used because of employee shifts to carpools and vanpools.

Several of Southern California's suburban workplaces are also unique for having introduced parking fees. Both the Warner Center and South Coast Plaza charge customers and employees going commercial rates for parking in their multilevel garages. Still, surveys indicate that fewer than one-third of all South Coast Plaza workers pay for parking, and among those who do, most receive at least partial reimbursement from their employer. As mentioned in Chapter Four, developers of the South Coast Plaza have also entered into a creative agglomeration agreement with the city of Costa Mesa that allows them to reduce their usual parking standards by sharing spaces with other projects. Specifically, daytime office workers are permitted to use available parking at a nearby theater and shopping mall, while customers of these businesses in turn are allowed to park in employee spaces on weekends. The desire to maximize the productivity of land in the Plaza area prompted private interests to negotiate this cooperative arrangement.

Other Traffic Mitigation Programs

Several additional programs round out Southern California's mounting offense against paralyzing suburban traffic. Of particular note have been the modified work schedules introduced by several major office park tenants. At the Warner Center, for instance, approximately 3,000 workers of two large insurance companies presently enjoy flex-time privileges. Several other Warner Center companies, moreover, have introduced four-day work weeks. In the increasingly congested west Los Angeles area, however, few flex-time programs have been launched, ostensibly because of the schedule interdependence of many aeronautics and engineering firms located there. The Southern California Association of Governments has estimated that rush-hour traffic could be reduced by 4 percent around LAX if 20 percent of the area's employees participated in modified work schedules—enough to free-up gridlock conditions at several key intersections and freeway interchanges.[24]

Southern California's leadership in the area of private commuter bus service has given regional planners additional cause for optimism in the quest to safeguard suburban mobility.[25] Already, over 100 buspools and subscription services operate throughout the Los Angeles basin, yielding handsome profits to enterprising private operators who deliver premium services to thousands of suburbanites in the market for convenient and comfortable commuting.[26] Within suburban office compounds, few Southern California developers anticipate operating their own shuttles, the notable exception being the developers of the Playa Vista project who plan to circulate a dozen mini-buses within the 926-acre village. The Irvine Company is considering on-site shuttle services within the massive Spectrum complex, although they are broaching the idea cautiously owing to the dismal ridership performance of past company-sponsored runs throughout the Irvine Ranch.

Lastly, an on-site child care center—which could serve as a possible reinforcement for other policies such as flexible work hours—is being proposed for at least one development. Members of the Warner Center Association believe a child care center will further enrich the mixed-use, village-like character of the 1.8 square mile development. In addition, day-care facilities could reduce the circuity of working parents' trips by providing a common terminus for child drop-off and their own commutes.

Case Study Summary

The expanding megalopolis along California's southern coast offers a richly textured setting for studying a host of suburban mobility issues. The term "suburban" must be used loosely here, however, as the bulk of office growth has been occurring in moderately dense, built-up areas, although still far from downtown Los Angeles. Building activities have been largely triggered by the sustained growth in Los Angeles's and Orange County's economies, primarily in aeronautics, electronics, and information-related industries. Many new office concentrations occupy in-fill zones and have emerged as important satellite "urban centers." As land and housing prices continue to soar throughout Southern California, however, many residents are being squeezed out onto the exurban fringes, widening the mismatch between where people live and work. Consequently, Southern California's commuting patterns can be expected to become even more diffuse and disorderly over the remainder of this century. Coping with the mobility dilemmas posed by this emerging settlement pattern will tax the ingenuity and resourcefulness of developers and planners alike.

Some of the specific case sites examined in this chapter, however, do inspire hope and confidence that Southern California's suburbs can successfully ward off suffocating traffic. In contrast to many other suburban office complexes taking form around the country, a growing number of Southern California's developments are being built at relatively high densities. Equally important, many suburban developers are emphasizing mixed-use planning, most notably the integration of either on-site or nearby housing. By creating more self-sustaining, village-like atmospheres, regional planners and developers hope considerable inroads can be made in narrowing the widening wedge between where Southern Californians live and work. Additionally, higher density, multipurpose work settings should help strengthen regional ridesharing and transit programs over the long haul.

Another prominent feature of several rapidly growing Southern California workplaces has been the recent ascendancy of transportation management associations. Southern California's TMAs have been particularly successful at promoting employee ridesharing. In some outlying settings, upwards of 40 to 50 percent of all workers presently commute in vehicles with two or more passengers. TMAs have also been lead players in financing critical roadway improvements throughout Los Angeles and Orange Counties.

Insightful lessons can also be learned from Southern California's experiences with traffic impact ordinances. By assessing oncoming developments based on the amount of traffic they are likely to generate, the city of Los Angeles and several Orange County municipalities hope to build a reservoir of funds to upgrade scores of regional highways. Fee offset provisions have been attached to all these ordinances to encourage private sponsorship of ridesharing and transit services. In addition to these ordinances, several multimillion dollar agreements have been negotiated involving joint cost-sharing of major roadway improvements in both Los Angeles and Orange Counties. To date, individual private financing of areawide highway and transit facilities has reached as high as $65 million in Southern California.

The impression should not be left, however, that all is "bright and sunny" in Southern California's suburbs. Strong neighborhood resistance, for instance, is stirring against the erection of high-rises in several outlying settings. Some homeowners feel threatened by what they view as the encroachment of city life into their traditionally rural-like neighborhoods. In reaction to one blossoming Southern California megacomplex, a citizens group has lodged formal protests against proposals to further expand the project, warning: "The whole plan was predicated on public transportation. What we're saying now is that development should slow down until public transportation catches up."[27] Major obstacles still hamper many Southern

California TSM programs, such as the tendency of most suburban employers to provide either free or subsidized parking and the predominance of inflexible working schedules. Furthermore, some developers have challenged recent traffic impact ordinances on the grounds that they are unfair and in violation of California's Proposition 13 tax restraint. Despite these and other outstanding problems, numerous unique and creative approaches toward safeguarding suburban mobility have recently surfaced in Southern California that could serve as exemplars for other regions of the country.

Notes

1. Southern California Association of Governments, *1984 Regional Transportation Plan* (Los Angeles: SCAG, agency report, 1984), Vol. 1, p. II-2.
2. Ibid., p. II-3.
3. Ibid.
4. Southern California Association of Governments, *LAX Area/Corridor Study* (Los Angeles: SCAG, agency report, 1984), p. 25.
5. Ruth and Going, Inc., *South Coast Metro Area Pilot Transportation Management Program* (San Jose, Calif.: consulting report prepared for the Orange County Transportation Commission, 1983), p. A-14.
6. Jan Klunder, "Warner Center Rising Up as Valley's Super Center," *Los Angeles Times* (January 29, 1984), p. 26.
7. As a precondition to rezoning the land, city officials made the developers agree to a two-level design of all structures with allowances for the possible phase-in of a future peoplemover, light rail transit station, and eventually a heavy rail station.
8. Irvine Industrial, Research and Development Company, "Irvine Spectrum: Design Guidelines" (Newport Beach, Calif.: Irvine Company, unpublished report, 1985).
9. This estimate is based on unpublished surveys of Irvine residents by the Irvine Company and was cited during interviews with company representatives, April 1985. Also see Raymond J. Burby and S.F. Weiss, et al., *New Communities USA* (Lexington, Mass.: Lexington Books, D.C. Heath, 1976) for an earlier account of Irvine's jobs–housing imbalance.
10. El Segundo Employers Association, "ESEA Origins and History" (Los Angeles: unpublished agency brochure, 1985).
11. Warner Center Association, "Warner Center Association: Background Information" (Los Angeles: unpublished agency brochure, 1984).
12. Eric Schreffler and Michael D. Meyer, "Evolving Institutional Arrangements for Employer Involvement in Transportation: The Case of Employer Associations," *Transportation Research Record*, No. 914 (1983), p. 47.

13. Ibid., pp. 46–47.

14. Southern California Association of Governments, *1984 Regional Transportation Plan*, p. II–10.

15. Ruth and Going, Inc., *South Coast Metro Area Pilot Transportation Program*, p. II–6.

16. Ibid., p. A–9. The survey also found that 83 percent and 45 percent of South Coast Plaza employees needed their cars for personal business and work-related purposes respectively at least once a week. On average, the weekly car use for personal business and work was 2.8 and 1.5 times, respectively.

17. City of Los Angeles, *Los Angeles Coastal Transportation Corridor Specific Plan* (Los Angeles: Departments of City Planning and Transportation, preliminary ordinance, 1985).

18. As in the Westwood Village area, the fee amount was derived based on the cost of public improvements necessary to accommodate a single rush-hour vehicle over the next 25 years, using Institute of Transportation Engineers (ITE) trip generation rates. For further discussion of Los Angeles's proposed ordinance, see: Kenneth J. Fannucchi, "Traffic Fees Could Cost Developers Millions," *Los Angeles Times* (March 21, 1985), p. 1.

19. Victor Carniglia, "Updating Industrial Zoning: The Irvine Business Complex," *Urban Land*, Vol. 44, No. 3 (1985), pp. 15–19. See Chapter Four for further discussions of Irvine's point system.

20. Ruth and Going, Inc., *South Coast Metro Area Pilot Transportation Program*, pp. II–17, II–28.

21. See: Orange County Transportation Commission, "San Joaquin Hills Transportation Corridor" (Santa Ana: report prepared for the California Transportation Commission, 1985); C. Kenneth Orski, "Suburban Mobility: The Coming Transportation Crisis?" *Transportation Quarterly*, Vol. 39, No. 2 (1985), p. 292.

22. Orski, "Suburban Mobility," p. 292.

23. David Curry and Anne Martin, "City of Los Angeles Parking Management Ordinance" (Washington: Paper presented at the Annual Meeting of the Transportation Research Board, January 1985).

24. Southern California Association of Governments, *LAX Area TSM/Corridor Study*, p. 15.

25. See Chapter Four for further discussions of commuter bus services throughout Los Angeles County.

26. Genevieve Giuliano and Roger F. Teal, "Privately Provided Commuter Bus Services: Experiences, Problems, and Prospects," *Urban Transit: Private Challenges to Public Transportation*, Charles A. Lave, ed. (San Francisco: Pacific Institute for Public Policy Research, 1985), p. 154.

27. Klunder, "Warner Center Rising Up as Valley's Super Center," p. 26.

6

Northern California Case Study

SAFEGUARDING MOBILITY
IN THE SAN FRANCISCO BAY AREA

Contextual Setting

The San Francisco Bay Area is widely known as an economically viable region that ranks high on most quality of life criteria. Even though its population grew faster than any consolidated metropolitan region outside of the sunbelt during the sixties and seventies, the Bay Area has avoided faceless urban sprawl so characteristic of many other rapidly developing regions. The region's varied topography, with the bay at its center and its encircling range of hills, has acted to contain physical expansion while restricting mobility to limited geographic corridors.

The Bay Area's overall transportation network clearly reveals the importance of San Francisco as the dominant employment hub. Physical limitations on vehicular access to San Francisco's CBD has resulted in, by American standards, a large resident workforce, high rates of transit usage and carpooling, and an extensive network of heavy rail transit (BART), bus and ferry systems, bridges and freeways, and commuter trains which focus mainly on the city's financial district. Although San Francisco continues to function as the region's economic nerve center, the makeup and location of business activities throughout the Bay Area are rapidly changing, altering commuting patterns in the process.

This case study highlights development and commuting trends in two areas experiencing the healthiest economic growth in the region—northern Santa Clara County and the central portions of Contra Costa and Alameda Counties along the Interstate 680 corridor, both shown in Map 6.1. Together, these two areas already account for 35 percent of the nine-county Bay Area's total employment and total population. Year 2000 projections call for an increase in the combined share of regional jobs located in northern Santa Clara and along the I-680 corridor to around 42 percent. Population, on the other hand, is expected to grow more slowly, reaching a relative share of 37 percent at the close of this century.[1]

Santa Clara outgrew all other counties in the Bay Area over the past two decades. Jobs almost tripled, increasing from 248,000 in 1960 to 699,000 by 1980, and population more than doubled, increasing from

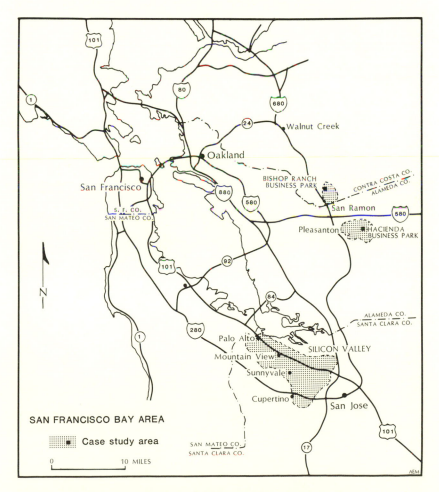

Map 6.1. Northern California Case Study Setting

642,000 to 1,295,000. The county is expected to add approximately 350,000 new jobs by the end of the century, more than twice as many as any other Bay Area county. Equally impressive job growth is anticipated along the southern I-680 corridor, exceeding 300 percent in Pleasanton and 235 percent in the San Ramon Valley over the next 15 years.[2] Sustained growth in two key sectors of the region's economy—high-tech industries and white-collar occupations—has fueled much of the recent job expansion and is expected to continue doing so in the future.

Over recent years, the Bay region's economic base has become geographically specialized. This trend has been largely propelled by the growing physical space requirements of the booming office and high-tech employment sectors and soaring downtown land prices. As San Francisco continues to assume a larger role as an administrative and financial hub, many businesses have begun decentralizing their data processing and clerical functions to fringe areas. One of the prime repositories for back office functions has been the I-680 corridor 35 miles east of San Francisco, where freeway access is generally good and large parcels of land are comparatively cheap and readily available. Proposed office park developments within the cities of Pleasanton and San Ramon alone are expected to generate as many as 75,000 additional jobs over the next 20 years.

Jobs in the high-tech and electronics fields have similarly clustered into a handful of areas. The Silicon Valley, located some 40 miles south of downtown San Francisco in the northern half of Santa Clara County, has become the world's densest concentration of high-technology industries and today accounts for 85 percent of the Bay Area's high-tech complex.[3] This amalgamation of scientists, engineers, researchers, and venture capitalists has been spawned by an industry undergoing rapid change that has grown dependent on face-to-face interaction for advancing knowledge and exchanging ideas. The demand for industrial land and office space in close proximity to Silicon Valley's high-tech complex remains strong despite dwindling supplies of vacant land and soaring property values. The extraordinary growth of the high-tech industry has transformed what only 20 years ago was prime agricultural land into a highly developed patchwork of office complexes, industrial parks, commercial strips, hotels, and restaurants.

The office settings presented in this chapter not only speak to some of the most pressing growth issues in the Bay Area, they also highlight new institutional arrangements that local governments and the business community have forged in an effort to resolve mounting mobility problems. Specific case settings examined are:

"SILICON VALLEY." Silicon Valley refers primarily to the concentration of electronics and high-technology firms in a roughly 400 square mile area of northern Santa Clara County. Although no formal boundaries exist, the Silicon Valley is generally considered to include the five cities of Palo Alto, Sunnyvale, Cupertino, Mountain View, and Santa Clara, plus a northern slice of San Jose. (See Map 6.2.) Although some major electronics firms are located outside this area, the overwhelming majority of Santa Clara County's 200,000 high-tech jobs can be found within these cities' boundaries. The Silicon Valley area presently contains over 96 million square feet of industrial space and about 11 million square feet in office use. The area of most intense development pressure has been the "Golden Triangle" bounded by three heavily traveled freeways: U.S. 101, State Route 237, and State Route 17. Estimates of job growth in this 400 square mile area alone are as high as 80,000 by the year 2000.[4] Because the Silicon Valley is characterized by a large number of freestanding, independent develop-

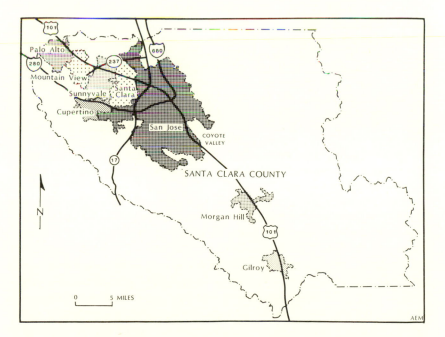

Map 6.2. Santa Clara County and the Cluster of Communities in the Silicon Valley

ments, no single project is examined in this chapter, but rather general mobility issues are discussed for the subregion as a whole.

PLEASANTON-SAN RAMON VALLEY. Comprising the central portions of Alameda and Contra Costa Counties along I-680, the Pleasanton-San Ramon Valley has become the primary recipient of regional office growth outside of San Francisco's financial district since the early eighties. Two major complexes currently being built are:

Bishop Ranch Business Park—a 585-acre, master-planned office and light industrial development fronting on Interstate 680 in San Ramon. At buildout, the site will house approximately 54 buildings totalling 8.5 million square feet. Construction began in 1982 and as of 1985 nearly one-quarter of the development has been completed. Present plans call for approximately 25,000 employees at buildout in 1995. Two corporations now constructing major headquarters on the site will ultimately employ half of Bishop Ranch's eventual workforce. Ownership of about 40 percent of the land will be retained by the developer, and at buildout will feature 3.5 million square feet of speculative office space and a 450-room luxury hotel.

Hacienda Business Park—a 860-acre master-planned, mixed-use complex located in north Pleasanton near the junction of Interstates 580 and 680. Construction began in 1981 on Phase 1, a 578-acre portion of the site that is slated for 200 buildings and 8 million square feet of space. At completion of Phase 2, expected in year 2005, total employment on the site will reach 45,000 and total constructed space will be around 11 million square feet. Hacienda's developers expect to attract primarily high-tech firms. Over 300 acres of Phase 1 have been zoned to allow both light industrial and office uses. A hotel is now under construction, 30 acres have been zoned for retail functions, and a developer-sponsored child care facility is currently in the final planning stages.

Table 6.1 presents background information on the types of uses and physical characteristics of the Northern California study areas.

At the outset, it should be noted that the specific projects and study settings discussed in this chapter are poles apart as far as their development profiles. The Silicon Valley case raises mobility issues associated with continued development pressure in a fairly mature suburban milieu. It also highlights the role of both public and private initiatives in shaping commuting practices once land use patterns are fairly well established. In contrast, the Pleasanton and San Ramon cases represent large master-planned projects in suburban communities undergoing rapid expansion. Since the Bishop

TABLE 6.1
Background Summaries of
Northern California Case Study Sites

Area and Project	Type of Development	Total Acreage	Total Building Square Footage (in millions, nonresidential)		Project Status	Expected Completion	Total Employment		Mileage From Downtown San Francisco
			Current[a]	Buildout[b]			Current[a]	Buildout[b]	
Pleasanton-San Ramon Valley									
Bishop Ranch Business Park	Primarily office; some light industrial; hotel and restaurant	585	4.0	8.5	First several phases completed	1995	4,500	25,000	35
Hacienda Business Park	Primarily office and light industrial; hotel and restaurant	860	1.2	11.0	First several phases completed	2005	4,000	40,000	38
Silicon Valley	Primarily office, R&D, and light industrial; nearby commerical	275,000	107.0	120.0	Approximately 90% buildout	2000	295,000	380,000	30–35[c]

a As of 1985.

b When project is completed.

c Distance to downtown San Francisco only. Distance to downtown San Jose is roughly three to eight miles.

Ranch and Hacienda projects are situated within five miles of each other, the collective impacts of some 70,000 employees at buildout from these two projects alone will needless to say affect surrounding communities tremendously. Important questions regarding the roles of coordinated strategic planning and employer commitments to transportation problem solving are raised in the Pleasanton-San Ramon Valley case study.

Key Mobility Issues in the Bay Area

Although the Bay Area is blessed with an extensive freeway and transit network, stop-and-go commuting is almost an everyday routine for many of its five million residents. Most of the region's freeways, along with the BART heavy rail system, are radially oriented, funneling commuters into downtown San Francisco and Oakland. Relatively few circumferential highways and cross-town connectors, however, are available for serving suburb-to-suburb trips. Consequently, traffic breakdowns and bottlenecks occur regularly at some 50 freeway locations spread throughout the region.[5] A recent survey of Bay Area residents revealed that nearly 60 percent believe traffic conditions on both local roads and the regional highway network have deteriorated markedly since 1975. Over one-quarter of the population, moreover, now rates chronic congestion as the region's number one problem. Frustrations over traffic have reached the point where residents in Walnut Creek, Sausalito, Mill Valley, Tiburon, and Corte Madera—all booming Bay Area suburbs—recently approved sweeping initiatives limiting future commercial growth.

The Bay Area's freeway conditions have deteriorated most markedly within the past several years, a period coinciding with rampant suburban building activities. Just within the period of 1982 to 1984, the total miles of congested Bay Area freeways—where the average speed drops below 35 mph for 15 minutes or more on a typical weekday—jumped from 166 to 212 miles. Moreover, the total hours of additional driving time resulting from congestion climbed from 29.1 million in 1982 to 47 million in 1984.[6]

Santa Clara County suffers from some of the worst traffic congestion in the Bay Area. Presently, over 25 miles of the county's freeways are regularly clogged during the six or so hours of morning and evening rush traffic. While the average ten-mile commute within the county takes around 30 minutes, daily one-way commutes of an hour or more are becoming more and more common.[7] Although a new LRT system is being built along San Jose's north-south Guadalupe corridor to help accommodate growing travel demand, the county's low density, coupled with the remoteness of many rail stations relative to existing employment sites, casts considerable doubt over the congestion-relieving potential of this one project.[8]

Santa Clara County's unbridled and somewhat unbalanced urban growth over the past two decades bears much of the responsibility for today's congestion mess. Since the early sixties, new jobs have been primarily concentrated in the northern half of the county, while much of the housing has been pushed southward toward several bedroom communities. By 1975, the northern tier of the county accounted for 243,000 jobs, yet only 129,000 housing units. During the late seventies, approximately 156,000 new jobs were created in the county, mostly within the Silicon Valley, while only 46,000 new housing units were constructed.[9] Regional planning projections portend an even grosser imbalance in the ratio of jobs to housing by the end of the century. As shown in Table 6.2, the county is expected to have 60 percent more jobs than dwelling units by the year 2000.

In addition to shortages, soaring housing prices have also forced many Santa Clara workers to search for residences in other areas of the region. The average cost of a single-family home in the county nearly quadrupled during the decade of the seventies in real dollar terms. The joint effects of critical housing shortages and escalating prices on the proximity of residences to jobs is revealed in Figure 6.1. In 1980, over 60 percent of all the work trips destined to the Silicon Valley were external, made mainly from the bedroom communities of Morgan Hill and Gilroy to the southeast. Commuting paths have also fanned out as far as Marin and Solano Counties, some 50 miles to the north. The scattering of trip ends in recent years has taken its toll on the county's mass transportation system—bus patronage currently accounts for only 3 percent of journeys to work within Santa Clara County. Moreover, the county averages fewer than 20 annual transit trips

TABLE 6.2

Ratios of Total Employment to Total Dwelling Units for Selected Northern California Suburban Settings

Area	Actual 1980	Year 1990 Projection	Year 2000 Projection
Santa Clara County	1.45:1	1.57:1	1.60:1
City of San Ramon	0.79:1	1.06:1	1.64:1
City of Pleasanton	0.81:1	1.29:1	1.86:1

Source: Association of Bay Area Governments, "Bay Area Economic Profile" (Oakland: agency report, 1983).

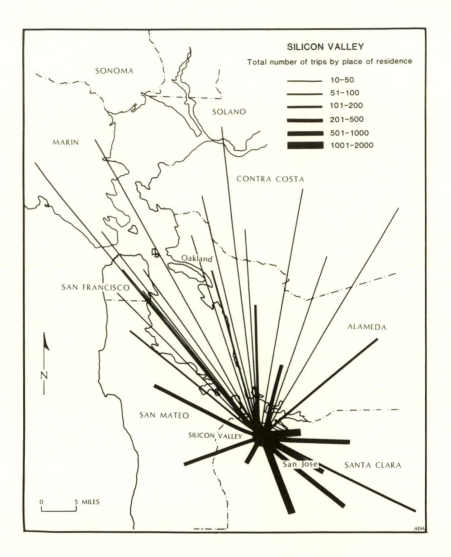

Figure 6.1.   1981 Desired Lines and Recorded Volumes of Daily Work Trips from the Entire Bay Area to the Silicon Valley.
(Source: Tabulated from journey-to-work census data and Bay Area Travel Survey Update provided on computer tape by the Metropolitan Transportation Commission, Oakland.)

per capita, one of the lowest rates among all U.S. metropolitan areas above one million population. Carpooling has fared much better, however—19 percent of countywide commute trips are made by auto passengers.

Regional forecasts suggest that traffic conditions may soon reach intolerable levels along Santa Clara County's most heavily traveled corridors. Nearly 70,000 new rush-hour vehicles have been projected for Route 101 within the next five to ten years, a corridor that currently labors at 95 to 100 percent of capacity from 7:00–9:00 A.M. and 4:00–6:00 P.M.. Bumper-to-bumper conditions are expected to last three and a half hours in both the morning and evening by 1990.[10] Overall, regional planners project that rush-hour volumes throughout the county will increase 40 percent by the early 1990s. Current funding, however, will only allow roughly a 10 percent expansion of roadway capacity over the next decade despite the recent passage of a local sales tax referendum dedicated to new highway construction.[11] As shown in Figure 6.2, traffic paralysis is expected to pervade the county's entire roadway system by 1990 if current trends continue.

In contrast to the Silicon Valley, traffic in the San Ramon-Pleasanton area currently flows with few restrictions during peak hours. Both the I-580 and I-680 freeways operate in the range of 65 to 75 percent of capacity during the peak throughout the area. Spot congestion currently plagues only a handful of intersections that feed into the Hacienda and Bishop Ranch Business Parks. These favorable conditions are not expected to last very long, however. Based on regional forecasts, commute volumes in the Pleasanton-San Ramon Valley area will probably triple over the next 15 years. Bishop Ranch alone is expected to generate about 90,000 average daily trips when it is fully completed sometime in the mid-1990s.[12] Future mobility will also be jeopardized by the widening imbalance in the location of jobs and housing projected for the area (see Table 6.2) as well as by shortages in affordable housing. (Only 25 percent of the area's recent housing additions, for example, have been targeted at moderate-income families.) Already, there is a significant in-flow of commuter trips from the far outreaches of Alameda and adjoining counties where housing tends to be cheaper and more readily available. (See Figure 6.3 for the current origin-destination pattern of commute trips to the San Ramon area.) Future trip patterns are expected to become even more dispersed since developing centers of affordable housing—Solano and Sonoma counties in the North Bay, and eastern Contra Costa and Alameda counties—are far removed from the new employment centers along the I-580/I-680 corridors.

As in other Bay Area suburbs, public transit plays only a marginal role throughout the Pleasanton-San Ramon corridor. In 1980, fewer than 4 percent of all journeys destined to Pleasanton and San Ramon were made by bus. Moreover, the area's future prospects for transit seem dim owing to its extremely low residential densities—on average, only 4.8 and 5.7 dwelling units per acre within the communities of San Ramon and Pleasanton respectively. The San Ramon Valley area does, however, match the national average for ridesharing—auto passengers accounted for 18 percent of all commute trips in 1980.

Overall, a potentially volatile traffic situation is brewing along some of the Bay Area's fastest growing suburban corridors. By the turn of the century, if trends continue, peak commute traffic will be at a virtual standstill not only throughout Santa Clara County but along major stretches of suburban freeways in the East Bay as well. The possible roles both design

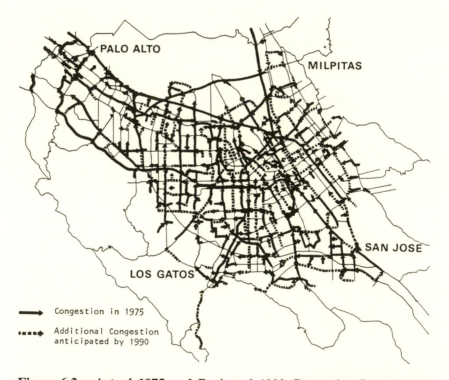

Figure 6.2. Actual 1975 and Projected 1990 Congestion Locations in Santa Clara County.
(Source: Santa Clara County Planning Department, General Plan: Santa Clara County, 1982.)

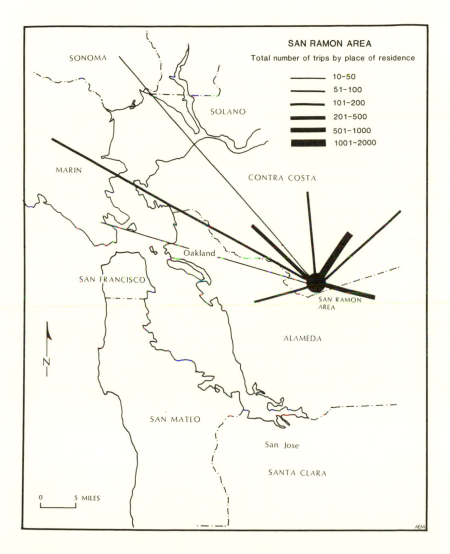

Figure 6.3. 1981 Desired Lines and Recorded Volumes of Daily Work Trips from the Entire Bay Area to the City of San Ramon. (Source: Tabulated from journey-to-work census data and Bay Area Travel Survey Update provided on computer tape by the Metropolitan Transportation Commission, Oakland.)

and traffic management strategies could play in averting a suburban mobility crisis throughout the Bay Area are examined next.

Design and Land Use Issues in the Bay Area

Project Scale and Site Characteristics

In contrast to the Southern California cases discussed in the previous chapter, recent suburban office construction along the Bay Area's fringes has followed more of a traditional low-density form. In both the Silicon Valley and the Pleasanton-San Ramon Valley areas, the overriding design objective of most recent office projects has been to create attractive working environments sensitive to the preferences of upscale and highly skilled professionals.

Silicon Valley. The Silicon Valley's 100 million square feet of high-tech research and industrial space has taken the form of both low to mid-rise buildings arranged into campus clusters, and predominantly single-story structures grouped into smaller business parks (see Photo 6.1). Employment densities throughout the Silicon Valley are consistently low. This is due, in part, to the logistics of high-tech manufacturing, which normally requires low-rise, horizontally scaled buildings for the mass production and distribution of highly specialized electronic components. Low densities can also be attributed to the selective tastes of widely sought tenants who are looking for spacious, attractively landscaped environments conducive to creative work and occasional relaxation.

Most larger R&D facilities in Santa Clara County have been modeled around the Stanford Industrial Park, one of the nation's first campus-style developments, and today considered the birthplace of the Silicon Valley's electronics industry. The original design concept behind the Stanford Industrial Park was to create a high-quality and roomy working environment capable of wooing top engineers to the electronics industry, which at the time was tied most closely to Stanford University. The low-density, estate-like character of the Stanford Park has become the design template for virtually all office parks and industrial complexes in the Silicon Valley during the post-WWII era.

In some instances, Santa Clara County's low office densities have been reinforced by zoning, as in the case of the Coyote Valley in eastern San Jose. In an attempt to expand its tax base, the city of San Jose recently

Photo 6.1. Varying Scales of Development in the North San Jose Section of the Silicon Valley.
These photos show the layout of buildings dotted along North 1st Avenue where San Jose's light rail transit system is being built. (Photos by the author.)

rezoned a large portion of the undeveloped Coyote Valley for high-tech industries. Although as many as 50,000 new jobs may wind up in this area, the "Campus Industrial" zoning limits building coverage to 30 percent of any site and employment densities to 40 workers per acre. Despite the intense demand for land throughout Santa Clara County, Coyote Valley's permitted densities are appreciably lower than those in Pleasanton and San Ramon, where office developments average around 55 employees per acre.

Suburban densities could quickly become a relic of the past in northern Santa Clara County, however. Over the past several years, the Silicon Valley has experienced mounting pressure to use land more intensively. Although there has yet to be a wave of high-rise building activity, the tight land situation has virtually eliminated any new single-story construction. In some parts of Santa Clara County, most notably along the planned Guadalupe Corridor light rail line, six- to eight-story buildings are beginning to sprout. Most office developers along the LRT corridor, however, have resisted attempts by city officials to lower the ratio of required parking spaces as an inducement to patronize transit. One recent survey found that minimum parking requirements are regularly exceeded in many of the business parks along the corridor, with ratios often as high as 5.0 stalls per 1,000 square feet of gross floorspace.[13]

Largely built-out suburban settings like the Silicon Valley limit the effectiveness of design approaches to transportation problem solving. Most new office projects going up are under 200,000 square feet in floor area, thus their marginal effects on local transportation conditions are quite small. Silicon Valley generally lacks the large-scale megaprojects that produce instant congestion as soon as they open. Although the Silicon Valley enjoys sustained growth and prosperity, the additional traffic generated by new office construction continues to appear gradually and without notice. Any effective intervention in mobility problems in more mature suburban settings like the Silicon Valley must almost by default concentrate on solutions that influence travel behavior rather than those that stress physical redesign.

San Ramon-Pleasanton Valleys. In contrast to the Silicon Valley, most new office parks in San Ramon and Pleasanton are being built at scales that could easily overwhelm surrounding single-family neighborhoods and the local infrastructure. The Bishop Ranch and Hacienda Business Parks will each have an eventual workforce larger than the present population of the community in which it is located. The gargantuan scales of the two parks—each over 500 total acres in size—will produce such long distances between on-site buildings and surrounding land uses that many employees will find few real alternatives to automobile commuting.

The site designs of both Bishop Ranch and Hacienda have been strongly influenced by their immediate environs, as the developers of both projects have sought to integrate their parks gracefully into the low-density, almost rural, character of the Pleasanton and San Ramon Valleys (see Photos 6.2 and 6.3). The goal of "fitting in" has figured prominently in decisions governing building design and placement, landscaping, and site organization. The delicate relationship between the built and the natural environment is particularly evident in Hacienda Business Park's design guidelines, which specify that interior zones of the complex should recall the "orchard or grove-like character typical of California farm communities."[14]

Strict height limits and zoning controls have been employed by both the project developers and community officials to enforce this low-profile design objective. In Bishop Ranch, building heights are restricted to four stories, although the current market could support taller, more intensive development. Hacienda allows six-story mid-rise structures, but only on two parcels at the center of the park. Hacienda's master plan seeks to control scale changes at the park's edges by zoning for lower densities and shorter building profiles around the periphery of the site, and reserving a handful of interior parcels for taller buildings. Hacienda's planning guidelines also specify that publicly accessible commercial, hotel, and office uses be placed along several major collector streets at the park's edge, thereby smoothing the transition between the business park and the surrounding land uses.

The massive scale of these two megaprojects has elevated transportation to a position of central importance from the time they were first conceived. The owners-developers of both Hacienda and Bishop Ranch placed a high premium on ease of access and on-site circulation during the earliest stages of project design. Both have also voluntarily initiated assorted programs aimed at reducing vehicular trips generated by their projects. While most traffic management efforts have focused on promoting ridesharing, each developer continues to view the overall design of the site—from building placement to the provision to pedestrian amenities—as integral toward guaranteeing good access and site circulation.

At Bishop Ranch, each of the major corporations purchasing land in the compound has been given a relatively free hand in the design of individual sites. While Bishop Ranch has positioned and built the roadways and pedestrian paths for the park as a whole, details regarding the location of parking and transit access lanes, the siting of buildings, and the provision of

Photo 6.2.   Features of the Hacienda Business Park in Pleasanton.
Upper photo shows the ornamental entrance of the park along
with developer-financed soundwalls used to buffer surrounding
residential neighborhoods. Lower photo shows new mid-rise
office towers with developer-financed transit shelter on the far
right. (Photos by the author.)

Photo 6.3. **Bishop Ranch Business Park in San Ramon, Designed to Blend into Surrounding Residential Neighborhoods and the Area's Hillscape.** (Photos by the author.)

197

preferential parking have been largely left to individual landholders. Specific transportation improvements are not required by covenant, but are evaluated as part of Bishop Ranch's architectural design review process. In addition, transportation improvements considered beneficial to the project as a whole are discussed at tenant meetings, although any actions taken by individual site owners are entirely voluntary.

By comparison, the developers of Hacienda Business Park have drafted an extensive set of design guidelines aimed at integrating each individual parcel into the larger development strategy of the park. These standards aim not only to ensure continuity in design, but also to visually define and emphasize the main circulation corridors by establishing consistent setbacks and landscaping styles.

The degree of control over individual parcels has varied between Bishop Ranch and Hacienda largely because of their vastly different tenant mixes. Bishop Ranch has attracted several large multinational corporations who have purchased major tracts of land. There, coordination of building design and the implementation of transportation programs has involved negotiations between a relatively small circle of landholders. Bishop Ranch developers own exactly one-half of the park's total acreage, retaining control over the physical appearance and organization of much of the park. Hacienda expects a much larger number of individual landowners by the time the project is completed, so more formal design guidelines have been drawn to coordinate individual design decisions.

Both projects' developers have elected not to build their compounds in one fell swoop, but rather to retain vacant parcels for future phases. At Bishop Ranch, a linear strip on the eastern portion of the site has been set aside for future expansion. At Hacienda, approximately one-third of the site is slated for later development as Hacienda Phase Two. In both places, conscientious phasing is expected to lead to a more compact built form that could bode favorably for transit, shuttle services, and vanpooling over the long run when employee densities begin to increase.

Land Use and Tenant Mix Characteristics

Compared to Southern California and several other parts of the country, relatively few large-scale office developments in the Bay Area have incorporated mixed-use activities. In the Silicon Valley, smaller business parks have been designed almost exclusively for research, office, or industrial uses, seldom including any tenant support services other than an occasional sandwich shop or deli. Larger corporate tenants often feature employee cafeterias, and a number provide jogging paths, basketball courts, or other facilities for employee lunchtime recreation. Although the Silicon Valley offers a wide assortment of retail and consumer services, most office complexes are not within walking distance of any restaurants, retail shops, or other supplemental services.

Silicon Valley's freewheeling market economy is largely responsible for this highly segregated land use pattern. Over the years, high-tech firms have clustered in close proximity to one another, outbidding retail and other uses for prime sites. Ancillary functions, such as printing services and equipment repair shops, have often nestled onto adjoining parcels, leaving few nearby tracts for restaurants, convenience stores, and other consumer functions. Strict exclusionary zoning at the municipal level has further reinforced the isolation of land uses.

Hacienda Business Park, however, is emerging as a notable Bay Area exception to the Silicon Valley style of insular office development. While Hacienda has been designed to compete head-to-head with the Silicon Valley for high-tech firms, it was originally master-planned and subsequently zoned as a mixed-use complex. Over 300 acres of Hacienda's 545-acre first phase have been zoned for light industrial uses to attract the expected spillover of high-tech jobs from Santa Clara County. An additional 150 acres have been reserved for office uses, leaving roughly 40 acres, or slightly over 10 percent of the site, for commercial development. A six-acre parcel of commercial land, on which the developer has constructed leasable retail space, is located in the heart of the project. This shopping area is conveniently situated near a six-story multitenant office building, expected to become the densest concentration of office workers at Hacienda. The remaining commercial land, located along a major collector street on the western edge of the park, will feature several high-quality restaurants and retail establishments oriented to the entire community of Pleasanton.[15]

Additionally, one of the Bay Area's largest shopping malls lies approximately one mile from the main entrance to the Hacienda Business Park. Hacienda's developers have widened several roadways and constructed a bicycle and pedestrian path spanning the entire distance between the park and the shopping complex. Project managers plan to operate convenient shuttle connections to the mall to serve workers, in particular those who have left their personal vehicles at home to join a carpool.

In nearby San Ramon, the massive Bishop Ranch complex will primarily house office and light industrial uses, although some allowances have been made for on-site customer services as well. Of the 8.5 million square feet of floorspace projected for Bishop Ranch at buildout, roughly 6.5 million will be devoted to white-collar functions. A 450-room luxury hotel, featuring the only full-size restaurant on the site, is also planned. Moreover, Bishop Ranch has placed delis in each cluster of offices it leases. No general purpose retail activities are planned on the site, although one bank recently installed an automated teller machine and additional financial services are expected within the near future.

Like Hacienda, a wealth of retail stores and restaurants have sprung up in close proximity to Bishop Ranch. A small shopping center with eateries, banks, and a variety of small retail stores lies just beyond the northern border of the site. Because of Bishop Ranch's enormous size, however, the round-trip distance between this shopping complex and the southern end of the park, where 13,000 people will be employed, is just over two miles—far beyond convenient walking distance for lunch-hour excursions. Since lineal distances to other retail outlets near Bishop Ranch are even longer, unless most workers are content to patronize the limited on-site services, a skirmish of midday vehicular travel to and from the complex can be expected.

The managers of both projects believe, however, that the high premiums placed on creating pleasant working environments may keep substantial numbers of employees on-site during lunchtime. Several of the office complexes at Bishop Ranch are designed around nicely landscaped inner courtyards where employees can congregate during lunch breaks. Similarly, several corporations within the park have built attractive employee cafeterias. One of the most impressive is Bishop Ranch's Pacific Bell complex, where the cafeteria is housed in a large pavilion overlooking a seven-acre lake (which also functions as part of the building's cooling system). For the recreational minded, both parks feature sinuous jogging paths as well as shower and locker facilities.

It should be noted that past attempts to further enrich the mixed-use characters of both projects by integrating housing have met stiff community resistance. Early in the planning process, the developers of Hacienda filed a petition to revise Pleasanton's General Plan to allow the construction of on-site housing. The request was denied, in large part because of a 2 percent annual growth limit placed on residential construction within the city of Pleasanton. Despite this setback, Hacienda's developers have proceeded to link the park with several abutting neighborhoods by building an integrated network of off-site trails in addition to financing other public amenities, such as areawide street lighting.

Public backlash to large-tract housing development at Bishop Ranch actually led to the creation of a new municipality. There, developers originally intended to transform their entire 585-acre vacant parcel into a planned unit development (PUD), but their request to change the existing "controlled manufacturing" zoning to allow residential development was denied. Local residents were so fearful of their community being gobbled up by land speculators that they gathered a petition to incorporate as the new municipality of San Ramon, which subsequently passed on a referendum ballot. Not surprisingly, any interest in building residential housing within the Bishop Ranch compound quickly waned.

Transportation-Related Design Features

Both Hacienda and Bishop Ranch stand out for their on-site circulation systems and transit amenities. Hacienda's hierarchy of major, secondary, and local roadways consumes roughly 15 percent of the entire 860-acre project. Six-lane parkways dissect the park from all four directions. Mindful of the need to encourage transit and shuttle usage, Hacienda has also provided bus facilities along roadways both within and outside of the park. Twenty bus turnouts with all-weather, glass-enclosed shelters have been constructed internally, and an additional 15 shelters and turnouts have been placed along major connecting roads off-site. Because Hacienda's shelters were sited prior to development of individual parcels, building entrances do not always bear a direct relationship to the location of bus stops. Still, most bus shelters are within 100 yards of a building entrance. Bus stops are not only used by a regional transit authority that operates inside the park, but also serve as boarding areas for Hacienda's own internal circulator shuttle.

At Bishop Ranch, bus shelters are being placed as buildings are constructed. To date, 16 shelters have been sited within the 585-acre compound. Although no turnouts have been provided along park roadways, direct bus access lanes have been designed into many of the larger buildings on the site. A three-building complex of rental office space constructed and owned by Bishop Ranch developers has been sited so that entrances to all three buildings are a maximum of 50 feet from a shelter located on a direct bus lane. The bus shelter is closer to the three buildings than any of the employee parking spaces. At the Pacific Bell compound, a reserved access lane conveniently connects a bus turnaround and employee drop-off circle directly at the building's front entrance.

Because developers of both Bishop Ranch and Hacienda are banking so heavily on ridesharing to reduce traffic, considerable emphasis has been placed on including special facilities for carpools and vanpools. Hacienda requires that a minimum of 5 percent of the parking spaces at the entrance of each building in the park be reserved for vanpools or carpools. According to park management, demand for preferential spaces has already exceeded this 5 percent minimum at virtually every occupied building in the development. Many preferential parking programs are also in place at Bishop Ranch. One of the most impressive is at the Pacific Bell complex, where all spaces within a 75-yard radius of the main building entrance are reserved for carpools and vanpools. The parking lot itself is roughly 200 yards on each side, and with solo drivers facing a walk anywhere from 75 to 200 yards, there is a perceptible convenience advantage to carpooling.

Both Bishop Ranch and Hacienda have also integrated bicycle pathways into their overall circulation systems. At Bishop Ranch, double-width sidewalks form the bikepaths, skirting most of the major roadways within the park. At Hacienda, an elaborate pedway system hugs the development's main parkways, consisting of an eight-foot wide shared bicycle and pedestrian pathway, gently curving to add visual interest and separated from traffic by tree-lined medians and landscaped berms. Hacienda's commitment to cycling is reflected by the extension of the bikeway system off-site along most of the major roads leading to the park. Pleasanton's generally flat terrain and favorable climate, coupled with the presence of 22,000 homes within a five-mile pedalling range of Hacienda, have combined to make cycling a potentially viable commute alternative.

Finally, both Bishop Ranch and Hacienda developers plan to build transit stations on-site if current proposals for constructing a light rail or busway alongside of Interstate 680 ever materialize. The proposed route is aligned along former Southern Pacific Railroad right-of-way, which runs directly through both office parks. Some regional observers believe the existence of two substantial anchors of at least 25,000 workers each at buildout augurs well for the future of LRT along this corridor.

Transportation Management

Transportation Management Associations

As in Southern California and elsewhere around the country, transportation management associations (TMAs) have become lead players in battling traffic congestion along rapidly expanding corridors of the Bay Area. In both Santa Clara's Silicon Valley and the Pleasanton-San Ramon Valley, fairly active employer coalitions have formed over the past five years.

The largest and oldest TMA in the Bay Area is the Santa Clara Manufacturing Group (SCMG). Created in 1978 by 34 of the county's leading business executives, the group currently represents about 65 percent of all manufacturing employees in the Silicon Valley and nearly 25 percent of all county employees. Financed by a voluntary fee (currently between $500 and $16,500 per year, depending on the number of employees in the company), the SCMG's transportation task force has been most active in coordinating the traffic management initiatives of individual employers, lobbying for assorted highway improvements in the county, and guiding land development in conjunction with major areawide transportation investments. SCMG has also worked closely with public officials on the planning of the Guadalupe LRT line to ensure it serves the commuting needs of high-tech employees along the corridor. The group was also instrumental in building a base of political support for the recently approved 1 percent sales tax earmarked for countywide highway improvements.

Rideshare promotion has also been a chief focus of the SCMG, which has worked primarily on getting individual companies to set up internal rideshare coordinator positions. So far, it has been successful in doing so. Currently, each of the 90 participating companies has a designated rideshare coordinator, most of whom spend around 10 percent of their work time on carpooling matters.[16]

Perhaps the most ambitious developer-initiated TMA in the Bay Area to date has been formed at the Hacienda business complex. There, covenants stipulate that all land purchasers and building lessees participate in the Hacienda Business Park Owners Association (HBPOA). Each company with 50 or more employees is also required to designate a rideshare coordinator. Five coordinators have been brought on board so far. In addition, the Association has hired a full-time manager to compile employee matching data, market ridesharing, and monitor progress. HBPOA's overall activities to date have been wide ranging, including aiding companies in relocating their employees, negotiating with BART to operate express buses between the park and rail terminuses, and assisting the city of Pleasanton in developing its trip reduction ordinance.

Similar to Hacienda's association, the Bishop Ranch TMA (BRTMA) was created by developers' initiative. The group represents the employees of companies that lease space from Bishop Ranch as well as employees of two of the park's landowner corporations. BRTMA's primary goals have paralleled those of the Hacienda association, namely to make the site more accessible and to represent the park on areawide transportation planning matters. All of Bishop Ranch's transportation services are provided by a central office run by a full-time manager. In addition to ridesharing promotion, Bishop Ranch's TMA has helped companies relocate their employees and has also worked closely with Contra Costa County officials in acquiring a stretch of abandoned railroad trackage for possible reuse as an LRT or busway corridor.

Although TMAs have gained a strong foothold in the Bay Area, their overall effectiveness has been limited by several factors. Notably, there has been little progress so far toward establishing TMAs at the subregional level. Most TMAs have concentrated on access issues along narrowly defined corridors. The Santa Clara Manufacturing Group, coordinating the initiatives of individual employers throughout the Silicon Valley, has been perhaps the one notable exception to this. But even there, the decision to work only with companies who physically manufacture products has created an artificial institutional boundary for dealing with common transportation problems. In the Pleasanton-San Ramon areas, Bishop Ranch and Hacienda have so far opted to work on most transportation matters independently, thus there has been little coordination between either of these megaprojects and the several dozen nearby small office parks of 500 employees or less. Because most developments have chosen to work in isolation of one another on transportation matters, a critical mass situation is not being exploited. Indeed, the possibilities for interproject coordination in the Pleasanton-San Ramon Valley corridor are enormous given the addition of 75,000 or so new employees who will be working there over the next 20 years.

Ridesharing and Commute Alternatives Programs

Ridesharing. The one area where there has been some degree of both regional and subregional coordination among Bay Area suburban employers has been ridesharing promotion. RIDES for Bay Area Commuters, a nonprofit chartered organization, has been at the forefront in coordinating regional ridesharing. RIDES annually registers about 50,000 employees throughout the Bay Area and has been credited with placing over 65,000 people in carpools or vanpools since its inception in 1977. Like Commuter Computer in Southern California, RIDES has concentrated primarily on promoting ridesharing among employers of at least 100 workers, providing not only matching services, but also assisting in the formation of approximately 750 third-party vanpools. RIDES has also set up ridesharing offices at several suburban employment centers, including the Bishop Ranch complex.

Several noteworthy company-sponsored ridesharing programs also thrive in the Silicon Valley area. At Stanford Industrial Park in Palo Alto, for instance, five of the largest employers have purchased vans for employee commuting. Presently, 45 percent of their employees share rides to work. In nearby Sunnyvale, Lockheed International offers various bonuses, such as monthly travel allowances, to employees who join pools, currently 36 percent of the company's workforce. A particularly interesting carpool marketing strategy is currently being pursued at San Jose's General Electric corporate offices. There, an in-house lottery program has been set up for rideshare participants, offering prizes such as free amusement park tickets to the winners of weekly drawings.

Among large-scale suburban office complexes, Bishop Ranch has launched one of the most successful ridesharing campaigns in the country. Around one-third of the project's current 4,500 employees commute via carpool or vanpool, and around 20 percent of them have registered with RIDES. One of Bishop Ranch's tenants, the Davy McKee Company, leases 15 vans from RIDES and underwrites one-half of the operating costs for employees participating in vanpools. The incentive has proven too hard to resist: over half of their 300 staff members vanpool to work. Another Bishop Ranch employer, Pacific Telephone, not only sponsors weekly cash drawings for employees who co-commute, it also offers low interest loans to enterprising staffers who own and operate vanpools.

Rivaling these programs have been some of the recent efforts at the Hacienda Business Park. In addition to sponsoring several ridesharing exhibition fairs for the employees of all tenants (billed as "TSM in action"), Hacienda's management team has embarked on a fairly personalized approach to carpool promotion. In 1984, 18 meetings were held with employees of one of the larger companies, American Telephone and Telegraph, to acquaint them with the advantages of ridesharing. Meetings were arranged by area of residence to encourage self-matching among those who are neighbors. The 400 attendees were lured by a $50 per employee cash bonus put up by the company. As a result of these and other efforts, around 25 percent of the park's 3,100 current employees have joined a carpool or vanpool to date.

Transit. Although carpooling and vanpooling have received stronger corporate backing in the Bay Area, mass transportation has not been totally ignored. In fact, some of the most ambitious privately sponsored suburban transit services in the country have been initiated in the Bay region. Most notably, both Bishop Ranch and Hacienda business parks provide shuttle connections between their respective sites and the nearest BART stations.[17]

Bishop Ranch currently owns two 41-passenger buses while Hacienda's developers have purchased three 28-passenger and two 49-passenger coaches. Both shuttles, operated by private contractors, run on thirty minute headways from 7:00–9:00 A.M. and 4:00–6:00 P.M. Bishop Ranch's shuttle is free to the employees of companies leasing office space.[18] To date, only 4 percent of the park's eligible employees have taken advantage of free shuttle connections, in large part because BART itself serves limited corridors outside of San Francisco and the densely populated communities of the East Bay. In comparison, Hacienda's shuttle is available to all employees working on-site since it is subsidized by all tenants and landholding companies. A 90¢ fare is charged for a one-way ride. Currently, less than 2 percent of Hacienda's total workforce has opted for transit commuting.

As a further inducement to transit usage, bus tickets and monthly passes are sold at Bishop Ranch and Hacienda as well as at a number of Silicon Valley companies. For example, the Syntex Corporation of Palo Alto and San Jose's IBM plant sell transit tickets and multiride coupons at a discount to their employees. Two other firms—Memora Corporation and Rolm Industries, both in Santa Clara—give away a month's worth of bus tickets to employees who patronize transit for three straight months. The most generous perquisites are offered to the employees of Shugart Associates in Palo Alto who receive free transit tickets for agreeing to commute by bus.

Other Commute Alternatives.   Employee cycling has also been actively promoted in the Bay Area's suburbs. The most successful programs have been introduced by several Silicon Valley firms. The Hewlett Packard Company headquartered in Palo Alto has helped finance an integrated network of bikepaths throughout the community. The company also provides brochures on cycling routes to workers, sponsors bicycle commuting classes, and offers a 10 percent employee discount on all equipment and accessories purchased at several local bike shops. Similar inducements can be found at the nearby Xerox research complex where around 20 percent of the company's 500 employees currently cycle to work.

Traffic Impact Ordinances and Legislation

While ridesharing and other TSM efforts are being voluntarily initiated by the Bay Area's largest suburban developers and employers, there are growing signs that municipalities themselves are anxious to prod these programs along by government fiat. As discussed in Chapter Four, the city of Pleasanton has enacted the most far-reaching trip reduction ordinance anywhere to date. Adopted in 1984, the ordinance requires all employers of 50 or more persons, as well as all employers in large office complexes like the Hacienda Business Park, to implement TSM programs. It further stipulates that these programs must achieve a 45 percent reduction in peak-period vehicular trips staged over four years,[19] assuming that all employees would normally drive to work alone. Whether the city can actually enforce this ordinance and monitor the progress of individual employers remains to be seen. To assist in this effort, a task force has been formed among representatives from large business complexes like Hacienda, the Downtown Merchants Association, local transit authorities, and the city at large. The task force wields a fair amount of clout. For instance, it can not only increase the commute trip reduction goals for individual employers, it can also require businesses to adopt specific TSM measures. Failure to provide progress reports required by the ordinance is subject to fines of up to $50, $100, and $250 for the first, second, and third infraction in a calendar year. Similarly, failure to comply with a task force requirement for TSM program revisions is subject to fines of $250 per day. As noted in Chapter Four, of Pleasanton's 36 employers with 50 or more workers, 34 of them met or exceeded the first year target of a 15 percent reduction in peak hour trips. Moreover, among the 3,100 employees working at the Hacienda Business Park in 1985, 28 percent got to work either in carpools or via transit, up from just 17 percent the previous year.

Presently, the Pleasanton ordinance is the only one of its kind in Northern California, although some local observers expect other areas to soon follow suit. Developers of the Bishop Ranch project have explored the possibility of an areawide trip reduction ordinance with Contra Costa County officials, one that would be consistent across municipalities and that would also offer carrots and not just sticks. Whether legislated TSM requirements spread to the Silicon Valley and other parts of the Bay Area will no doubt hinge largely on how successful Pleasanton is in enforcing its ordinance.

Cooperative Financing of Transportation Improvements

Private sector cofinancing of freeway interchanges, street widenings, and other major infrastructural improvements has become fairly prevalent around the Bay region. In this area as well, the city of Pleasanton has again emerged as a leader. Through an assessment district created for the northern half of the community, Pleasanton expects to collect an almost unprecedented $110 million for financing major highway and infrastructural improvements. The bulk of funds—$80 million—will come from the owners of the Hacienda Business Park. All monies collected will go toward constructing two new freeway interchanges, widening existing freeways, upgrading areawide traffic signals, and installing sound barriers around surrounding neighborhoods. The Bay Area's second largest single private-sector contribution has come from the owners of Bishop Ranch where more than $10 million has already been committed toward building a new freeway interchange, widening several overcrossings, and rebuilding a couple of critical intersections. Other significant private sector roadway contributions in the Bay Area include $20 million pledged to the city of Fremont by five separate developers for various interchange improvements and $19.3 million donated by several landowners for interchange reconstruction and railroad grade separations near the Oyster Point complex in San Mateo County.

Parking Management Programs

Fairly progressive approaches to reducing on-site parking can also be found at Bishop Ranch Business Park. Notably, a parking phasedown program has been instituted at Bishop Ranch that is indexed to the success of TSM actions. In the initial stages of the project, code-required parking of five spaces per 1,000 square feet of floorspace was supplied. In subsequent phases, however, parking has been steadily reduced to a current level of 3.2 spaces per 1,000 square feet owing to the success of company-sponsored vanpooling. Bishop Ranch hopes to attain an ultimate parking goal of 2.6 spaces per 1,000 square feet, almost unheard of in the suburbs. In that the developers of Bishop Ranch have financed the entire project solely on their own, they have been free to depart from industry parking standards without having to answer to private lenders. Given the abundance of available free parking found at virtually every suburban office complex in the Bay Area, Bishop Ranch's seminal approach toward phased parking reductions deserves close regionwide attention.

Modified Work Schedules

Several successful flexible work hour programs have also been instituted among large Bay Area business complexes. At the Stanford Industrial Park, over 80 percent of all employees presently enjoy flextime privileges between the hours of 6:00 A.M. and 9:00 P.M.. Nearly two-thirds of the Stanford Industrial Park's employees arrive at work prior to 7:00 A.M., and thus manage to avoid the morning rush hour. A similar flextime program at the

Moffet Industrial Park in Sunnyvale has been credited with reducing peak traffic volumes generated by the complex by one-third. And as noted in Chapter Four, the widespread introduction of flex-time among the Hacienda Business Park's employers in response to the Pleasanton ordinance has allowed over half of the complex's employees to miss the afternoon rush period.

Outside of the Silicon Valley and Pleasanton, relatively few Northern California suburban employers have adopted flextime. According to several rideshare coordinators, most Bay Area employers have shied away from flexible working arrangements because they fear that overall productivity will suffer. A number of high-tech firms have also cited the schedule interdependence of their individual corporate functions as their reason for maintaining set working hours. To ensure that work schedules overlap, several Silicon Valley companies have instead opted for programs like staggered work hours and variable work shifts. Overall, less than 3 percent of all Northern California suburban office workers currently enjoy the luxury of commuting to work outside of the traditional 7:00–9:00 A.M. and 4:00–6:00 P.M. periods.

Case Study Summary

The Bay Area's office park settings illustrate the delicate relationship that exists between land development decisions and traffic conditions in rapidly growing areas. In the Silicon Valley, almost ubiquitous rush-hour congestion seriously threatens its very economic future. Thirty miles to the north in Pleasanton and San Ramon, the future marketability of both existing and planned business parks also rests crucially on developers' and local governments' abilities to control rapidly multiplying traffic volumes. Throughout the Bay Area, public and private interests are teaming together to forge creative responses for dealing with the looming suburban mobility crisis.

Growing concerns over employee and customer access problems are beginning to influence design decisions at major suburban workplaces like Bishop Ranch and Hacienda. Developers of both business parks have been resolute in their commitment to reinforce ridesharing and transit programs through conscientious design practices. In particular, careful attention has been given to the strategic placement of bus shelters throughout the respective parks, the provision of integrated networks of cycling and pedestrian paths, and the preferential siting of carpool and vanpool loading and drop-off zones near building entrances. The unusually high rates of employee vanpooling in both places suggest that some of these progressive design strategies are beginning to pay off.

The dominant focus of traffic mitigation efforts in the Bay Area's suburbs, however, has been less on physical and design solutions than on establishing programs aimed at changing employee commuting habits. Spearheading these efforts have been several recently formed transportation management associations. By providing a unified voice for dealing with wide-ranging mobility issues, TMAs have proven to be powerful forums for getting transportation programs off and running in the Bay Area's suburbs. Ridesharing tops the list of TMA activities in Northern California. In the case of Bishop Ranch, aggressive rideshare marketing and the initiation of various employee incentive programs have lured over one-third of the business park's employees to carpools and vanpools. Alliances like the Santa Clara County Manufacturing Group have also actively lobbied for areawide roadway improvements, new rail transit projects, and the establishment of dedicated highway funding programs.

The passage of Pleasanton's pioneering trip reduction ordinance could signal a trend toward stronger public intervention in protecting suburbs from the threat of gridlock. Pleasanton's ordinance mandates up to a 45 percent reduction in solo commuting for all developments—large and small ones alike. By spreading the burden of relieving traffic congestion to everyone, Pleasanton's program scores high marks as far as equity is concerned. The jury is still out, however, on whether the Pleasanton approach is fully enforceable. The fact that Hacienda's developers and other major employers have been fully supportive of the ordinance since its inception suggests that enforceability may be a moot issue. So far, most companies seem inclined to reduce peak hour trips in compliance with Pleasanton's ordinance by flexing work schedules, largely because they recognize the ability of ridesharing programs to reduce travel has been stretched to the limit.

Joint cost sharing of areawide local transportation improvements has also gained popularity throughout the Bay Area's suburbs. The single most outstanding example of this has been in Pleasanton where the Hacienda Business Park has pledged over $80 million toward off-site roadway construction. Without this commitment, there simply would be no way Pleasanton could accommodate the park's 45,000 workers at buildout, even with trips reduced 45 percent by the ordinance. As in Southern California, cooperative financing is being increasingly looked upon as the only practical way of building the infrastructure necessary to keep up with the Bay Area's soaring demand for intersuburban commuting.

Some of the underlying causes of suburban mobility problems facing the Bay Area are not easily addressed. Despite the fact that acute jobs-housing imbalances are known to be at the heart of Santa Clara County's traffic woes, new office buildings continue to cluster in areas devoid of affordable housing. Moreover, the sprawling layouts of most new office park additions have given the private automobile a distinct advantage over its competitors in places like Pleasanton despite the passage of an ordinance that emphatically discourages private auto usage. Community pressures to maintain low employment densities are largely responsible for this auto-oriented design emphasis. To date, Northern California's suburbanites have stonewalled most attempts to introduce higher density, more urban-like office complexes. The comparatively low price of land on the fringes of the Bay Area has also removed some of the incentive for developers to vertical-ize structures and cluster buildings, such as is being done in suburban Southern California. Combined with the general absence of restaurants and other on-site consumer services, the sprawling, low-density designs of most Bay Area suburban complexes have made access to a private vehicle almost imperative for anyone who has even an occasional need to leave his office during the day.

Finally, while ridesharing has been embraced by many suburban Bay Area employers, several impediments still stand in the way of its widespread adoption. Without question, free parking throughout the Bay Area's suburbs heads the list of deterrents to carpooling, transit usage, and other commute alternatives. In most outlying settings, the promise of a convenient, no-cost parking spot has been an open invitation to drive alone. Additionally, there has been little progress in encouraging ridesharing among employees of different suburban workplaces. In the Pleasanton-San Ramon Valley, for instance, by concentrating almost exclusively on corporate-level ridematching, most local employers have failed to exploit the critical mass of some 50,000 office employees presently working in the area. This tendency toward individual employers solving their own "front door" access problems is certainly not generic to the Bay Area, however. Clearly, TMAs offer the most effective framework for building a united front to deal with subregional mobility problems.

All in all, several novel approaches to transportation management have emerged in the Bay Area in recent years that, through emulation, could benefit other regions of the country. While traffic conditions continue to worsen along several outlying corridors, many local observers believe that the collective impact of such actions as company-sponsored vanpooling, flex-time programs, cooperative financing of new infrastructure, and employer TSM requirements will restore suburban mobility over the long run. Many will undoubtedly be watching the Bay Area's progress toward warding off suburban congestion over the next decade to see whether such tactics as mandatory trip reduction ordinances are indeed viable options.

Notes

1. Association of Bay Area Governments, "Bay Area Economic Profile" (Oakland: agency report, 1983).
2. Ibid.
3. California Department of Economics and Business Development, "California Technological Future: Emerging Economic Opportunities in the 1980s" (Sacramento: agency report, 1982).
4. Metropolitan Transportation Commission, "Initial Findings of the Interstate 680 and Interstate 580 Corridor Study" (Oakland: unpublished technical report, 1984).
5. League of Women Voters of the Bay Area, "Inner Ring Freeways: Problems and Prospects," *Bay Area Monitor* (May 1984), pp. 1–3.
6. Elliot Diringer and George Snyder, "Suburbs in Uproar Over Growth-Snarled Traffic," *The San Francisco Chronicle* (October 21, 1985), p. 4.
7. Santa Clara County Industry and Housing Management Task Force, "Living Within Our Limits: A Framework for Action in the 1980's" (San Jose: Santa Clara County Planning Department, agency report, 1979).
8. Robert Cervero, "Light Rail Transit and Urban Development," *Journal of the American Planning Association*, Vol. 50, No. 2 (1984), pp. 133–47.
9. Santa Clara County Planning Department, "General Plan: Santa Clara County" (San Jose: agency report, 1982).
10. Ibid.
11. Ibid.
12. Metropolitan Transportation Commission, "Initial Findings of the Interstate 680 and Interstate 580 Corridor Study," p. 25.
13. San Jose Department of City Planning, "Horizon 2000: General Plan for the City of San Jose" (San Jose: agency report, 1984).
14. Fee and Munson, Inc., "Hacienda Business Park: Design Guidelines" (San Francisco: consulting report, 1983).
15. A portion of these parcels will be occupied by financial services, including bank branches. A two-story hotel complex and family-style restaurant are also nearing completion on ten acres of the commercially zoned site.
16. Several Bay Area companies have hired full-time coordinators, including the Rolm Corporation of Santa Clara, the Hewlett Packard Company of Palo Alto, and Lockheed Corporation in Sunnyvale.

17. Both Bishop Ranch and Hacienda run their shuttles to nearby commercial areas during noon hours as well. Bishop Ranch also operates a midday shuttle service to the Walnut Creek BART station and downtown San Francisco. These services are targeted to employees who have to take care of out-of-the-workplace midday business.

18. One large company, Pacific Telephone, has signed a contract with a private company to operate its own two buses as commuter shuttles. The shuttle presently makes three runs in the morning and four in the evening. Although still heavily subsidized by the company, a $1.00 per trip fare is charged.

19. In the first year, a 15 percent reduction is required. Vehicular volumes must continue to decline by at least 10 percent each year until the 45 percent reduction goal is achieved in the fourth year.

7

Unlocking Suburban Gridlock

RISING TO THE CHALLENGE

The Do-Nothing Versus Intervention Alternatives

The mobility challenges facing suburban America are immense. Years of explosive and unconstrained growth have flooded the rims of our cities with cars and trucks they are ill-equipped to handle. The situation has begun to reach crisis proportions on the outskirts of Houston, Los Angeles, and a dozen or so other major metropolises across the country. Graphic accounts of the nerve-wrenching commutes facing more and more suburbanites have been chronicled in a flurry of recent newspaper articles on the subject of suburban congestion.[1] Some observers now venture that, under current trends, crippling traffic tie-ups outside of downtown "may well be the major transportation problem of the late 1980s and early 1990s."[2]

There certainly are no ready-made solutions to the problem. Just as it has taken years for traffic buildup to reach a point where suburbanites are beginning to take notice, it will no doubt take years to turn the situation around. We currently have the technical expertise and engineering know-how to deal with traffic congestion regardless where it surfaces. Finding the money to do so remains a major hurdle. The most difficult obstacles, however, are behavioral and institutional—getting people to change their travel habits and getting governments and private industry to respond to emerging mobility dilemmas efficiently and creatively.

Because both individuals and institutions are so resistant to change, some argue that the best course of action is to let the problem take care of itself—i.e., the "do-nothing alternative." Indeed, mounting congestion is apt to force both behavioral and institutional changes as well as give rise to

214

technological innovations. Those with the lowest tolerance for traffic jams will eventually move to quieter environs. Others will relocate close to their jobs. More and more businesses will stagger work hours and purchase vans to guarantee their employees a hassle-free commute. Advances in the telecommunications field might allow increasing numbers of data processors, clerical staff, and others chiefly involved in handling information to work at home rather than fight morning commuter traffic. In the true American tradition, the argument goes, the market itself will work for change and innovation.

An apropos question at this point is: Are we doomed to letting the congestion problem get so bad that it ultimately forces residents, developers, and elected officials into changing where they live, how they build, and what public programs they initiate? Or can we effectively head off impending mobility crises through artful public-private intervention? Are we better off operating in more of a passive/reactive mode, or is there indeed a role for proactive planning in the battle against suburban congestion?

Good arguments can certainly be made on both sides. The do-nothing alternative relies on the proven prowess of the marketplace to guide the locational and behavioral choices of residents and business such that a steady-flow traffic situation ultimately prevails. Proponents of this approach note that many of today's transportation solutions—mass transit, ridesharing, preferential carpool lanes, and the like—were designed to relieve inner-city congestion and that trying to make them work in the suburbs is both futile and wasteful. Some point to the dismal track record of many publicly sponsored transportation programs over the past several decades to support this position. Indeed, many of today's public initiatives run contrary to the travel preferences of most city and suburban dwellers. In aggressively pursuing TSM programs, we are asking Americans not only to alter commuting habits but to change a set of values cultivated over the past 30 to 40 years that give preference to the private automobile for its privacy, comfort, and convenience. Thus, supporters of the "do-nothing" option contend we are waging a losing battle in trying to force motorists out of their cars, and that suburban mobility can only be achieved incrementally through individually inspired changes in the marketplace.

Compelling arguments for market intervention, however, can also be made. Regional immobility is largely a systemic problem, symptomatic of how land uses are organized over physical space. The saturation of many freeways and major arteries during rush hours, for instance, can be largely attributed to the gross imbalances in where jobs and homes are located. The piecemeal, laissez-faire pattern of land development that has taken place in many parts of the country bears considerable blame for the mismatches in where people live and work, and thus for today's congestion woes. Some note that these problems are not the result of market failures, but rather planning failures—specifically, a failure of government to perform its duty in protecting and defending the public interest.[3]

The case for public intervention can also be made on conservationist grounds. The explosion in cross-town and perimeter commuting threatens the very livelihood and physical well-being of many established suburban communities around the country. In some instances, increases in through-traffic have transformed what were once ideal environments for raising families into noisy, blighted neighborhoods. Suburban sprawl and the helter-skelter commuting it produces also pose serious threats to surrounding agricultural land, open spaces, watersheds, and other natural ecologies. Indeed, a persuasive argument against the "do-nothing" alternative is the pressing need to protect productive agricultural land from encroachment. To rely on residents dispersing farther out into the hinterlands as a solution to deconcentrating trips and relieving suburban congestion is to invite endless leapfrogging and environmental disaster. There is obviously a finite limit to how far a metropolis can expand outward without devouring prime cropland and endangering the natural habitat. Realistically, there can only be so many cycles any one region can go through of spillover growth induced by congestion on the fringes. Sooner or later, the spread of tract housing and office complexes must be contained and traffic predicaments dealt with directly.

Weighing the "do-nothing" and "public intervention" alternatives, one is left with the sense that there is merit in both. Obviously, a community cannot "do nothing" and "intervene" at the same time. Still, both market principles and planning doctrine have something to offer toward the preservation of suburban mobility. Fortunately, choosing a course of action is not an either-or proposition. We need to rely both on the marketplace and creative public-private initiatives if we are to be successful in fending off suburban traffic paralysis. Congestion itself can be a powerful force in prodding developers, employers, and the populace at large into changing their customary practices. But there is also a need for assertive government intervention to guide the locational choices of individuals and firms within the larger public interest and to protect farms, greenbelts, and fragile ecologies from encroachment. Public-private alliances represent the most logical forums for bridging together the creativity and resourcefulness that the marketplace has to offer and the public welfare interests of governments.

Community Reactions to Traffic Buildup

Growing public anger over the intrusion of traffic into once tranquil suburban communities could very well be the impetus to sweeping public-private initiatives and reforms. Many suburbanites are beginning to realize the high price that goes with economic progress and rapid expansion. Combined with critical housing shortages, unsightly fast-food strips, increasing decibel levels, and deteriorating air, the traffic melee that chokes many rapidly growing suburbs has prompted sharp cries for action. Increasingly, neighborhood associations, citizens clubs, and environmental watch groups are demanding that their communities be restored to the kind of place that attracted them there in the first place.

Many suburban policymakers find themselves in a quandary of sorts. On one hand, they want the expanded tax base that new businesses offer. On the other, they want to maintain a quiet, family-oriented place in which to live. Communities like Pleasanton, California, have responded by introducing trip reduction ordinances, while others have passed no-growth laws, restricted building height limits, and stiffened zoning requirements. Many others are still trying to walk a tightrope between banning growth and total capitulation.[4] For every public official leery of growth, however, there is at least another who unabashedly welcomes it.[5] In the words of one commissioner in a county outside of Atlanta which recently spent $100,000 to campaign for new development: "I hesitate to say 'limit development' because why would I want to limit a trend that has kept our economy growing?"[6]

The heated debate over whether to control or encourage growth has in many cases led to political impasses, forcing many homeowners to fend for themselves in the wake of development pressures to sell out. Over the past several years, builders have bought entire housing subdivisions, sometimes paying double the market price, in the suburbs of Atlanta, Houston, and Washington, D.C.[7] Not all outlying neighborhoods have caved in, however, to intense real estate pressures to sell. One well-to-do Washington suburb, for example, recently won a court battle to halt a parcel-sale of an entire residential neighborhood to a builder of townhouse offices over fear that the community at large would eventually be devoured by office towers and shopping centers.[8] Even there, however, neighbors remain split over what to do, resulting in disinvestment along some blocks and a gradual deterioration of the housing stock. According to one homeowner: "There's a feeling that we shouldn't fix the houses up because we are in the path of change."[9]

A much stronger antigrowth consensus has formed in other parts of the country. Residents of rapidly growing Lakewood, Colorado, just west of

Denver, recently voted down three major office-commercial projects that had been approved by the local planning commission. And in Southampton, Long Island, the city council has just instituted a maximum five-acre zoning rule for the remaining 26,000 acres of undeveloped land as a hedge against advancing suburban sprawl.[10] Along the outermost reaches of the Bay Area, the communities of Livermore, Pleasanton, and Petaluma have already placed caps on the number of building permits issued annually, while residents of Pleasant Hill recently passed a measure requiring ballot approval before any structure over six stories is allowed. Even higher levels of government are considering drastic action to curb unbridled growth. Atlanta's regional council of governments has drafted legislation to restrict new office and commercial building in certain outlying areas under the threat of a possible state-imposed moratorium on development.[11]

One of the most unusual and strictest growth control measures anywhere was recently imposed by Walnut Creek, in the heart of the Bay Area's booming Interstate 680 corridor. There, citizens approved a proposition that halts all future commercial and office projects over 10,000 square feet until peak traffic volumes at seventy-five critical intersections fall below 85 percent of capacity. In that nearly all these intersections currently operate at or above capacity during rush hours, most observers believe that unless drastic action is taken, growth in Walnut Creek soon will come to a screeching halt. What makes Walnut Creek unusual is that the citizen backlash was in reaction to the recent completion of mid-rise office towers around the city's BART rail station, something that regional planners have long been striving to achieve. The problem is that fewer than 2 percent of the workers at these offices ride BART, simply because it goes nowhere close to where most of them live. Thus, rather than filling up rail cars, Walnut Creek's new mini-downtown has flooded local streets with new traffic—a classic case of the jobs-housing rift rearing its ugly head.

From both a transportation and regional point of view, the imposition of height limits and growth ceilings could thwart efforts to lure motorists out of their vehicles. Both higher densities and mixed-use environments are essential if mass transit and vanpooling are to effectively compete with the private automobile. Height limits could spread buildings so thinly as to make walking and the pooling of trips impractical. The banishment of retail functions from certain areas, moreover, could force suburban workers into driving their own cars for accessing restaurants and shops during lunch periods and after work. Sweeping bans on all growth, in particular, seem doomed to failure. They are flawed because they fail to attack the problem, which is traffic, not growth per se. If new office growth is not allowed in

Walnut Creek, for instance, it simply will go somewhere else, most likely in the form of a sprawling, auto-oriented office park rather than efficiently stacked in towers near the BART rail station.

Perhaps a more prudent, evenhanded course of action would be to carefully phase-in mutually compatible growth rather than restrict new construction carte blanche. More suburban communities should index building permits to the availability of affordable housing to encourage a stronger integration of where people live and work. Performance zoning might also be used to both promote mixed-use developments and specific TSM actions, like company-sponsored vanpools. Allowances of higher building densities in return for specific programs that remove employee vehicles from local streets could produce an incentive system whereby individual developers and companies self-regulate local traffic through assorted TSM initiatives. Performance zoning that allows densification could also lead to self-sustaining transit and ridesharing programs by creating substantial clusters of customers. The real advantage of incentive-based zoning is that it prods builders and realtors into dealing directly with specific problems, in this case, traffic congestion. Alternately, the Pleasanton approach to traffic control could be invoked whereby growth is permitted as long as developers and employers assume the responsibility for regulating the number of vehicles accessing their sites. The key is to modulate auto traffic as opposed to blindly halting all growth. On this note, one official of the 100-member West Houston Association recently remarked: "If it's *traffic* you're worried about, then *traffic* ought to be the thing you control—not the type of development or the height of the building."[12]

Equity Considerations

Excruciating traffic jams have not been the only problems created by the regional dispersal of jobs and housing in recent years. Suburbia's increasing popularity as an employment and commercial site has also heightened inequities in Americans' abilities to access different economic, social, and cultural opportunities. For the nation's transportation underclass (e.g., those without a car, the physically disabled), the scattering of workplaces, shopping malls, and recreational centers along the suburban fringes has physically isolated them more than ever, denying them the chance to fully enter into society's mainstream and take advantage of its offerings. Given the dearth of convenient public transit connections in most suburbs, the nation's window of opportunity is being slammed shut on those who cannot drive a car because they are too poor, too young, or too infirm.

Some critics also note that the suburbanization of workplaces has aggravated the persistently high jobless rate among inner-city minorities.[13] Quite often, there are no reverse-direction or cross-town transit runs connecting core neighborhoods with outlying business parks and office centers during peak periods. In some cases, the only connection between minority neighborhoods and outlying areas is an occasional "domestic workers shuttle" carrying housekeepers and gardeners to fairly affluent suburban neighborhoods. Discrimination, unconsciously or not, has undoubtedly influenced regional transit routing decisions in some parts of the country. With regard to New Orleans's transit services, a journalist recently observed:

> Jefferson, by far the most populous of the [region's] suburban parishes, is plagued with the bane of many suburbs: A madhouse of strip commercial development with a resulting mass of automobiles. Yet legislators from Jefferson have always been the most vocal opponents of aid to New Orleans' transit system. Few will say it for the record, but most New Orleans officials say racism is a factor in the opposition of Jefferson leaders. If some of New Orleans' blacks could commute easily between the city and the suburbs on transit, the suburbs would not be so lily-white, they say. The suburban bus lines do not run on Sunday and usually close down at 9 P.M..[14]

Exorbitant housing costs and shortages in rental units have likewise prevented some inner-city residents from moving closer to where the jobs are. A recent *Wall Street Journal* article chronicled the plight of a black, unemployed teacher from Brooklyn who does not own a car:

> To reach suburban job interviews, she typically rides two and one-half hours each way on subways, trains, and buses. Although she wants to be a corporate trainer or public-relations specialist, she has rejected job offers in Westchester, N.Y., and Piscataway, N.J., because she felt she couldn't support herself in either locale with a yearly salary of under $29,000. "Sometimes I really think it's unfair and a hardship" that so many jobs exist outside New York, she complained.[15]

Suburban employers also are finding it increasingly difficult to fill low-paid service and clerical jobs because few suburbanites are unemployed. To help redress the mismatch in where minorities live and where jobs are available, Washington, D.C. recently announced a $100,000 plan to transport residents to suburban workplaces in city-owned vans and to provide public transit subsidies.[16]

It is important for both public and private suburban interests not to lose sight of the distributional consequences of the actions they take. In the battle to stamp out suburban congestion, it is easy to focus all energies and resources on making a transportation system operate efficiently while ignoring who gains and who loses in the process. Increasing the opportunities for the nation's poor and disadvantaged to access burgeoning suburban employment and commercial centers deserves priority attention at all levels of government.

Building Responsive Institutional Structures

A recurring theme that seems to cut across almost all the topics discussed in this work is the need to build a solid institutional foundation for effectively responding to the impending suburban mobility crisis. Jobs-housing imbalances, what many would argue is the root cause of metropolitan-wide traffic congestion, can be blamed largely on the absence of a strong regional voice for guiding land use decisions. Similarly, downstream traffic tie-ups can in most cases be attributed to the failure of individual municipalities to coordinate their respective traffic management programs. Regional governance, many political scholars would argue, is essential if spillover problems like countywide traffic jams are to be seriously dealt with.

The numerous institutional voids and bureaucratic snags that stymie efforts to respond creatively to emerging transportation problems are all too familiar to most employers, developers, and planners. In suburbia, where myriad smaller municipalities and unincorporated villages often ring a large core city, decision making tends to be highly fragmented and narrowly focused. Many individual jurisdictions are too small in size and too short in funds to launch any meaningful transportation management program. Some lack the authority and organizational capacity to provide even the most basic public services. Where growth is incessant, small traffic engineering departments and county agencies are oftentimes overwhelmed and invariably ill-prepared, in both staff resources and management experiences, to handle the explosion in traffic. In many cases, a byzantine structure of special-purpose authorities exists, with each bureaucracy working independently on its particular area of responsibility, be it transportation, pollution, housing, education, or public health. Overlapping authorities and multiple agency involvement can bog down even the most routine assignments.

Lines of authority sometimes also become muddled in suburbia. Federal agencies, state highway departments, regional planning councils, county governments, and special authorities may all have some say-so on transportation matters in outlying settings, particularly in unincorporated places. Deciding who is to do what can be a trying, drawn-out process. Where gray areas of responsibility exist, bureaucratic footdragging and inaction often follow.

Politically, many suburban jurisdictions tend to be conservative, preferring traditional approaches to traffic problem solving, such as widening roads and retiming signals, over programs aimed at modifying travel demand, like parking reduction ordinances. There is also usually a strong conviction toward market principles and a distaste toward government "meddling" into private business affairs. Some students of regional politics have found the majority of suburban governments to be timid and inclined toward procrastination.[17] Policymaking is generally limited to what are considered to be "safe," noncontroversial issues as a way of avoiding political conflicts and open confrontations. Decisions are all too often put off in hopes that issues die out on their own.

The diffusion of decision making throughout suburbia has more often than not hindered efforts to engage in meaningful cooperation on problems that transcend municipal boundaries. The intense competition for new industries among neighboring jurisdictions has also been an impediment to joint problem solving. Some municipalities are unwilling to consider regulatory programs like trip reduction ordinances and mandatory traffic impact fees over fear that companies will take their business to adjoining communities that have no such controls—"voting with their radials," if you will. Inconsistencies in transportation policies across neighboring jurisdictions not only undermine the effectiveness of specific regulatory measures, they also remove the incentive for municipalities to innovate and try out fresh approaches toward traffic management.

The absence of regional cooperation also hinders efforts to balance jobs and housing throughout suburbia. There becomes little incentive to promote residential subdivisions that sap treasuries in lieu of office projects that fatten them when most municipalities act within their own narrow accord, catch-as-catch-can. If an enlightened board of aldermen behaves responsibly and zones for balanced housing, others will no doubt respond by permitting even more office and commercial development than they perhaps otherwise would have. Accordingly, in the absence of a strong regional framework for balancing jobs and housing, most suburban municipalities have seen fit to zone principally for office, commercial, and light industrial uses, sometimes forcing home builders out onto an amorphous rural fringe. Such fiscal zoning has more often than not physically fractured regions.

Communications channels between central cities and suburban municipalities are perhaps even more jammed than they are among individual suburbs. A city-suburb schism afflicts many regions of the country. Fiscal disparities are largely to blame for these political rifts. Already wealthier—average family income was over $27,800 in 1983, compared to $21,650 in central cities—suburbs are expected to widen this margin.[18] As suburbs become more self-sufficient and politically powerful, urbanologists note, their willingness to aid struggling cities often erodes.[19] Many transportation programs, such as regional transit services, evolve along distinct city-suburban geopolitical lines, with each side fighting for its own respective interest as far as routing, scheduling, and service expansion decisions. In the case of the Southeast Ohio Regional Transit Authority (SORTA) in the Cincinnati area, for instance, the control of the transit board by city interests has resulted in a funding package that places a large share of the system's financial burden on suburbanites. There, the introduction of peak-period surcharges, zonal fares, and a payroll tax dedicated to transit (collected on the basis of where people work) has resulted in suburbanites paying over twice as much for their transit services on a per-mile basis as city dwellers.[20] Political infighting has prompted outlying communities to split off from regional transit authorities in San Diego County, the Bay Area, Chicago, and a dozen or so other places around the country, and to form separate suburban transit districts. Geographical biases flow in both directions, however. In the New York area, for instance, the suburban counties of Nassau and Suffolk now have as many representatives in the State Legislature as do Manhattan and Brooklyn. Suburban politicians have resisted increases in New York City's commuter tax and have been able to vote millions of dollars in state funds for commuter railroads while New York's subways deteriorate.[21]

A commonly prescribed antidote for such regional problems is city-county consolidations. While a handful of areas such as Indianapolis, Nashville, and Jacksonville successfully consolidated five to ten years ago, nowadays few suburban communities find anything to gain from such mergers. Fiscal disparity laws, such as the tax-base sharing system in effect in the Minneapolis-St. Paul area, might stand a better chance of acceptance, however no other region of the country has managed to mimic the Twin Cities' program to date. As long as suburban communities remain the clear fiscal losers in any consolidation scheme, strong resistance can be expected.

Political pressure must no doubt come from the state level, such as in the Twin Cities' case, for any institutional mergers to succeed.

With regard to suburban mobility, however, it is not absolutely essential that there be a unified government structure; what is much more important is the emergence of a visionary regional planning function. As long as land use decisions are made on an ad hoc, piecemeal basis among geographically and functionally fragmented governments, dilemmas like jobs-housing imbalances will be impossible to resolve. The past 20 years of suburban evolution have taught us that the collective impacts of individual municipalities operating within their own narrow interests can be environmentally disastrous. Without a regional focus, individual suburban communities often lapse into a "band-aid" style of problem-solving—trying to put out fires by widening an intersection here and retiming signals there, oblivious to how all the pieces fit together to impact areawide mobility. Most regions of the country have councils of government (COGs) and metropolitan planning organizations (MPOs) of some shape or form. Like suburban municipalities, however, COGs and MPOs tend to operate in a collaborative planning style, choosing to deal largely with noncontroversial issues and to set broad, vaguely worded policy agendas.[22] Since COG boards are made up of elected officials who remain primarily loyal to the local constituents who put them into office, regional decisions are often compromised by what local councils want to do. MPO staffs frequently end up deferring to local planners on site-specific issues. Some serve as yes-men to municipal planning directors. Others find themselves functioning mainly as mediators who spend most of their time resolving interjurisdictional disputes.

The major reason why so many COGs and MPOs remain toothless, of course, is that there is no political consensus over what the comprehensive land use and transportation goals should be for a region. While metropolitan political bodies can agree upon such incontestables as the need to "improve air quality" and "reduce congestion," they are usually at loggerheads when it comes to deciding whether compact or low-density development is the optimal built form or even over whether scarce resources should be best spent on new expressways or expanded transit services. While many urban planners argue passionately for contained growth and higher densities, most Americans prefer large lots and single-family homes.[23] The net result of this disunity is usually nonaction and political passivity.

Arguments for stronger regional planning, by themselves, are vacuous. There is little disagreement over the need for closer cooperation among governments. Saying it and doing it, of course, are two different things.

There is certainly no instant potion for concocting a successful regional planning program. Many of the essential ingredients for success are imponderables. Having forceful and savvy leaders who embrace regionalism as part of their political platforms unquestionably helps. Gaining the support of local power-brokers and elites, such as news publishers and corporate leaders, is equally important. However, the stewardship of regional planning must begin with higher levels of government. State legislators must provide the enabling authority that empowers municipalities to form intermediate levels of government for dealing with cross-boundary problems. Incentives, such as cash grants and state revenue sharing, might also stimulate greater local interest in regionalism. Minnesota's state legislators paved the way for the Twin Cities' adoption of tax-base sharing and suprametropolitan land use planning, for instance, by enacting special enabling legislation and creating fiscal incentives. While needs and circumstances differ around the country, lessons from the Twin Cities offer a logical starting point for those seriously interested in pursuing regional planning.

Lastly, any enduring institutional response to the looming suburban mobility crisis must stress public-private cooperation. Whether through transportation management associations (TMAs) or individual developer cofinancing of roadway expansions, the intimate involvement of the private sector in arresting suburban congestion must be actively sought and promoted.

In recent years, metropolitan-wide mobility has gained wide recognition as a shared responsibility of governments, businesses, and developers. The concept of public-private partnerships, however, has come to mean many things to many people. In its purest sense, it means working together for common objectives—which in the suburbs include enhanced mobility and desirable places in which to live and work. However, it is much more than a mere slogan of esprit de corps. It is businesses and governments lining up deals to finance new interchanges; public officials and employers working closely together in drafting special ridesharing legislation; land speculators and economic development agencies jointly reaping the rewards of higher property values induced by a new transit terminus; and so forth.

As a team, the public and private sectors blend nicely. Governments provide legal authority and borrowing capabilities, while private interests offer a wellhead of financial resources as well as fresh entrepreneurial approaches to problem solving. Such alliances will endure because of their inherent superiority to most other institutional formats. A key to sustaining effective partnerships, however, is the equitable sharing of costs and benefits among all parties. As long as this can be accomplished, a win-win situation will ultimately prevail.

Agenda for Action

The "bottom line" of any crusade to safeguard suburban mobility, of course, is what actually takes place in the field. The following agenda for action is proposed.

Parking Reforms

Experts in the transportation field are almost unanimous in denouncing abundant, free parking as a major stumbling block toward making ridesharing, transit, and other commute alternatives work in suburbia.[24] There is very little incentive to bunch into buses or vans when a convenient, fully subsidized parking spot awaits you.

Current suburban parking practices need to be overhauled. Minimum parking requirements have produced an oversupply of land-hungry asphalt spaces that more often than not become permanent fixtures to the landscape. Any attempt to introduce ridesharing and transit incentives where there is excess parking is often for naught.

Parking charges should be enforced, set at market-clearing price levels. The full capitalized cost of providing parking should also be passed on to those who opt to drive to work. Further, stringent zoning requirements should be relaxed to give developers greater flexibility in gauging their individual parking needs. Given the freedom to respond to market demands, builders and employers might be more inclined toward clustering parking into decked structures when appropriate. Additionally, incentives such as preferential parking and vanpool substitution should be encouraged. A gradual phasing-in of parking reductions based on the relative success of assorted TSM programs over time makes the most sense.

Current tax laws should be revised to redress inequities between parking and transit/ridesharing policies. Presently at the federal level and in most states, employer subsidization of workers' bus fares is treated as taxable income while the provision of free parking is considered a tax-free, in-kind contribution. Thus, some employees face the choice of either parking free with no tax responsibility or receiving subsidized bus passes for which they have to reimburse Uncle Sam. Moreover, under current IRS rules, businesses can write off a maximum of $15 per month for each employee who participates in employer-supported vanpools and carpools. However, no limits are set on the amount that can be deducted for parking subsidies. Needless to say, today's tax laws are heavily stacked in motorists' favor. Parking reforms, then, need to be aggressively pursued not only at the local level, but at state capitals and in Washington as well.

Active Employer and Developer Participation

Employers and developers must become lead players in the war against suburban gridlock. Little government prodding will be needed since private interests fully recognize the high financial stakes posed by chronically clogged highways. Perhaps municipalities could best stimulate wide private involvement by paring down those regulatory controls, such as bans on mixed-use zoning and the prohibition of for-profit vanpools, that foil many progressive transportation initiatives.

The recent emergence of TMAs is hopefully a bellwether of future private sector involvement in suburban transportation. TMAs remain the linchpins to successful ridesharing. Experiences show that workers take pooling seriously only when encouraged to do so by their bosses. Combined with containment of parking, employer-sponsored and TMA-coordinated ridesharing holds considerable promise for arresting suburban congestion. Here again, federal tax revisions are called for. As nonprofit organizations, TMA purchases of vans and buses do not qualify for investment tax credits. While under 1985 tax laws individual employers can take such deductions, the exclusion of TMAs has discouraged intercompany purchases of fleets for coordinated ridesharing.

TMAs are particularly important along corridors populated by dozens of freestanding, loosely organized developments. A large share of new work centers sprouting along urban fringes are not massive megaprojects but rather small, unrelated complexes. Many projects are financially and organizationally incapable of sustaining successful ridesharing programs or sponsoring new interchange construction. TMAs provide an ideal forum for coordinating activities among myriad small developments whose collective road-clogging impacts sometimes surpass those of mammoth supercomplexes.

TMAs also offer the greatest hope for recasting the standard design mold of most suburban business centers. The architectural styles chosen by developers and builders principally reflect the preferences of their clients. TMAs are clearly in the best position to influence current corporate thinking on what is a preferred working environment. To the extent corporate leaders are willing to embrace higher-density, more pedestrian-oriented built forms, the development industry will no doubt respond with more intensive designs.

Balanced Growth

Little more need be said about the importance of balancing jobs and housing as well as intermixing land uses as the most fail-safe cure for regional traffic woes. Although perhaps today an overused phrase, the central message behind balanced growth remains as sound and unequivocal as ever. Travel is a direct function of how we organize our communities, and if we physically segregate activities and fail to zone certain areas for a mixture of uses, chronic traffic breakdowns are inevitable. It is imperative that jobs and housing be matched geographically as well as demographically, and that more self-sufficient, village-like working environments be built. Admittedly, finding the right institutional formula for bringing this about poses a monumental task. Vital first steps, nonetheless, are a forceful, resonant regional voice and an unwavering local commitment to intermunicipal problem solving. Clearly, any serious assault on suburban gridlock must begin with careful, strategic planning of land uses with regional objectives in mind.

Expanded Paratransit

Although most attention is usually given to carpools and vanpools as palliatives for suburban congestion, the potential roles of different paratransit modes—from shared-ride taxis and for-profit employee jitneys to private commuter buses—should not be overlooked. Paratransit fills the wide gap between conventional bus and auto commuting, offering travelers a rich mix of in-between service and price options. To date, paratransit's presence in both central cities and suburbia has been stymied by excessive and oppressive local regulation. There is no logical reason why enterprising employees should not be allowed to operate profitable vanpools or run noontime shuttles between office complexes and nearby shopping facilities for a small fee. Although governments have a role to play in guaranteeing driver fitness and indemnity, they have overstepped their bounds by restricting the entry of taxis, jitneys, and buspools. The primary reason they have done so is to protect deficit-riddled public transit operators from what some fear would be predatory and ruinous competition. Yet, most industry observers agree that competition is just the kind of jolt transit needs to shake it out of its doldrums and to force industrywide innovations. Competition has proven its prowess in other sectors of the economy. There is no reason why it would not do likewise for suburban commuter markets.

While paratransit's future in suburbia is promising, unfortunately the same cannot be said about conventional transit. In general, densities are too low for it to successfully compete. Transit's greatest hope for survival in suburbia is through the reconfiguration of radial route structures into more grid-like, timed-transfer networks that ease the hassle of transferring. Given the chance, paratransit could provide valuable feeder connections into out-lying transfer centers. Disturbingly, however, many American communities experiencing some of the most intense suburban growth pressures anywhere seem more inclined to build new, modern fixed-guideway systems than to rejuvenate their ailing bus systems. A large number of these projects smack of civic boosterism more than they do of a genuine interest in correcting regional mobility problems. In light of current demographic and employment trends, many of today's fixed-guideway proposals seem wrongheaded and imprudent.

Demand Management

All things considered, measures that regulate travel demand, rather than expand roadway capacity, should be exploited to the maximum extent possible in suburbia. In general, the regulation and management of travel demand seems to be in harmony with the growth control sentiments of many suburbanites. Trip reduction programs, such as Pleasanton, California's pioneering ordinance, are particularly appealing for this very reason.

As long as residential and employment densities remain low throughout suburbia, the role of many TSM measures such as ridesharing toward reducing rush hour traffic, although important, will be somewhat limited. It is unlikely that many suburban communities can raise their current ridesharing rates of 20 percent of the commuting market very much higher. While there are spatial constraints in modifying travel behavior (and thus reducing rush hour trips), fortunately there are usually few temporal ones. Notably, flex-time and staggered work arrangements—whereby changes are made *when,* not *how,* commuters travel—have yielded significant immediate-term dividends in the few suburban areas where they have been aggressively pursued. Among the many demand management programs available, flexible work schedules probably offer the greatest potential payoff toward unclogging suburban streets.

Responsible Financing

Despite the compelling case that can be made for abating suburban traffic congestion primarily through containment of demand, additional roadway capacity must nevertheless be provided in many settings. The optimal approach to financing new highway investments is to pass on construction costs to those most directly benefiting from improved access. In most cases, this will be land developers, who in turn will pass on the extra costs to their tenants. Responsible financing is absolutely pivotal to achieving balanced suburban growth and instilling a market discipline. To the extent developers internalize the costs of their projects, the scale and design of new office and commercial facilities will be moderated to ensure reasonably good site access and compatible growth.

Negotiated private financing of off-site roadway improvements has gained momentum in recent years, and because of its inherent flexibility and proven track record, will likely become a standard way of practice in many places. Responsible financing, however, does not only entail paying for new freeway interchanges and overpasses next to one's own property; it also means assuming responsibility for both the upstream and downstream traffic impacts of a project. Because of the need to pool monies for area-wide improvements in fast-growth settings, some communities have enacted laws requiring developer contributions to subregional trust funds, usually with the proviso that they can credit any specific near-site improvements they pay for against their obligation. Notwithstanding the thorny problem of trying to measure the congestion costs associated with a specific development, the creation of trust funds and assessment districts is the fairest and most prudent approach yet devised for financing new areawide infrastructure.

Showcasing Exemplary Programs

All levels of government could play an important role in safeguarding suburban mobility by widely publicizing those traffic management, site design, and funding programs that have proven to be the most successful. The federal government, in particular, would perform a valuable service by setting up a clearinghouse of "best practices"—a collection of model trip reduction ordinances, mixed-use suburban projects, employer-sponsored vanpool programs, and so on, available for others to imitate.

Summary

Stiff resistance can be expected to most of these prescriptions for change. There are clear winners and losers associated with each. Still, the likely cumulative effect would be to restore mobility to many traffic-choked suburbs and to work for orderly and environmentally sound growth.

Auto disincentives, such as mandatory ceilings on parking supplies, have historically proven to be far more effective at getting people to alter their commuting habits in urban areas than have transit and ridesharing incentives. There is no reason why this would not also be the case in suburbia. Most developers and employers resist parking controls because of the popular perception that ridesharing and mass transportation are unworkable in the suburbs. In a sense, this becomes a self-fulfilling prophecy. Critics of other auto disincentives, like mandatory trip reduction ordinances, decry the dampening effects such actions could have on future economic development. They sometimes ignore, however, the irrevocable damage that prolonged and unrestrained increases in traffic can do to a community's image. Although popularly used within professional circles, the term "auto disincentive" is actually a misnomer. More accurately, most of these programs are "auto equalizers"—they aim to remove many of the built-in biases that encourage single-occupancy commuting, thereby placing vanpools and other travel modes on more equal footing.

The notion that incentive-based programs like ridesharing are token gestures in sprawling suburban settings also does not hold water. Time and again, American commuters have shown just how resilient they can be. One of the most graphic demonstrations of this was the 1984 Los Angeles Olympics when, to the surprise of many alarmists, traffic flowed smoothly despite dire predictions that insufferable tie-ups would force motorists to abandon their cars on freeways. A combination of staggering working hours, self-initiated carpooling, stepped-up transit services, and rescheduling of deliveries outside of normal business hours turned what was to be a miserable week of commuting into a pleasurable one. Although it is doubtful whether such abrupt behavioral changes could be sustained over any length of time, the adage "when there's a will, there's a way" certainly seems to hold as far as regional commuting goes.

Although changes in land uses and employment densities are usually even more subtle and drawn-out than changes in commuting, the past decade has shown that the built environment is just as malleable as are people. Only a decade or so ago, the thought of twenty-plus story office towers far removed from the cores of cities like Houston, Los Angeles, and

Denver was the stuff science fiction movies were made of. Today, vibrant, high-rise villages dot the perimeters of at least a dozen North American cities. In a few instances, run-of-the-mill office parks have been transformed into lively multipurpose complexes, complete with restaurants, theaters, shops, and health spas within a few short years. The salvation of transportation, whether in a central city or exurbia, is that people and their environments are indeed adaptable. The challenge rests with builders, employers, planners, and policymakers to capitalize on this adaptability by crafting creative programs that promise to make suburbs better places in which to live, work, and travel.

Notes

1. See: Christopher Conte, "The Explosive Growth of Suburbia leads to Bumper-to-Bumper Blues," *Wall Street Journal* (April 16, 1985), p. 37; Joann S. Lublin, "The Suburban Life: Trees, Grass Plus Noise, Traffic and Pollution," *Wall Street Journal* (June 20, 1985), p. 29; and William Trombley, "Suburbs Gear Up to Beat Traffic," *Los Angeles Times* (December 28, 1984), p. 24.
2. Trombley, "Suburbs Gear Up to Beat Traffic," p. 24. Also, see: C. Kenneth Orski, "Suburban Mobility: The Coming Transportation Crisis?" *Transportation Quarterly*, Vol. 39, No. 2 (1985), p. 285.
3. David E. Dowall, *The Suburban Squeeze* (Berkeley: University of California Press, 1984).
4. Lublin, "The Suburban Life," p. 29.
5. Lawrence D. Maloney, "America's Suburbs Still Alive and Doing Fine," *U.S. News & World Report* (March 12, 1984), p. 61.
6. Ibid.
7. See: Lublin, "The Suburban Life," p. 29; and Maloney, "America's Suburbs Still Alive and Doing Fine," p. 61.
8. Lublin, "Suburban Life," p. 29.
9. Ibid.
10. Maloney, "America's Suburbs Still Alive and Doing Fine," p. 62.
11. Lublin, "The Suburban Life," p. 29.
12. Thomas Hazlett, "They Built Their Own Highways . . . and Other Tales of Private Land-Use Planning," *Reason* (November 1983), p. 27.
13. Lublin, "The Suburban Life," p. 29.
14. Jim Seale, "New Orleans—Where Bad Weather Makes Good Transit," *Mass Transit* (July/August 1978), p. 6. Quoted in: Donald O. Eisele, "Suburban Service in North America Today—Which Way Will We Go?" *Journal of Advanced Transportation*, Vol. 18, No. 1 (1984), p. 33.
15. Lublin, "The Suburban Life," p. 29.

16. Ibid.
17. Bryan T. Downes, "Problem-Solving in Suburbia: The Basis for Political Conflict," *The Urbanization of the Suburbs,* L.H. Masotti and J.K. Hadden, eds. (Beverly Hills, Calif.: Sage Publications, 1973), pp. 281–312; Peter Bachrach and M.S. Barazt, *Power and Prosperity: Theory and Practice* (New York: Oxford University Press, 1970).
18. Maloney, "America's Suburbs Still Alive and Doing Fine," p. 62.
19. Ibid.
20. Robert Cervero, "Examining Recent Transit Fare Innovations in the U.S.," *Transport Policy and Decision Making,* Vol. 3, No. 1 (1985), pp. 23–41.
21. Maloney, "America's Suburbs Still Alive and Doing Fine," p. 62.
22. David W. Jones, "Transportation in the Bay Area: A Challenge to Institutional Reform," *Public Affairs Report,* Vol. 19, No. 2 (1978), pp. 1–9.
23. Alan Altshuler, *The Urban Transportation System: Politics and Policy Innovation* (Cambridge: MIT Press, 1981), pp. 377–78.
24. This was a consensus position among the one hundred plus attendees of the Conference on Mobility of Major Metropolitan Areas, held in Los Angeles in November 1984, and sponsored by the U.S. Department of Transportation, Urban Mass Transportation Administration. For additional discussions on the role of parking as a determinant of mode choice, see: Donald C. Shoup, "Cashing Out Free Parking," *Transportation Quarterly,* Vol. 36, No. 3 (1982), pp. 351–64.

Selected Bibliography

Altshuler, Alan. *The Urban Transportation System: Politics and Policy Innovations*. Cambridge: The MIT Press, 1979.

Cervero, Robert. "Managing the Traffic Impacts of Suburban Office Development." *Transportation Quarterly* 51, 3 (1985): 533–50.

Clark, S.D. *The Suburban Society*. Toronto: University of Toronto Press, 1966.

Culver, Lowell W. "The Politics of Suburban Distress." *Journal of Urban Affairs* 4, 1 (1982): 1–18.

Donaldson, S. *The Suburban Myth*. New York: Columbia University Press, 1969.

Dowall, David E. *The Suburban Squeeze*. Berkeley: University of California Press, 1984.

Downs, Anthony. *Opening Up the Suburbs*. Washington: The Brookings Institution, 1973.

Dunphy, Robert. "Urban Traffic Congestion: A National Crisis?" *Urban Land*, 44, 10 (1985): 2–7.

Eager, William R. "Innovative Approaches to Transportation for Growing Areas." *Urban Land* 43, 7 (1984): 6–11.

Galehouse, Richard F. "Mixed-Use Center in Suburban Office Parks." *Urban Land* 43, 8 (1984): 12–16.

Gauldin, R. "Developing a Suburban Office Park." *Mortgage Banker* 40, 2 (1979): 42–49.

Hazlett, Thomas. "They Built Their Own Highway . . . and Other Tales of Private Land-Use Planning." *Reason* (November 1983): 22–30.

Huth, Mary Jo. "Toward a Multi-Nodal Urban Structure." *Transportation Quarterly* 37, 2 (1983): 245–62.

Lake, Robert W. *The New Suburbanites: Race and Housing in the Suburbs*. New Brunswick, N.J.: Center for Urban Policy Research, Rutgers University, 1981.

Lynch, Kevin and Gary Hack. *Site Planning*. Cambridge: The MIT Press, 1984.

Masotti, Louis H. and John K. Hadden, eds. *The Urbanization of the Suburbs*. Beverly Hills, Calif.: Sage Publications, 1973.

McKeever, J. Ross. *Business Parks*. Washington: The Urban Land Institute, Technical Bulletin 65, 1970.

Meyer, John R. and Jose Gomez-Ibanez. *Autos, Transit and Cities*. Cambridge: Harvard University Press, 1981.

O'Mara, W. Paul and John A. Casaza. *Office Development Handbook*. Washington: Urban Land Institute, Community Builder's Handbook Series, 1982.

Pushkarev, Boris and Jeffrey Zupan. *Public Transportation and Land Use Policy*. Bloomington, Ind.: Indiana University Press, 1977.

Joint Economic Committee. *Location of High Technology Firms and Regional Economics*. Washington: U.S. Government Printing Office, 1982.

Lave, Charles A., ed. *Urban Transit: The Private Challenge to Public Transportation*. San Francisco: Pacific Institute for Public Policy Research, 1985.

Orski, C. Kenneth. "Suburban Mobility: The Coming Transportation Crisis?" *Transportation Quarterly* 39, 2 (1985): 283-96.

Porter, Douglas R. "Research Parks: An Emerging Phenomenon." *Urban Land* 43, 9 (1984): 6-9.

Reichert, James P. "Wanted: National Policy on Suburban Transit." *Transit Journal* 5, 3 (1979): 37-42.

Schneider, Jerry B. *Transit and the Polycentric City*. Washington: U.S. Department of Transportation, Urban Mass Transportation Administration, 1981.

Shoup, Donald. "Cashing Out Free Parking." *Transportation Quarterly* 36, 3 (1982): 351-64.

Urban Land Institute. *Development Review and Outlook*. Washington: Urban Land Institute, 1984.

Valente, P. R. "Public Transportation in the 1980's: An Era of Change." *Public Management* 64, 7 (1982): 8-14.

Index